UNRAV
THREADS

The Life, Death, and Resurrection of

The Singer Company,

America's First Multi-National Corporation

by

Jack Buckman

First published by Dog Ear Publishing
4011 Vincennes Rd
Indianapolis, IN 46268
www.dogearpublishing.net

ISBN: 978-1-4575-4661-7

This book is printed on acid-free paper.

Printed in the United States of America

To

Henry W. Broude

and

Jacques Ehrsam

Table of Contents

The Beginning of the End

May 1978

The former Singer Company CEO loved his horses. He was a skilled rider, instinctively assuming the erect military posture he had learned from General George S. Patton, his mentor and idol. Donald P. Kircher had served as a tank commander under Patton in World War II, and he spoke often of Patton's bearing, management philosophy, and leadership skills.

It was a beautiful spring day in the country. Kircher was sure that most people who drove through New Jersey along the factories and oil refineries of the New York Harbor had no idea of what was hidden in the hills. The estates ran next to each other, so intimately joined that Kircher could ride from one to another without ever encountering a stranger. It was no accident that the interstates passed around this island of wealth and culture. This was where success was recognized by those who truly mattered, and Kircher felt at home there, among the elites who had populated the New Jersey hills for over a century— -the Astors, the Dukes, and the Blairs. And they had kept coming—DeLorean, Pfizer, King Hassan, even Jackie Kennedy, and then the Kirchers. As *Forbes* magazine put it, "The New Jersey hunt country would appeal to anyone with aristocratic tendencies. After all, it's a place where men don't wear Polo; they play it."

The Singer board had entrusted Kircher with an American icon, one of the most famous of American brands, known in even the smallest villages throughout the world. Singer represented the efforts of talented and creative Americans who, over the course of more than a century, had created a company that had emerged from the industrial revolution to grow into a company that impacted even remote parts of the world. It had created great wealth for both its founders and Kircher's predecessor CEOs. And Kircher had become the guardian of that legacy.

It had been clear to him that the world was changing in ways that could challenge the very existence of the company. If management did not recognize and plan for those changes, the company might not survive. Many in the investing community believed that the sewing machine was a product in decline. The trends seemed obvious; the women who had traditionally used the sewing machine no longer needed it at home. They had become used to working in the war effort factories and looked forward to continuing their growing independence and enjoying their extra income. They no longer had the time to shop nor were they at home for the door-to-door salesmen. Besides, why should they bother with the hassle of fabrics, patterns, cutting, and sewing when there were so many attractive and inexpensive ready-made clothes suddenly available? No, the future market for sewing machines was in doubt, and something had to be done if the company was to survive. Kircher had been selected as the agent for that change.

As he rode along on his favorite horse, the gentle pace and perfect morning allowed him to reflect on what had happened. He was not supposed to be in retirement. As beautiful as his life was in New Jersey, it was unfulfilling, incomplete. He had planned his career so well that when the sudden end came, he was totally unprepared. He had been on the verge of completing the plan he had worked so hard to conceive. The board had committed to his concepts, and he had assembled a talented team ready and able to carry the plan to a successful conclusion. He had seen the threat to Singer's existence and warned the board. He had analyzed what would be needed to succeed, and the board had enthusiastically provided full support. He had made the difficult choices, and he and the board had run the gauntlet together. They had been on the verge of overcoming the threats, just a short dash from success.

But it had all ended so abruptly, so unexpectedly. The charade that he was "taking time off for medical reasons" fooled no one. Even skeptical journalists had used quotation marks. Time had tempered the explosive anger he had felt at the time. But now, two years had passed and had given him the time to think more objectively about what he had accomplished and where he had gone wrong. Nonetheless, he couldn't shake the bitterness he still felt about how quickly everyone had turned against him, without warning or compassion. *Why had the board suddenly rejected the man charged with bringing the company into the twentieth century, who had prepared it for the twenty-first?* Kircher asked himself. He had devised and implemented Singer's diversification program, invented a new corporate concept, the Transnational Enterprise, worthy of recognition in the *Harvard Business Review* and a presentation at Columbia University. He had been honored by the *Financial Times* and invited to White House dinners. Admittedly, the board and he had hit a few bumps in the road, but that was not unusual, and the board had always supported him before as they moved forward together. He had identified the critical problems the company had faced and already taken the necessary steps to solve them, the same steps that would now be credited to his successor. He had proposed technology as the obvious solution to the company's dependence on the retail business cycle of the sewing machine. It was obvious that the sewing business was in sore need of modernizing if it was to respond to the new retail realities, and the management he had put in place was well-equipped to manage that change. He had carefully selected these board members and supported them for election. He had toiled for twenty-three years to save the company, and he could finally see the finish line. Whatever happened to loyalty? What had gone wrong? To make matters even worse, what had made the board choose Flavin, a mediocre Irishman, as his replacement? At the very least, they could have chosen someone of appropriate stature as a successor. Flavin didn't belong in hunt country and never would.

Kircher should have seen it coming. He had let the glamour of his own press convince him that Singer needed a more prestigious board than the one he inherited. It needed, he felt, other members of the high-profile CEO club he had just joined. As was often the case, however, his new recruits paid scant attention to the details of the company, content to just draw their fees and routinely approve his recommendations.

By 1972 he had expanded the board from eleven to fourteen seats, by adding two new outside board members and creating one vacancy. But he had taken his eye off the ball. With the combination of retirements and new board seats, he would never again have a controlling majority of insiders. He needed an inside appointment to at least establish parity. It had become difficult to promote anyone from inside the company to the board without setting off internecine warfare in his executive dining room. It was one thing to watch them joust over lunch, an amusing but inconsequential occurrence. It was quite another to bless one or two of them with the ultimate promotion, giving them coveted status over the others. But he had bit the bullet and made an internal appointment, ending up with a fourteen-member board that consisted of seven each of inside and out-side directors. It would turn out to be a serious oversight.

Initially, nothing seemed amiss and he had planned to correct the imbalance as the outside directors each retired. But before he had the opportunity to act, he was completely blindsided by massive losses from Friden, one of his divisions. He found himself with a board whose loyalty did not include going down with the ship. The outside directors knew a shareholder revolt was likely, and collectively they felt obliged to act swiftly to preserve their own reputations of success. Their directors' fees were an infinitesimal portion of their total compensation, but it was their reputations that were in jeopardy, and the circumstances were such that they couldn't resign without giving the appearance of walking away from their respon-sibilities. The Singer name was huge, and failure to act responsibly would be a blot on their personal histories, difficult to erase. So they acted.

With his dismissal, Kircher's own reputation had been trashed. Friden had been his groundbreaking acquisition, signaling the progress he had made in leading

Singer out of its dependence on the sewing machine and setting the stage for the completion of his technology strategy. Friden had its problems, but they were solvable. It wasn't the unmitigated disaster it had been made it out to be. His successors' strategy was obvious—announce every little problem facing the company as threatening to Singer's future and set up a huge reserve to cover the costs of correcting or discontinuing those businesses. Err on the downside, and if the reserve proved to be too large, it could always be brought back into future earnings. The announcement of the largest write-off in U.S. corporate history made Kircher appear the fool who had led the company astray and Flavin the technology genius who would save it. This was the work of a numbers juggler who had already mentally written off the core of the company's activities, convinced that it was not a question of if, but when the market would die completely and Singer along with it. The jury was still out on the sewing business, with some believing that it would come back stronger than ever. Selling sewing machines was a difficult business, but the managers Kircher had had in place had shown time and time again that they knew how to adapt to difficult circumstances and survive.

Deep in thought, Kircher finally approached the stable on his 132-acre property and saw a figure in the distance. It was Charles Moeller, his wife Lois's brother. Lois and Don Kircher had been married in 1965 and had two children, a son and a daughter. Lois's brother had been unstable and couldn't countenance Kircher's material success. Whatever conversations the two had had were usually disagreeable and openly hostile. Notwithstanding the uncomfortable relationship, Kircher had supported Lois's family for years. Charles's father had worked on the estate as a caretaker and lived in a guesthouse, while Charles, who had been unemployed since an accident several years earlier, had until recently lived rent-free in another guesthouse on the grounds. Unwilling to undertake any chores in return for his housing, Moeller had been asked to leave and, in defiance, had complied by moving in with his father in the other guesthouse, as if to give notice that he would not be that easy to get rid of.

The history of jealousy and bad blood between him and Kircher had once again surfaced. It was likely that, as he had no visible source of income, Moeller had been borrowing living money from his sister, and Kircher either had been aware of or strongly suspected that he had been the indirect source of Moeller's income. Before coming up to the main house that day, Moeller had told his father that he was going to return an iron he had borrowed from his sister, but his father thought he was actually on his way to ask his sister for more money. When he encountered Kircher, the two had a conversation that almost certainly turned to money and escalated into a fierce argument. Whether Moeller felt that Kircher had more money than he deserved and asked for a "loan," or he thought that, as Moeller's brother-in-law, Kircher was obliged to support him as family, we will never know. In a rage, Moeller had departed for his father's house and quickly returned to find Kircher now returning to his house on foot. With but a few words, Moeller produced a pistol and shot Kircher twice in the chest. He died almost immediately. He was sixty-three years old.

CHAPTER ONE

Tinkerer, Capitalist, and Machine Come Together

Isaac Merritt Singer, the Reprobate Tinkerer

Isaac Merritt Singer, 1850[1]

Adam Singer, Isaac's father, was born in Germany in 1753 and came alone from that country to the United States in 1769 at the age of sixteen. He settled in Troy, New York, and in 1788, married Ruth, a Quaker descendant of Dutch immigrants who had come to this country almost a century earlier. Adam's trade was believed to be a millwright, and following Isaac's birth in 1811 the family settled on the shores of Lake Ontario in Oswego, New York. By the time of the Singer family's arrival, Oswego had grown from being wild forest, deep in unsafe Indian Territory, to a fully functioning village, with a church, a newspaper, and a village square. If he was, in fact, a millwright, Adam's timing should have been provident. This was still considered to be the far west, the wheat-growing country that preceded the opening of the Great Plains and the midcentury migration of farming to what is now the Midwest. Tens of thousands emigrated from Europe to America in the belief that prosperity was there for the taking. There is no evidence that Adam was either significantly successful or a failure. For reasons that are unclear, however, the Singer family had become an unhappy one, and in 1821 Ruth divorced Adam and left the home. As the only grounds for divorce in New York State at that time was adultery, one can only conclude that Adam's behavior was the source of Ruth's unease, as he married again soon after. Ruth and her family retired to Albany, where she died in 1851 at the age of ninety-six.

Meanwhile, young Isaac was having difficulties of his own. He did not get on with his stepmother, and at the age of twelve he left home without resources, friends, or education, possessing only a "strong constitution and a prolific brain." (Brandon, 1977, p. 5). He followed the western migration as far as Rochester, which had become something of a boom town following the opening of the Erie Canal. With a population of more than thirteen thousand, Rochester had, in only eighteen years, acquired all of the attributes of a thriving town, with all of the requisite government, commercial, financial, religious, and cultural institutions. There,

Singer was able to finally attend, albeit fitfully, to a more formal education than he could have received at home. The family seems to have been preoccupied with its own survival, with little time to spend on the education of their youngest son. Survival was the prime motivation of most immigrant families as they made their way farther and farther west in search of fortune. These migrants were not part of the middle class that had preceded them, and in their new home they were valued primarily for fulfilling the increasing demand for unskilled labor.

Isaac Singer stayed in Rochester for seven years, alternately working at whatever came his way and attending the common public schools. He never acquired what might be considered a formal education but became a voracious reader, focused especially on the arts and anything mechanical, developing at an early age a desire to acquire the cultural trappings that characterized the middle class in the early nineteenth century. As he approached the age of nineteen, he realized that in order to earn a consistent living with the promise of improving his station in society, he would have to learn a trade. The private education that the middle class enjoyed was not available to him, so he combined his interest in things mechanical with the traditional educational route for the working classes and apprenticed in a machinist's shop. There, he learned to make and repair the tools and machines that the craftsmen and farmers required for their livelihood. So quick was he at learning the necessary skills that, within four months, convinced that he was as skilled as those who had served a full apprenticeship, he set out on his own. It is also likely that he became bored with the apprenticeship routine and, following the vagabond's impulse that would characterize the rest of his life, moved on to the next opportunity. Even at this early time in his life, Singer displayed an innate inability to establish satisfactory relationships with others, whether they be romantic or economic.

Prior to the nineteenth century, mobility was relatively rare. Most people in Europe lived within a short distance from their place of birth and had to make the most of what opportunities existed there. Theirs was a routine that had been duplicated by scores of generations before them. Young men would undertake to learn one of the traditional crafts, often that practiced by their fathers. The thought of moving in order to find an opportunity to improve one's quality of life never occurred to them. Life was stable, fixed, and unchanging, and they lacked the aspiration to even consider the possibility of a better life. The act of leaving an apprenticeship to learn a trade was a contradiction of the very nature of a craftsman and would have brought disapproval from the community.

In the United States, however, life was different. Those who immigrated there shared many traits in common, both positive and negative. They were risk-takers, willing to sail into the unknown hoping for a better life. They were strivers, disappointed with the lack of opportunity in the "old country" and drawn to America, where everything was open. They often tended to be "loners," prepared to depend only on their own skills and resources for survival, and in many cases they had experienced discrimination based on their religion or ethnicity. They were restless and attracted to the "new." Here, a willingness to strike out on one's own was evidence of adventurousness and self-reliance.

Born in the United States, young Isaac Singer embodied many of the characteristics of the new immigrants, restlessly moving from job to job, easily bored, lacking perseverance, and always drawn to the novel. In fact, Singer's lifelong dream at this early age was to become an actor. If self-reliance and ambition were well regarded by early nineteenth-century society, acting was not and was condemned by the clergy and the community leaders. Permanent theaters were the exception outside of the "Sodom and Gomorrah" of New York City. Acting was discouraged, not to say totally suppressed if possible. Still, the theater had a broad risqué appeal for many, and audience and actors always seemed to find ways to meet. If they could not set up shop permanently, actors would move, and traveling road shows became popular substitutes.

Outwardly, Singer appeared made for the theater. He was good-looking, over six feet tall, big and blond with considerable charm and magnetism—not to say salesmanship. However, in Rochester, Singer was regarded as an uneducated young mechanic from the sticks at a time when a successful actor had great cultural awareness and was able to recite almost endless passages from Shakespeare. Convinced of his acting ability, Singer auditioned for an itinerant theater troupe visiting Rochester. He was asked to recite a few lines of Shakespeare, and after performing a few lines from *Richard III* he was invited to join the company for its stay in the city. His performances were greeted with loud and enthusiastic applause, primarily from the many friends he had invited, and on the strength of this he joined the company on its tour.

Singer's reception in towns other than Rochester, where he was unable to "pack" the audience, was decidedly less rousing. By now it had become part of his nature to always seek the center of attention, shouting when a normal speaking voice would have sufficed and preceding every point he wished to make with a swear word. His acting mirrored his behavior outside the theater. His performances were characterized as "crude and bombastical," and he was dismissed from the company in Auburn due to a "lack of suitable parts" for him. He would later boast of his theatrical achievements as "one of the best Richard's of the day" (Brandon, 1977). This pattern of alternating between jobs in any way related to the theater followed by the need to make a living as a mechanic was to continue for another decade and a half.

While still in Rochester, Singer met and married the fifteen-year-old Catherine Maria Haley. Notwithstanding his limited success as an actor, Catherine probably saw him as a glamorous and physically attractive young man who had just landed the lead with a touring theater group. In retrospect, the wedding was a curious step for Isaac. He was apparently completely uninterested in the ceremony itself, and it soon became apparent that Singer's notion of fidelity was in no way related to the institution of marriage, but rather an intense need to have a physical relationship with virtually every pretty woman he encountered, married or not. In Catherine's case he likely could have bedded her without the necessity of a legal complication. In relationships, Singer was becoming used to having whatever he wanted, a personality trait that was to prove equally strong in his business relationships. Although they later separated, Catherine would remain his wife for thirty years until she finally divorced him in 1860.

For a while, the couple stayed with the Haleys in Rochester and then moved to a house of their own. Taking whatever opportunity came along, Singer worked just enough to feed and clothe his family until either the work came to bore him or another acting opportunity appeared. In 1834 they moved to Port Gibson, where their first son, William, was born. Here, the family would remain while Singer was seldom at home, continuing his quest for an acting career. He would take whatever job a troupe could offer in order to be connected with the theater, always in search of recognition.

Singer's romantic success with women, despite the way he treated them, was a mystery. It was obvious to all that his interest was primarily, not to say exclusively, physical. His behavior was openly crude by the standards of the day and would continually embarrass his friends and business associates. The opinions of others had no effect on Singer. For the most part, the ladies he became involved with, even to the point of having his children, had the choice between his chosen lifestyle and nothing. He would maintain affection for all of them and their children, supporting them for his entire life.

In 1835 or 1836, the family moved to New York City. Singer found work for a short time in a press shop, but in 1836 he once again left his job and family to act as an advance man for another acting company. The tour took them to Baltimore, where Singer noticed a beautiful young girl in the audience. Eighteen-year-old Mary Ann Sponsler was the daughter of the prosperous owner of an oyster-packing company. He visited her and eventually stayed with the family. Apparently they thought that Singer was an attractive, bright, and ambitious catch, and by the end of his stay they were engaged. Singer overlooked the fact that he already had a wife and family in New York.

He promised Mary Ann that they would be married in the fall and hurried back to Catherine, doubtless considering how he was to arrange an increasingly complicated life. While considering his available choices, he made Catherine pregnant again and their second child, a daughter, Lillian, was born in 1837. Despite the new child, their relationship grew increasingly quarrelsome and they separated. Singer waited for Mary Ann's arrival in New York while Catherine returned to her parents in Palmyra. In due course, Mary Ann arrived alone, and without giving a reason to defer the actual marriage ceremony, Singer invited her to live with him. Following an additional wedding delay, he admitted, not that he was married, but that he had a child by another woman who was claiming to be his wife. He said that they had separated and neither had the desire to ever see the other again, asking Mary Ann to come live with him as man and wife until he could find a satisfactory legal solution to his predicament.

Singer had presented Mary Ann with a fait accompli. She had left home with the announced intent to become Mrs. Isaac Singer. In Victorian society she could hardly return home and announce that there was a problem. She was obliged to continue the charade, and they returned triumphantly to Baltimore as man and wife. In July 1837, their first child, Isaac Augustus Singer, was born (Brandon, 1977). The seven-year difference in their ages does not seem great by today's standards. However, by Victorian standards, the cultural differences were significant. He called her by her first name while she addressed him as "father" at home and "Mr. Singer" in public. No sooner was Augustus born than Singer headed once again for the road, treating Mary Ann much as he had treated Catherine before her. Mary Ann, however, would have none of it, and she returned to Baltimore, saying that her husband had deserted her.

There is little information about how Singer spent the next two years. In all likelihood, he returned to his habitual pattern of seeking acting jobs and, when none were available, earning a subsistence living at whatever was available at the time. The next time we encounter him, in 1839, he is working as a laborer in Chicago, where his brother was a contractor working on the new Lockport and Illinois Canal. As the West continued to expand, with canals opening seemingly every few months, the demand for unskilled labor increased. The Industrial Revolution had yet to provide the labor-saving technology that could have satisfied that demand, and the enormous labor effort required to dig the canals attracted the new immigrants. In this environment, Singer invented his first labor-saving device, a machine for drilling rock, using the ancient Chinese method of rope-drilling artesian wells. It "operated…by a crank, and its appendages, in such a manner, that the drill is raised the same height at each successive stroke, without altering, or setting, any part of the machinery, from the commencement of its hole to its termination, other than removing the drill, for the purpose of clearing the hole" (Brandon, 1977). The machine was driven by horses, walking in a circle to turn the crank. The inventor claimed that the drill bit was such that "the hole will be round, and true...avoiding those three-cornered holes usually made with a flat drill." Historians have called this the forerunner of the rotary drill press. Singer patented the machine in 1839 and was able to sell the patent for the considerable sum of $2,000 ($43,000 in 2014 dollars), the most money he had ever had in his life (Brandon, 1977; Clark, 1982). This concrete evidence of his ability to aspire to greater things with other inventions was to become his motivation for life. He would be driven by two overwhelming desires, notoriety and the accumulation of wealth.

Despite, or perhaps because of, the financial success of his first invention, Singer returned again to his dream of becoming a famous actor. With his new-found wealth he formed his own acting troupe, the Merritt Players of Chicago. By now, Mary Ann had returned and she would stay with him for a total of thirty years, during which time she would bear him ten children. The group produced Shakespearean stage plays for five years, when their popularity ebbed and they found themselves once again penniless in Fredericksburg, Ohio. While there, Singer invented his next machine, a device for carving wood-block type, and in 1849, Singer moved to New York, desperately in need of both the funds and space necessary to pursue a patent for his wood-carving machine.

Edward Cabot Clark, the Accidental Venture Capitalist

Edward Cabot Clark, 1850[2]

There is very little written history of the Clark family prior to Edward Clark's becoming famous as Isaac Singer's partner. The following section is derived from a late nineteenth-century genealogy produced by one of Clark's descendants.

Samuel Clark came to Wethersfield (CT) in 1636; "one of a company of restless and dissatisfied men" who forsook the colony; and was one of twenty men who bound themselves May 16th, 1640, to establish a home for themselves at Rippowams, now Stamford, CT. Samuel Clark born perhaps, about 1619, in Devonshire, came with company from Wethersfield. Four generations later, we find Nathan Clark, born in Cornwall, Orange Co., N.Y in 1787. Nathan married Julia Nichols, who was born in Waterbury, CT., July 8th, 1793, and died in Athens.... Mr. Clark was among the earliest residents of that village, and led nearly all of its important enterprises. He… "….established the Athens Pottery Works, which has gained a national reputation for its wares…." (Clark, 1982)

Nathan and Julia Clark had but three children: Edward, Nathan Henry, and Nathan. Nathan Henry died before his first birthday. Nathan was a senior warden in the Episcopal Church and well-respected in the community. He would live for most of his son, Edward's life. In 1880, at the age of ninety-two, he predeceased his eldest son by two years. He was described in his obituary as "one of the sturdy, active but modest men who make their mark in American life without creating excitement." The Athens Pottery Works was, indeed, highly successful. In a precursor to Edward's eventual market strategy with Singer, Nathan virtually monopolized the sale of pottery in upper New York State, and then established branches farther west to increase the size of his market. He helped build the local church and was well-known for his generous giving to charity and inspired in his descendants an acute consciousness of the needs of the community.

Edward had his own tutor before going to a local academy to learn Latin. The academy was run by E. King, Esq., one of the first alumni of Williams College, which Edward would later attend. At the age of twelve, he began four years at the Academy in Lenox, Massachusetts, continuing his study of Latin as well as Greek. He was a voracious reader and devoured every one of the five hundred books in the school library. However, he found life away from his parents so difficult that he left school and went home, only to be returned by his father the next day. Nonetheless, Edward was transformed during those years in Lenox. He became more outgoing, endured the toughness of the teachers, and developed physically from being slight and delicate, almost sickly of constitution, to a strong and well-trained athlete.

In the fall of 1826, at the age of fifteen, Edward Clark went to Williams College, graduating in 1831. In the early nineteenth century, one did not attend a school to enter the legal profession, one trained by preparing legal papers at an existing law firm. Edward began his legal training at the firm of Ambrose L. Jordan, in Hudson, New York, and was admitted to practice three years later, setting up his own office in Poughkeepsie. Thus, Edward's early life followed the contours of the emerging upper middle class, resembling the characters created by Henry James, as a predictably secure member of the new establishment.

In 1835, Edward married his former boss's eldest daughter, Caroline, and, in 1837 he returned to Hudson to form a partnership with his father-in-law. In 1838, they moved the firm to New York City, where Ambrose Jordan became the state's attorney general and Jordan & Clark soon became one of the City's most prestigious firms. In 1836, Edward and Caroline Clark had their first child, a son they named Ambrose Jordan Clark. In 1838, their second son, Edward Lorraine

Clark, was born; in 1841, he was followed by a sister, Julia, but she lived for only two months. Their fourth and last child, Edward Corning Clark, was born in 1844.

The Crucible

Sewing has existed for over twenty thousand years. In that time no one has devised a better way for joining two flexible materials than with a needle and thread. Methods such as gluing or heating failed to produce a joint as flexible, durable, or, in the case of clothing, as comfortable as a sewn seam. Although the sewing machine existed as an imperfect device over much of the period of the Industrial Revolution, it did not become a practical household product until the middle of the nineteenth century. Once it became both technically and commercially viable, the household sewing machine altered the lives of women as significantly as did their entry into the workplace following World War II. The daily routine, which until then had been largely devoted to food preparation and the making and mending of garments for the family, was now open to other choices.

The actual creation of the first practical sewing machine was not a single "Eureka" moment, but the result of a series of solutions to seemingly intractable challenges over the better part of a century, each solution necessary for the next. Each "inventor" in this series, building upon the efforts of his predecessors, was convinced that his latest effort was the best. Frustratingly, each new variation lacked one or more of the essential components necessary for a commercially viable product. At the end of this chain of creation were Elias Howe and Isaac Singer, both of whom claimed final authorship. However, Howe lacked the economic understanding of the product's significance, as well as Singer's taste for the jugular. Partnering with Edward Clark, Isaac Singer created the Singer Sewing Machine Company.

The Singer Company was born at the intersection of three epic changes in American culture; the use of new technology from the Industrial Revolution to create technologically sophisticated products for mass markets; the liberation of women, for better or for worse, from the drudgery of the household; and the rise of entrepreneurism, as the accumulation of great wealth would no longer be conditioned by land ownership and inherited fortunes. The Singer Company would prosper in this environment through the creation and sale of America's first mass-produced home appliance using a unique business model, which would remain singularly successful the world over for more than a century. If there was a single element at the source of the Company's success, it was the development of the Singer brand itself. By the end of the nineteenth century, Singer had become synonymous with quality, reliability, and technology. By the middle of the twentieth century, the Singer brand would be instantly recognized in the over 190 countries where it conducted its business.

The Industrial Revolution began in Europe in the mid-eighteenth century and brought the application of power-driven machinery to manufacturing, changing virtually all aspects of the economic and social structures of a country. The same Revolution arrived in America somewhat later in the nineteenth century and was characterized here by the development of unique manufacturing processes that came to be described as the "American System" (Hounsell, 1984). This "Second Industrial Revolution" in America is described as lasting from 1820 to 1870, when in reality it began much earlier. Hand and home production moved to the machine and the factory. Muscle power was replaced by water power and then by steam, and a generation of inventors produced machines such the cotton gin, the sewing machine, the steel plow, and the reaper. Although it would eventually follow the same changes that had occurred in England, the evolution here saw the development of two processes that were uniquely American: interchangeable parts and mass production.

The term *mass production* has become an ingrained part of the American industrial vocabulary. In the first half of the nineteenth century, as England evolved through its Industrial Revolution, manufacturing in the United States was developing along its own distinct lines. So different was the evolution that English engineers visited to observe the new production methods and came to call it the *American System* (Hounsell, 1984) of manufacturing. The development of these unique processes culminated in the early twentieth century with what eventually was called *mass production* (Hounsell, 1984). Some historians identify the *Second Revolution* with a series of important inventions such as the cotton gin and interchangeable parts (Eli Whitney), weapons (Samuel Colt), the reaper (Cyrus McCormick), the sewing machine (Elias Howe and Isaac Singer), the light bulb (Thomas Edison), the telephone (Alexander Bell), and others.

The system originated with the United States Ordnance Department, which recognized the need for interchangeable parts as a prerequisite to the quality and quantity of arms that the young nation would require to assure its own security. The prime movers that brought about the development of machine-made interchangeable parts were the national armory at Springfield, Massachusetts, and the experimental rifle factory at Harper's Ferry, Virginia.

During its early years, the United States was often at risk of being drawn into one of the many conflicts that seemed frequently to erupt in European countries. In North America, the new country was barely free of the British, who were still invading Virginia in 1781. Jefferson had been appointed Ambassador to France in 1875 and his continuing preoccupation with the possibility of another war with England manifested itself in his curiosity about anything military that could assure the probability of victory in any such conflict. He was particularly interested in work being done by the French military to improve both the quality and quantity of its arms production capabilities. He became convinced that the French were on to something, and in 1785 he wrote a letter to John Jay, the then Secretary of State, in which he suggested that the United States pursue a system of interchangeable parts in its arms manufacture.

> An improvement is made here in the construction of the musket which it may be interesting to Congress to know, should they at any time propose to procure any. It consists in the making every part of them so exactly alike that what belongs to any one may be used for every other musket in the magazine. The government here has examined and approved the method, and is establishing a large manufactory for this purpose. As yet the inventor (Honore Blanc) has only completed the lock of the musket on this plan. He will proceed immediately to have the barrel, stock and their parts executed in the same manner. Supposing it might be useful to the U.S., I went to the workman. He presented me with the parts of 50 locks taken to pieces and arranged in compartments. I put several together myself taking pieces at hazard as they came to hand, and they fitted in the most perfect manner. The advantages of this, when arms need repair, are evident. (Hounsell, 1984, p. 26)

Until then muskets, as well as every other mechanical device, were made by hand, with each part handmade by a skilled artisan to fit into a unique end product. When any of the component parts failed, which was often on the battlefield, the entire device had to be returned to the craftsman, who would then fabricate a replacement part. The implications of this method on the volume of inventory that had to be maintained were enormous.

The War Department had established federal armories at Springfield, Massachusetts (1794), and Harper's Ferry, Virginia (1798). The possibility of war led the United States to issue cash-advance contracts for the production of arms. Two vendors, Simeon North and Eli Whitney, expressed interest in the possibility of producing arms and were both awarded the earliest cash-advance contracts. Both Whitney and North had considered mechanizing their arms production facilities. Whitney was the more public advocate of the idea of interchangeability, but North was the more successful, focusing on division of labor as a necessarily successful first step, rather than the development of specialized machinery. Using the logic that if each individual part was manufactured repetitively to fit a single standard of measure, rather than attempting to fashion a set of parts into a finished weapon, then all of the parts so manufactured would be interchangeable. In order to achieve the volumes required in a War Department contract, the parts fabrication could no longer be done manually. North turned to the other principle at the core of the American system of manufacture, the use of special-purpose machinery, and in 1816 devised the first known milling machine. Prior to his invention, the only way to remove metal to achieve a desired shape was by hand with files, with the result that each successive part was slightly different, no matter the skill and effort of the worker. A milling machine removed metal by the use of a hardened steel cutter that passed uniformly over a piece of iron, removing the same amount of metal in the same form as that of the cutting device. Although not yet combined into a system with division of process performed by a succession of machines, each having but a single objective in the process, North had created the elements of mass production.

Eli Whitney, although generally credited as the pioneer of the American system, has less of a claim to that position than Simeon North. Whitney claimed to have invented the cotton gin and incurred enormous debt in efforts to enforce that claim and successfully manufacture it. With the help of another Yale graduate, Whitney won an arms contract with sufficient advance payment to stave off impending bankruptcy, not because of any particular interest in the arms business. While Whitney had proposed that he could manufacture thousands of arms by adapting the methods and machinery he used in the manufacture of the cotton gin, which reduced the labor content by using water power, he neglected to note that he had not yet been able to successfully manufacture that product using machines. In October 1798, ten months after the actual contract began, Whitney received from the treasury a pamphlet describing Honore Blanc's treatise on the subject of interchangeability of parts in arms manufacture. By then, Whitney had used the greater part of his arms contract advance defending his legal claims to the cotton gin, and by the contract fulfillment date he had not delivered a single weapon. His excuse was that he was working on a complicated new manufacturing process that employed both the cost savings of power mechanization and the fabrication of uniform parts. Whitney never did achieve this objective in his own facility, but subcontracted the arms manufacture while he attended to his continuing difficulties with the cotton gin. He finally completed his 1798 contract in 1809. With the advent of the War of 1812, despite Whitney's reputation for wretched quality and poor delivery, he was awarded another contract. By this time he realized that his hoped-for success with the cotton gin was not to be, and he finally began his career as an arms maker. Whitney's pioneering reputation as an innovative arms maker eventually survived, largely because of his entrepreneurial abilities rather than because he understood the implications of combining mechanization with interchangeability.

Within the Ordnance Department, the first steps toward true interchangeability began at the Springfield armory with the development of the Model 1816 Musket. Starting with the creation of a "standard" production model, against which all production would be compared, the engineers soon realized that the standards had to be maintained at the individual part level to realize true interchangeability. The result was an elaborate system of gauges, to measure each part. The master armorer kept a complete set of master gauges and both the foreman and inspector had a set of gauges for the part or parts under his responsibility to be used while the part was being made.

Samuel Colt was to make significant advances in the processes of manufacture. Colt had received a patent for his revolving pistol in 1835 and had, with other investors, formed the Patent Arms Manufacturing Company in Paterson, New Jersey, for the purpose of making revolvers for the government. After several years of small orders and unsatisfactory quality, Colt concluded that it was not possible to obtain the necessary uniformity or accuracy with hand labor, and in 1842 Patent Arms Manufacturing Company ceased operations. In 1847, Colt had a second opportunity to manufacture his revolvers for the U.S. forces in the Mexican War. Determined not to repeat the errors of the past and lacking both the time and financial resources to fulfill the contract on his own, Colt subcontracted the task of making patent pistols with acceptably interchangeable parts to Eli Whitney. Colt would own any special purpose machines that Whitney designed for production of the revolver. In 1848, Colt moved his new machinery and tools to Hartford, Connecticut, where he transformed an empty mill into his own gun factory, which produced both guns and machine tools, to establish two new Colt armories for truly interchangeable parts. Colt's manufacturing system employed all of the features of the "American System" of arms production, and improvements toward the realization of a true mass production system would be in degree, not in kind.

While Colt and others engaged in arms production, tethered to government funding, another industry was about to apply the principles of the "American System" to a commercial marketplace, driven only by the customers' demands and available resources. Prior to 1800, the wooden clock industry had operated in the United States by essentially producing custom-made clocks upon demand. From 1800, the industry began to specialize with companies producing either movements, cabinets, or assembling both. Specialized machines were then developed that enabled much larger production of individual parts. The difference between clockmakers and arms makers was that clockmakers were not working toward parts interchangeability; they were working toward minimum cost. While clockmakers used gauges and other measuring devices, the requirements for precision bore no relationship to that needed for arms manufacture. As clocks became cheaper, demand increased, and the absence of the need for arms-like precision, reduced dramatically the capital required for entry. Connecticut became the center of clock making in the United States, producing thirty-eight thousand clocks a year by 1837. Clock-making thus became the first significant industry to adopt a variation of the "American System" driven entirely by market demand. When demand declined, a new model was introduced, made of brass instead of wood, smaller and more convenient to place in the home, or with a new cabinet whose style could be altered to respond to the fashion of the time—a truly *consumer* product. This emphasis on marketing to drive manufacturing, rather than the reverse, would come to characterize another American industry, that of the sewing machine.

The Invention of the Sewing Machine—Not as Easy as It Looks

Although the impact of the practical sewing machine on society was revolutionary, the creation of a sewing machine for household use was evolutionary. The potential gain in productive time that might be achieved by a mechanical sewing system had been apparent to anyone who had witnessed the daily household routine of women in the seventeenth century. By the time Singer arrived at the end of the development chain, inventors had been working for almost a century trying to find the secret to a practical, affordable working household sewing machine.

The Essentials

There are ten critical features necessary for a successfully functioning household sewing machine:

1. A straight needle with an eye-point

2. A horizontal table

3. An overhanging arm

4. Continuous thread

5. A shuttle for the secondary thread

6. The lock-stitch

7. A pressure foot

8. Continuous synchronous feed

9. Thread or tension controls

10. The ability to sew in either straight or curving lines

1. The Needle—First Version (1755)

No one knows who invented the common needle, a thin shaft with a point at one end and a thread-carrying eye at the other. We know only that it had been used for thousands of years and had been made variously from bone, silver, bronze, or steel.

**Primitive Needle, bronze
Egyptian, 30 BC-AD642[3]**

2. The Horizontal Table;
3. Overhanging Arm; and 4. Continuous Thread (1790)

Thomas Saint[4]

Saint's machine, 1790[5]

The earliest known attempt to create a mechanical device for sewing was made by Thomas Saint, an English cabinetmaker, who was granted a patent for his machine in 1790. The machine produced a chain-stitch using a completely different method than that used by the single- and double-pointed needles. No working model of the machine was ever found.

Although impractical and never commercially developed, Saint's design did incorporate three of the features that would be incorporated in the practical machines of the nineteenth century; a horizontal sewing surface, an overhanging arm carrying a straight perpendicular needle, and thread.

Barthelemy Thimmonier[6]   **Thimmonier's machine[7]**

The earliest evidence of a machine being put into commercial operation was by a French tailor, Barthelemy Thimonnier, who invented a machine that operated much as Saint's did. He received a French patent in 1830, which made a chain-stitch using a barbed or hooked needle and incorporated an overhanging arm. Thimonnier's machine was basically an attempt to mechanize embroidery, but he also saw a more practical application for making clothing. He found financial backing, set up a workshop, and within a year had eighty seamstresses using machines capable of doing one hundred stitches a minute.

In 1841, fearing that the machine would destroy their livelihood, a mob of tailors broke into his shop and destroyed his machines. Thimonnier fled to Paris, where he developed an improved machine and organized the first French sewing machine company. He patented the machine in France in August 1848, and in the United States on September 3, 1850.

5. The Lock-stitch (1832–34)

Walter Hunt[8]

At the same time that Thimonnier was developing his chain-stitch machine in France, an American inventor, Walter Hunt, was working on a completely different kind of sewing machine. Sometime between 1832 and 1834, he invented a machine that also used an eye-pointed needle, but produced a double-threaded lock-stitch, instead of a single-threaded chain-stitch. The disadvantage of the chain-stitch was that if the thread broke, a pull on the end of the thread would cause the entire stitching to come undone. The lock-stitch required two threads, one passing through a loop in the other and locking in the middle of the fabric. In Hunt's machine the second thread was carried on a shuttle working in combination with the needle. Hunt's was the first machine that did not attempt to replicate the motions of the hands in making a stitch. Although in retrospect the lock-stitch was used in virtually all subsequent machines and was clearly a significant development toward a practical home sewing machine, Hunt did not see the significance and sold a half-interest without even trying to patent it.

He gave three reasons for not pursuing the patent: he had other business; the expense of patenting; and the supposed difficulty of introducing them into use, saying it "would have cost two or three thousand dollars to start a business." Hunt's failure to procure a patent would have momentous consequences a few years later.

6. The Intermittent Feed—The Howe Machine (1846)

Elias Howe, Jr.[9]

Interest in the financial potential of a successful machine grew, and efforts to create a new or improve an existing machine multiplied. Between 1820 and 1845, a succession of inventors tried to develop machines. However, none incorporated all of the necessary elements for a practical home sewing machine

Finally, in 1846, Elias Howe Jr., having probably ascertained that Hunt had never patented his machine, added two devices of little consequence that were later abandoned, and received a patent for a sewing machine that...

...used a grooved and curved eye-pointed needle carried by a vibrating arm, with the needle supplied with thread from a spool. Loops of thread from the needle were locked by a thread carried by a shuttle, which was moved through the loop by means of reciprocating drivers. The cloth was suspended in a vertical position impaled on pins, which moved intermittently under the needle by means of a toothed wheel. The length of each stitching operation depended on the length of the baster-plate, and the seams were necessarily straight. When the end of the baster-plate reached the position of the needle, the machine was stopped. The cloth was removed from the baster-plate, which was moved back to its original position. The cloth was moved forward on the pins, and the seam continued. (Cooper, 1968)

The machine was capable of sewing 250 stitches a minute, roughly seven times faster than hand sewing, and before obtaining a patent, Howe set up a display in the Quincy Hall Clothing Manufactury in Boston. While the machine was a demonstrable technical success, there were no orders for it. The objections were much the same as they had been for Thimonnier and Hunt, that the machine would put individual tailors out of work. While Howe has been generally credited with the invention of the practical sewing machine, the description of his first machine, above, adds only the intermittent feeding mechanism, while incorporating the previously successful lock-stitch, shuttle, and continuous thread. It abandons the horizontal sewing surface for a vertical one, the overhanging arm and the straight needle for a grooved and curved one. Although Howe never claimed to have invented the eye-pointed needle, the court upheld his claim to control the use of the eye-pointed needle in combination with the shuttle to form a lock-stitch. This judgment was later interpreted to give him control of the eye-pointed needle itself. Although Hunt had made a working machine in 1834 or 1835, it was only in 1853, following the patenting of a machine by Howe, that Hunt belatedly applied for a patent. His application was refused, by reason of an Act of Congress in 1839, which provided that inventors could not pursue a claim of patent priority unless the application was made within two years from the date when the first sale of the invention was made.

Having obtained his patent, Howe spent the next three years trying to interest manufacturers in both the United States and Britain in building his machine. A major inconvenience, however, was that the machine was expensive to build and had to be sold for $300 in lots of thirty or forty to justify their manufacture. Finally, he sold the British patent rights and returned home, without funds. Upon his return, Howe discovered that other inventors had been hard at work, correcting the deficiencies of his machine, and that sewing machines were being manufactured for sale. Howe began a series of patent suits to sustain his rights. His interest was no longer one of manufacturing sewing machines for sale, but rather protecting his royalty rights. His ability to use the threat of litigation to obstruct any subsequent inventor would give rise to the first patent pool, the great Sewing Machine Combination.

Howe's patent model, 1846[10]

7. The Pressure Foot (1849)

Morey & Johnson's machine, 1849[11]

Although the chain-stitch had been in use since Thimonnier, Charles Morey and Joseph B. Johnson were the first to patent it in 1849. Although it was not claimed in the patent description, they also invented the first pressure foot, described as "a bar device for stripping the cloth from the needle. This bar had a slight motion causing a yielding pressure to be exerted on the fabric." Jotham S. Conant improved on the Morey and Johnson patent, which offered a slight modification of the cloth bar and of the method of keeping the cloth taut during the stitching operation. While an improvement, this modification was never used.

8. Continuous Synchronous Feed (1849)

Batchelder's patent model, 1849[12]

A second and more important improvement of the Morey and Johnson patent was issued in 1849 to John Bachelder for the continuous, rather than intermittent feed by means of an endless feed belt.

Although the machine employed a horizontal supporting surface, a vertically reciprocating eye-pointed needle, and a yielding cloth pressure foot, none were claimed in the patent. He never manufactured machines, and in the mid-1850s, he sold the patent to I.M. Singer. It was to become to become one of the most valuable patents of the many that Singer acquired.

9. The Shuttle and Thread Tension (1849)

Also in 1849 Sherburne C. Blodgett and John A. Lerow patented a sewing machine using a completely different principle, the continuously rotating circular shuttle. Rather than reciprocating, as in earlier machines, the shuttle movement was continuous, revolving in a circle. Automatic tension was introduced, restraining the slack thread from interference with the needle. Although the machine was produced commercially, it had one outstanding flaw that could not be corrected. As the shuttle passed around, it put a twist in the thread at each revolution. This caused the thread to constantly break, a condition that could not be corrected without changing the fundamental design of the machine.

Blodgett & Lerow's machine, 1850

Other inventors patented machines that incorporated modifications to existing features, but that still failed to combine all of the features necessary for a practical household sewing machine. In 1850, Allen B. Wilson invented a double-pointed shuttle. In 1851, Grover & Baker obtained a patent for a machine using two needles, one passing through the goods and the other operating beneath the cloth. Although by this time, factories had been built that were producing hundreds of machines and although territorial rights for these machines had been sold, none could produce a machine that would successfully do continuous stitching. These machines were a disappointment to those who purchased them and bankrupted many who sought to manufacture them. At one point, Blodgett told Singer that he was a fool for trying to sell the machines, that the only money to be made was by selling the territorial rights.

10. The Ability to Sew in a Straight or Curving Line (1850)

Isaac Singer[13]

In 1850, Isaac Singer produced a machine that corrected the thread-breaking deficiency of the Blodgett and Lerow machine by means of a reciprocating shuttle, the motion of the needle, the control of the thread, and the engagement of the bobbin. Singer had already acquired the continuous feed patent from Bachelder. Finally, the machine incorporated some of the successful features of the Howe machine for which he would later be sued. This machine was the first to combine all of the elements necessary for a successful commercial sewing machine: It had the ability to sew in either a straight or a curving line. His next task would be to create a company that could make and successfully sell his machines.

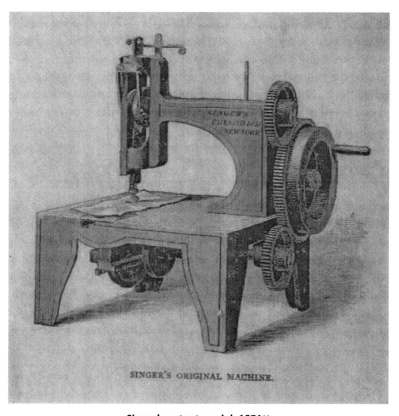

Singer's patent model, 1851[14]

CHAPTER TWO

Creating a Business

As we join Isaac Singer and Edward Clark on their journey, it gradually becomes clear that they, especially Clark, had instinctively considered all of the elements that might today be used to construct a successful business model. Isaac Singer finally had a product, but now he needed a business. Over the next thirty years, he and Edward Clark would create a succession of modifications to their initial business, developing a core model that would dominate the worldwide sewing machine market for the next century. In the early years, Singer would constantly innovate, improving the technical features of their machine to stay one step ahead of the competition, while Clark would add to or modify the basic non-technical features of the original business in such a way as to always maintain a competitive advantage. Other manufacturers would copy, give up, or eventually allow themselves to be acquired by Singer. During the last half of the nineteenth century, over two hundred companies competed in the manufacture of sewing machines in the United States. By 1910, only six remained independent of Singer. Even after the passing of both Singer and Clark, the company's management proved extremely adept at identifying changes in the market or the competition and modifying its business accordingly.

We Need Money—Venture Capital, Nineteenth-century Style

America in the mid-nineteenth century was the land of opportunity. Tinkerers with a particularly inventive bent found new ideas everywhere, particularly in the creation of labor-saving machines. The differing attitudes between Europe and America toward labor-saving devices were striking and long-established. Visitors from the United States were struck by the lack of heat in dwellings, antiquated household equipment, and an absence of labor-saving devices. European companies appeared uninterested in labor-saving machinery to improve productivity. Visitors to America from England were equally struck by the preoccupation with gadgetry and automation. In 1820, the economist Friedrich List noted that:

> Everything new is quickly introduced here, and all the latest inventions. There is no clinging to old ways, the moment an American hears the word 'innovation,' he pricks up his ears. (Brandon, 1977)

In the decade of 1820–1830, patents in the United States averaged 535 annually—almost four times that of Britain, the most advanced industrial nation in the world.

In the new continent, labor was scarce, particularly skilled labor. The prospect of cheap land and high wages led the working man to expect to become his own master within a few years. Americans considered working for someone else to be an unpleasant experience, to be shed as soon as possible. With this kind of business environment, any new machine that held out the prospect of reducing labor effort was welcome. Still, the United States was a relatively small country that was growing faster than the old economies of Europe, and the labor effort required for that growth was coming from machines, not men. The psychology of the new was attractive to the inhabitants of the United States, especially to the recent immigrants who witnessed all of the possibilities around them. The United States was the route away from the old ways of Europe, a route to the creation of new ways of doing things. De Tocqueville described Americans as living in a country where:

> Restlessness of character seems to me to be one of the distinctive traits of these people. The American is devoured by the longing to make his fortune; it is the unique passion of his life; he has…no inveterate habits, no spirit of routine; he is the daily witness of the swiftest changes of fortune, and is less afraid than any other inhabitant of the globe to risk what he has gained in the hope of a better future, for he knows that he can without trouble create new resources again… Everybody here wants to be rich and rise in the world, and there is no one but believes in his power to succeed in that. (Tocqueville, 2000)

The economic potential of the market for a practical sewing machine was obvious to everyone with an inclination for invention. The sewing machine could not fail. Everyone who wore clothes must sew or employ people to sew. In 1850, there were an estimated five thousand shirt sewers in New York City alone. Both employers and employees would welcome a machine that was easy to operate and did boring, laborious tasks better than by hand. The potential savings in time and effort were enormous, as shown by the data prepared by the Wheeler and Wilson Company at the time.

Time necessary to:	By hand	By Machine	Ratio
Make a man's shirt	14 hrs 26 min	1 hr 16 min	11.4:1
Make a frock coat	16 hrs 30 min	2 hrs 30 min	6.6:1
Make a merino wool dress	8 hrs 30 min	1 hr 0 min	8.5:1
Sew a man's hat	15 min	1 min	15:0:1

Practically speaking, the only essential difference between the venture capitalists of the postwar twentieth century and the private equity investors of the mid-nineteenth century was the source of funds. The motivations seem identical. The only skill that most of the early investors lacked was the ability to connect a realizable idea with a potentially significant market. The only unavailable resource in the nineteenth century was the existence of pooled funds looking for a realizable idea. The only source of funding for these inventors was the limited universe of individual investors with both the necessary appreciation of market potential and the discretionary funds. The essential features of a successful new product were its unique ability to fill a perceived need, well known in the case of the sewing machine, and the funding necessary to bring it to market. It had taken a succession of inventors over sixty years to develop and combine the essential features of a practical working household sewing machine. Howe's machine worked, but lacked the final features necessary be successful in the household market: ease of use and reliability. Both Elias Howe and Isaac Singer lacked the financial resources to complete and bring their products to market. Howe lacked the conviction necessary to convince financing sources that he possessed both the creative instinct and the requisite conviction to see the development of his product through the idea stage to a successful and cost-effective manufacturing model. Singer invented the final necessary features but lacked funds.

In 1844, Elias Howe constructed a rough model of his sewing machine out of wood and wire that was sufficient to convince him that his design would work. Aside from the fact that his machine still lacked some of the essential features, Howe had a major problem with manufacturing cost. A good mechanic, with only his ordinary tools, could not construct a sewing machine in less than two months, at a cost of not less than three hundred dollars. The retail price of such a machine would begin to approach, even exceed, the average annual family income.

Forced to return to the question of how to feed and clothe his family, Howe had moved to Cambridge, Massachusetts, and was staying with his father, who had moved there to help his brother develop an invention of his own, a machine for cutting palm leaves in strips to use in the fabrication of hats. Apparently made also of wood, the machine was destroyed in a fire. The move to Cambridge, however, proved fortuitous. An old school friend, George Fisher, happened also to live there. Fisher had just inherited some money, and he was willing to invest in Howe's machine. They set up the machine for demonstration in Quincy Hall, successfully demonstrating the machine's ability to compete with five seamstresses. Notwithstanding this impressive performance, the orders did not flow in. The cost of fabricating his machine by hand was so costly that only professional tailor's shops could possibly be interested, and even they would have to buy at least thirty machines at a cost upwards of three hundred dollars each in order to generate a profit. Howe had developed an industrial sewing machine rather than one for home use, which had to be sold in great quantities for which relatively few prospective customers existed. Despite this disappointment, Howe and Fisher proceeded with the patent application, which was granted in September 1846.

Howe, unwilling to give up, had his brother Amasa Howe cross the Atlantic to search for new funding. In England, Amasa met a William Thomas, a corset manufacturer, who expressed interest in the machine. Thomas had a substantial operation, employing up to five thousand people to manufacture a wide range of corsets and other clothing accessories. Thomas bought the single machine for two hundred fifty pounds, a verbal agreement to the patent rights in England, and the promise to pay Howe a royalty of three pounds for each machine sold. Thomas succeeded in having the machines manufactured and sold locally, taking a royalty of 10 pounds for himself while never making any payments to Howe.

With nothing but the original two hundred fifty pounds from Thomas to show for his efforts, Howe was obliged to abandon the English market until Thomas's patent would expire fourteen years later. Nevertheless Howe and his brother, enticed by an offer of 3 pounds a week, returned to England to work for Thomas on the adaptation of the machine for corset making. Howe worked on the necessary modifications for eight months, after which his usefulness to Thomas was exhausted. Thomas fired him and in April 1849, Howe and his family returned to New York essentially penniless. As if that wasn't enough, his furniture was lost in a wreck off Cape Cod and he never again worked on his sewing machine. When Howe returned from England, he was surprised to find that sewing machines had become very popular and that several companies were making them, apparently ignoring Howe's rights under his patent. While unsuccessful as an entrepreneur, Elias Howe would eventually find success as a litigant, successfully pursuing infractions of his patent and selling the manufacturing rights to others, such as Singer.

In 1849, Singer had arrived in New York, patent in hand, looking for the funds and time required to construct a prototype of his machine, except that this was not the sewing machine; it was the wood-carving machine. There he connected with A.B. Taylor & Co., who agreed to advance him money and provide a room in which he could work on his model. In February 1850, a boiler exploded there, killing sixty-three people and taking Singer's just-completed machine with it. Taylor would no longer advance him any money and the model was lost. In an encounter as serendipitous as Howe's meeting with Fisher, Singer met George B. Zieber, the unsuccessful owner of a book publishing and sales business in Philadelphia, who was interested in getting into a new business. In 1849, prior to the explosion, Zieber had been to see Singer's completed type-carving machine on display at Taylor's. Singer contacted Zieber in the hope that he might finance another model. Zieber convinced two friends, Stringer and Townsend, to lend him $1,700, on the condition that Singer set up a large-scale machine with Zieber in Boston.

In the spring of 1850, the two signed an agreement under which Singer would receive a total of $3,000, $600 upon signing, with the balance to be paid from the proceeds of sales and the exclusive rights for the State of Massachusetts. Singer soon burned through the advance, Zieber loaned him another $50, and the two set off for Boston. In 1850, Boston was one the most important manufacturing centers in the United States. The development of transportation and communications systems, along with extensive "free" water power in New England, served to increase the desirability of Boston as a business center, especially for the traditional manufacture of textiles and shoes. The area had also become a center for the manufacture of automatic machines, which replaced the use of skilled labor in the factories.

Singer and Zieber rented space at the steam-powered machine shop of Orson C. Phelps. They set up their machine there and waited for the customers to come, but there was little interest. Singer and Zieber had both spent all of their time and funds on a product that had no market. It was technologically ingenious, but wood would soon be replaced by metal. In yet another serendipitous encounter, the shop where they had landed was flourishing, engaged in the manufacture of sewing machines for a machine patented in 1849 by J.H. Lerow and S.C. Blodgett. By 1850, a number of sewing machines had been patented, each with a significantly different feature. Howe had actually visited Phelps's shop in 1856, but Phelps was then a journeyman making scientific instruments in a shop school. Howe had asked for help in "getting up a machine" (Brandon, p. 42), but had not disclosed the nature of the machine. Phelps learned later that it was a sewing machine.

By 1850, Phelps was manufacturing the Lerow and Blodgett machine. It was a curiously complicated machine, lacking several of the elements for a successful machine. It had a curved needle, a bowstring-type thread loop with a taut thread when it penetrated the fabric, and a shuttle that moved in a circular motion rather than back and forth. In short, it was clumsy and didn't work, with only eight or nine machines working at first use out of 120 machines produced. Phelps was well aware of the technical shortcomings of the machine and believed that a successful machine could be developed with sufficient ingenuity and capital. Singer and Zieber lacked the capital, but assured Phelps that it was not a problem because Singer had the inventive ability and Zieber had more than sufficient funds to complete the project. Not having been previously involved with either Singer or Zieber, Phelps had no reason not to believe them and tried to interest Singer in improving his sewing machines. Singer assured him that he was not only interested, but convinced that he could correct the deficiencies of the Lerow and Blodgett machine, which was the fact that it had a curved needle and the shuttle moved circularly, rather than back and forth. On the basis of Phelps's interest, Singer went back to Zieber for more money. With serious misgivings, Zieber continued to advance Singer the funds necessary to continue. A contract was drawn up between Singer, Phelps, and Zieber in which it was agreed that Zieber would contribute the forty dollars necessary to complete a working prototype. For that forty dollars, Phelps would fabricate a complete machine and Singer would contribute his inventive genius. Inexplicably, it was further agreed that the patent curiously would be taken out only in the names of Singer and Phelps, while each (to include Zieber) would receive a one-third interest in the ownership of the patent. There being no remaining financial resources, the success of the enterprise was all up to Singer.

As all of the parts had to be handmade and either retooled or completely redesigned after each unsuccessful attempt, the forty dollars was quickly consumed by labor costs. Frustrated by series of failed attempts to produce even stitches without the thread breaking, Singer finally realized that he had failed to readjust the thread tension after each attempt. The successful machine was completed in the night of the eleventh day, and the next day Singer proceeded to New York, where he employed Charles M. Keller to obtain a patent. On November 7, 1850, Singer and Phelps placed an ad in the newspapers announcing:

"SEWING BY MACHINERY"

To "the Journeyman Tailors, Seamstresses,

Employers, and all others interested in

Sewing of any description."

(Brandon, 1977, p. 50)

On the day this advertisement appeared, the *Boston Daily Times* commented:

> At the common prices for plain sewing, one of their machines will net its proprietor five or six dollars a day. Its price complete with all appendages for operation is $125. (Brandon, 1977, p. 51)

In fact, the machine had a significant advantage over the other machines on the market in that it worked successfully in practice. Singer had solved the main problem with the Howe machine, the fact that the fabric was fed through the machine by means of a "baster plate" to which it was attached. Because of its limited size, one could sew only until one reached the end of the plate. Then it had to be brought back, with the result that it was impossible to sew a long continuous seam, to sew curved seams, or to turn corners. Singer's machine did all three. He had finally perfected a machine that incorporated all ten of the elements essential for a working household sewing machine.

When Elias Howe returned from England, he noticed that sewing machines were being manufactured and prominently advertised by several companies. The Lerow and Blodgett machine had been the basis for Singer's machine. A.B Wilson made another, which eventually became the basis for the Wheeler and Wilson Sewing Machine Company. Howe made it his business to inspect these machines and became convinced that they were an infringement on his patent. His primary occupation for the next several years became that of suing patent infringers for royalties. However, he would soon discover that litigation, like invention, could be an expensive proposition. Suits could take years to resolve, and successful patent lawyers didn't work on credit. Searching for a new source of funding, he approached his old friend George Fisher, who, desiring to limit his losses, agreed to sell Howe his half of the patent for what it had cost him. While this did not provide Howe with the funds necessary to aggressively pursue his litigation strategy, it did provide him with a resource with which to approach other sources. George W. Bliss was willing to take the gamble and agreed to advance the money for lawsuits for Fisher's one-half share and a mortgage on Howe's father's farm.

Singer continued to work on his machine, perfecting existing features and seeking new ones. He evolved a packing case that could double as a table and incorporated the treadle instead of the hand crank. In Boston, Singer and Phelps were having violent arguments over who should apply for the patent on the new machine. Singer was absolutely determined that the patent should be his alone, not joint, and Zieber convinced Phelps to submit, rather than risk a continuation of Singer's rage. Phelps was a quiet man, out of his element in dealing with Singer, and he probably conceded just to make the matter go away and maintain the peace. Zieber had by now exhausted his funds in order to pay for the patent and the first two or three machines. Singer had promised the first two machines to a clothing store in New York for $125 each. Having successfully isolated Zieber and Phelps from any possibility of interference in the control of his "invention," Singer immediately took his new machine to New York. His son delivered the machine to Smith and Conant's, a clothing shop where he demonstrated the machine in the window. When a second machine arrived, the son was joined by a young woman, and together they showed how one could do both simple and complicated sewing on the machine.

Singer was still desperately short of funds, having exhausted the resources of both Zieber and Phelps, and this shortage would become very expensive over time. Elias Howe, in his search for litigation opportunities, had heard of Singer's machine and had actually seen it demonstrated in Smith and Conant's window. Howe claimed patent infringement and demanded $2,000 for the exclusive rights to use his patent. Such a right would insure Singer and Zieber a virtual monopoly of the sewing machine business; however, they barely had money to live from day to day, much less the sum that Howe demanded, and so they declined his offer. Desperate, the partners advertised in the *Boston Daily Times* for a partner with $1,000, and they were willing to part with a one-fourth interest for that sum.

Phelps continued to manufacture machines as fast as possible, with several sold and ten or twenty under construction. In late December 1850, Singer returned to Boston to inform Phelps that they must halt production for lack of funds. Singer had led Phelps to believe that Zieber had $80,000, to which Singer replied that it was all in liquid real estate. As orders were finally beginning to come in, Phelps refused to stop making machines. By now, ever more convinced of the eventual success of his machines, Singer had decided that he had one partner too many and that Phelps had to go. On the strength of an order for thirty machines at $100 each from a firm in New Haven, Connecticut, Singer received an advance of $1,200. He gave $200 to Zieber and kept the rest for himself. Puzzled, Zieber and Phelps did not object at the time, since it did not create a problem in manufacturing. Soon thereafter, Singer proposed to Zieber that they buy Phelps out, but Zieber refused. Singer became increasingly argumentative and insulting to Phelps, creating such an unpleasant atmosphere that Zieber eventually agreed in order to simply keep the peace. They proposed to buy Phelps out for $1,000 plus $3,000 to be paid in installments, along with assurance that the shop would be kept busy for at least the duration of the partnership, which was five years. In effect, they offered Phelps a deal precisely suited to his personality, cash and security in return for high risk and profits. The new contract was signed on December 24, 1850, and Phelps was also appointed to be a traveling agent for the firm.

No sooner had Singer engineered the Phelps buyout than he found another investor interested in becoming a partner. Barzillan Ransom, a manufacturer of cloth bags for packaging salt and an early buyer of the machine, bought the one-third interest, despite the fact that Singer's son, Gus, had removed the end of Ransom's finger during a demonstration of the sewing machine. Under the terms, Ransom would pay a total of $10,000, of which $8,000 was to be used in the business and $2,000 would be paid in a series of notes of $250, $750, and $1,000, the first two due in three months and the last in four months (Brandon, 1977, p. 80). By the spring of 1851, Singer had once again concluded that he had an unsatisfactory partner. Ransom had become ill and was of little help in promoting or managing the business, and, more importantly, the promised capital didn't exist. Singer employed the same strategy that had worked so effectively with Phelps, that of creating an extremely hostile environment. Ransom quit in May 1852, receiving forty sewing machines for his interest.

By this time, Singer had concluded that his personal skills did not include legal and financial affairs, and in anticipation of legal problems with Howe, he decided to search for a partner with such skills. In 1851, Singer proposed that Edward Clark be taken into the firm without any payment, receiving an equal share of the business in return for assuming responsibility for managing the legal affairs of the company. Edward C. Clark was the junior partner of the highly reputable law firm of Jordan, Clark, and Company. Ambrose Jordan, the senior partner and Clark's father-in-law, had just been appointed attorney general for the State of New York. Singer could never have afforded the services of such a firm except by bartering a significant ownership position. Although Clark had earlier taken a three-eighths interest in the unprofitable patent rights to Singer's carving machine for the same legal services, perhaps Clark saw a much larger market opportunity in Singer's sewing machine. Singer had finally found his venture capitalist, even if the capital was in the form of a resource that would eventually overcome all of the substantial legal obstacles to his success.

Taking Stock of the New Company

At this point, Isaac Singer brought little to the enterprise other than technology. He was able to recognize the elements necessary for a successful household sewing machine and acquire them, either through his own patents or by purchasing many of the key patents of others. Unable to acquire a critical patent right, he ignored the holder's patent and fabricated a prototype that he could show to prospective customers, exposing himself to substantial litigation risk. Singer had exhausted all of his funding sources, but he had either bartered or bought his way out of his co-ownership obligations. Fortuitously, Singer had met Edward Clark, who, in return for a substantial interest in the company, had agreed to assume the responsibility for dealing with patent litigation. Singer lacked both manufacturing and distribution relationships and he had to rely on subcontracted fabrication by hand and his own sales skills.

The household sewing machine responded to a universal need and, if manufactured and distributed in quantity sufficient to lower its price to an affordable level relative to household income, offered staggering profit potential, as the sewing machine successfully mechanized the labor-intensive act of joining fabric materials for making or mending clothing and other household articles. Singer sought to either create or acquire the technology necessary to provide a sewing machine that was always ahead of the competition.

The initial market was roughly half of the population of the United States, all women who sewed by hand; however, distribution was limited by Singer's financial resources to personal visits, customer by prospective customer, in order to capture the equivalent of the sales commission in a larger organization. Manufacturing, and its profit margin, was contracted to a third party. The sales/customer relationship was directly by the company owner, but it had to be as brief as possible, due to the necessity to generate the necessary sales volume and cash flow.

The cost of manufacture was high as a result of the obligation to subcontract. Singer could not both fabricate and sell. The cost of distribution in its earliest stages was a function of Singer's personal time (sweat equity) and travel expense. Since the product was unique and had almost universal application, it could be priced sufficiently high to leave a considerable contribution over manufacturing cost. However, the resulting high price had the effect of limiting the market to commercial customers or home-sewing customers with substantial personal resources. Clark had by this time minimized the exposure to litigation cost, which would either have driven the price higher or consumed the existing margin. Singer and Clark did not yet have a profitable business model.

Monopoly, the Perfect Business Model: The Patent Wars

It is difficult to imagine two more different personalities than Isaac Merritt Singer and Edward Cabot Clark. Singer was an upstart, brash, crude, and frequently blasphemous. Clark was the patrician head of a very respectable upstate New York family whose origins in the United States dated from the eighteenth century. The Clarks had been settled in Cooperstown for several generations, where Edward

Clark had been a Sunday school teacher. Their talents, on the other hand, were almost perfectly complementary. Singer was an inventive genius, with extensive mechanical ability, wildly optimistic, overconfident, and with boundless drive and energy. Clark was the cool wise-head, deliberately planning and cold-bloodedly assessing the available options before moving ahead. There was never any secret about Singer and Clark not getting on. Given Singer's self-deification, he surely must have regretted having to share his good fortune with anyone, even Clark. However, it was Clark's skill at exploiting the patent that enabled the business to develop as it did.

Zieber had learned of Clark's involvement in a distinctly unfortunate way. He had joined forces with Singer in the hopes of paying off some debts he had incurred in some of his previous business transactions. Now that he and Singer were the sole owners of I.M. Singer & Co., Zieber thought that he would be in a better position to deal with his creditors if he could show them a written agreement attesting to his ownership position. Consequently, in May 1851, he went to Singer's house in search of such a document, only to be greeted by a raging Singer, who told him that, in the absence of a written agreement, he would have no part of Phelps's claimed ownership interest. Shocked, Zieber decided to go see Edward Clark, since it had been Clark who had drawn up the agreement between Singer and Ransom, who was by now deceased. Clark merely confirmed that, in the absence of a written agreement concerning the disposition of Phelps's one-third interest, there was little Zieber could do. Zieber then referred to the original agreement of the three partners in Boston to share equally in any benefits of the future patent obtained by Singer, only to be told that any agreement about a patent before it was issued is not binding in the law.

The patent in question was finally granted on August 12, 1851, and it claimed the three final features necessary for a successful sewing machine, the motion of the shuttle, the control of the thread, and the engagement of the bobbin. The *Scientific American,* in its November issue, concluded that "This machine does good work" (Brandon, 1977, p. 85). Now that the patent had been issued, the rights were legally assignable and were divided equally between Singer and Clark. They presented Zieber with a paper, drawn up by Clark, in which they agreed to give Zieber one-third of the profits in return for his full attention to the business. In December 1851, Zieber was taken ill and confined to bed. By this time, the profits of the business were approximately $25,000. Clark visited Zieber, followed by Singer the next day, who noted that, in the doctor's opinion, Zieber would be unable to continue in the business, and offered to buy out his interest. Concerned about the friends from whom he had borrowed money, Zieber agreed to a price of $6,000 ($168,000 in 2014 dollars). Clark drew up the agreement and Singer brought it back, where Zieber signed it. As it turned out,

Zieber recovered his health and later learned that Singer did not actually know Zieber's doctor, who had apparently made no observation about the outlook for his long-term health.

In early 1852, Howe once again appeared at Singer's to demand settlement of his patent claims. This time, he increased his demand from $2,000 to $25,000 ($700,000 in 2014 dollars), and once again Singer refused him. Whether Singer had felt emboldened by his new partner's presence or whether both Singer and Clark seriously underestimated Howe, their refusal to deal with him would eventually cost far more than even his second demand. Clark's assessment of Howe was that he was pretty much of a gadfly, suing everyone in sight who was making sewing machines, and if they ignored him he would go away. Apparently the others in the industry didn't consider Howe to be a gadfly and, by 1853, four of the five largest manufacturers (excluding Singer) had come to terms with Howe and were operating under his license.

Howe continued to pursue I.M. Singer & Co., using the strength of his other agreements to threaten litigation, a threat that consumed significant amounts of Clark's attention. For the next three years, the resources devoted to battling both Howe and the other manufacturers consumed virtually all of the firm's profits and severely hindered the company's ability to compete. The battle soon attracted an interested public, accustomed to the sensational journalism of that period's tabloids, creating a second front to the war being waged in the courts. Advertisements were taken out by both sides, with the sole intent of diminishing the reputation of the adversary. On July 29, 1853, Howe advertised:

> The Sewing Machine—It has been recently decided by the United States Court that Elias Howe, Jr., of No. 305 Broadway was the originator of the Sewing Machines now extensively used. Call at this office and see forty of them in constant use upon cloth, leather, etc., and judge for yourselves as to their practicability. Also, see a certified copy, from the records of the United States Court, of the injunction against Singer's machine (so called) which is conclusive. He has a suit now pending against the two-needle machines, so called, and is about commencing suit against all others offered to the public except those licensed under his patent. You that want sewing machines, be cautious how you purchase them of others than him or those licensed under him, else the law will compel you to pay twice over. (Brandon, 1977, p. 90)

Not to be outdone, Singer carried his version of events on the very next day:

> Sewing Machines—For the last two years Elias Howe, Jr., of Massachusetts, has been threatening suits and injunctions against all the world who make,

use or sell Sewing Machines—claiming himself to be the original inventor thereof. We have sold many machines—are selling them rapidly, and have good right to sell them. The public do not acknowledge Mr. Howe's pretensions, and for the best of reasons. 1. Machines made according to Mr. Howe's patent are of no practical use. He tried several years without being able to introduce one. 2. It is notorious, especially in New York, that Howe was not the inventor of the machine combining the needle and shuttle, and that his claim to that is not valid.... Finally—We make and sell the best SEWING MACHINES—and the only good ones in use; and so far from being under injunction, we are ready to sell and have the perfect right to sell our Straight Needle, Perpendicular Action Sewing Machines—secured by two patents in the United States—at the very low price of $100, at our offices in New York, Boston, Philadelphia, Baltimore and Cincinnati. (Brandon, 1977)

Howe thundered back:

Caution. "ALL PERSONS ARE CAUTIONED against publishing the libelous advertisements of I.M. Singer && Co. against me as they will be prosecuted to the fullest extent of the law for such publications. I have this day commenced action for libel against the publishers of the said Singer & Co.'s infamous libel upon me in this morning's *Tribune.*" (Brandon, 1977)

Singer and Clark might have seen themselves as defending the battle for inventors against those who would steal the fruits of their inventions without just compensation. On the other hand, they might in turn be viewed as opportunists, as they were professing an opinion unsupported by a judgment while Howe had an actual court opinion. As we have seen, there are ten essential ingredients for a practical, working sewing machine and while Singer could lay credible claim to the last three, it was also true that a machine could not work without at least three of Howe's features. Singer and Howe found themselves between a rock and a hard place. The sewing machine was an aggregation of the fruits of nearly a century of inventors. If they could prove that the sewing machine had been invented prior to Howe's patent, that patent would logically be as much of an infringement by Howe as Howe claimed by Singer. Searching through the complex history of the sewing machine, Singer and Clark came across the efforts of an inventor we have already discovered, Walter Hunt and his 1834 machine. Hunt had produced a workable, if imperfect, machine that incorporated a lock-stitch, formed by using a shuttle. If proven, the Hunt machine would predate Howe's by twelve years and negate Howe's infringement claim. The problem was to find Hunt and one of his machines and demonstrate that it worked.

Hunt was still alive and in business, but he had no records and an imperfect memory of his machine. He had the pure imagination of an inventor, who worked for the discovery, not the profitability of his invention. Once invented, he had no further interest in the machine and he had no idea where one might be found. Hunt had sold a half-interest in his machine to George Arrowsmith, but apparently no one had gotten around to patenting it. After searching at Arrowsmith's shop, they found a few pieces that Hunt declared were the remains of his original model, but he was unable to reconstruct a working machine from the parts. Notwithstanding the absence of a working machine, his lawyers convinced Hunt to make a belated application for a patent, and he announced his intent on September 19, 1843, in the *New York Tribune*:

> TO THE PUBLIC—I perceive that Elias Howe, Jr.., is advertising himself as the patentee of the Original Sewing Machine, and claiming that all who use machines having a needle or needles with an eye near the point, are responsible to him. These statements I contradict…. Howe was not the original and first inventor of the machine on which he obtained his patent. He did not invent the needle with the eye near the point. He was not the original inventor of the combination of the eye-pointed needle and the shuttle, making the interlocked stitch with two threads, now in common use. These things, which form the basis of all Sewing Machines, were first invented by me, and were combined in good operative Sewing Machines which were used and extensively exhibited, both in New York and Baltimore, more than ten years before Howe's patent was granted …I have taken measures as soon as adverse circumstances could permit, to enforce my rights by applying for a patent for my original invention. I am by law entitled to it, and in due course no doubt will get it. (Brandon, 1977)

While no one actively opposed Hunt's claim to having invented the machine, there was strong opposition, particularly in the *Scientific American,* to the notion that, having neglected to pursue a patent for that invention, the inventor could come forward and apply for a patent ten years after the fact, in effect voiding an existing patent by another inventor. It was nimble-footed lawyership, but it seemed a bit beyond the pale. Nevertheless the case of *Hunt vs. Howe* eventually went to trial on May 24, 1854. The then commissioner of the Patent Office had the same problem with excessively belated patent applications as had the *Scientific American*, noting that an inventor's failure to bring his invention to useful activity during a period of eighteen years, resurrecting it only after another has made it practically useful, should be decided in favor of the inventor who gave the invention a useful life. Encouraged by the testimony, Howe brought suit to refrain two firms in Boston from selling Singer machines, and on July1 the judge confirmed that "The plaintiff's patent is valid" (Brandon, 1977, p. 95).

Singer was ordered to pay Howe $15,000, and Howe threatened to sue Singer in both New York and New Jersey. With little possibility of success, Singer negotiated a settlement with Howe, under which he agreed to manufacture under license from Howe and pay a twenty-five-dollar royalty on each machine sold. Howe's income from his machine increased from a few hundred dollars a year to over $200,000. In 1860, he applied for an extension of his patent, and when it expired in 1867, his total earnings were nearly $2,000,000 ($33 million in 2014 dollars). No sooner was the Howe case settled than the remaining manufacturers began to sue each other, in the belief (and fact) that the sewing machine had evolved over almost a century and that no single inventor could claim to have produced an entire working household sewing machine. Every sewing machine then manufactured had to confront the fact that a complete working sewing machine was the never the product of the efforts of a single unaided person. Recognizing this, by 1856 I.M. Singer & Co. had acquired the rights to twenty-five different patents and the original inventions of nine different inventors. Perhaps thirty of these patents were valuable, considering the fact that by 1867, almost nine hundred patents had been issued for improvements in the sewing machine. For the most part, these patents were valueless, made in the early years of the machine. Only ten or so had real value and were made during the machine's early introduction.

The judge's decision had effectively given Howe control of the entire sewing machine market. No one could manufacture without taking out a license from Howe. On the other hand, the landslide of patented improvements precluded Howe from manufacturing on his own without infringement of a subsequent patent. There was no useful device connected to the basic machine that did not have a patent claimed by more than one person. The circular nature of the enormous number of litigations that followed the Howe decision drained everyone's profits. It eventually became obvious that it was in no one's interest to continue the circle of litigation, except that of Elias Howe, who continued to collect twenty-five dollars for every machine sold by one of his licensees. An exception to this point of view was Orlando B. Potter, president of the Grover and Baker Company. Although not obvious to anyone else in the industry, Potter had the blindingly obvious idea that, rather than engage in endless legal battles between themselves, why should the major players in the industry not join forces by pooling their patents? Anyone able to afford the costs of establishing a facility capable of producing extremely complicated pieces of machinery without major legal challenge, would be better disposed to cooperate on their respective patent rights. The core idea was simple. All of the interested parties would pool the patents they held. For a fee of fifteen dollars per machine, they agreed to license any machine of the sewing machine combination to use any of the devices patented by them. Part of the pooled fees would be reserved for litigation with Howe, and the rest would be divided equally among the members of the pool. The only problem with the combination was Elias Howe. The agreement could only work if he could be persuaded to join it. Since he already received a substantial income from his royalty agreements, Howe had little incentive to join the agreement. In the end, he agreed to join, on the condition that he receive five dollars for every machine sold in the United States and one dollar for every machine exported and that the other then-existent sewing machine manufacturers be a part of the agreement in order to prevent the formation of a monopoly. Perhaps inadvertently, Howe was the first to recognize the dangers inherent in such pools, the ability to kill off competition before it could thrive and to dictate the terms of trade in the industry. In addition, Orlando Potter had created a new industry for lawyers, which would eventually give rise to the Anti-Trust Division of the United States Department of Justice. The formal organization was known as the Sewing Machine Trust and/or the Sewing Machine Combination. The important patents contributed to it were (Cooper p. 41):

1.   For a fee of $5 on every machine sold domestically and $1 for every machine exported, Elias Howe contributed his 1846 patent on the grooved, eye-pointed needle used with a shuttle to form the lock-stitch;

2.   Allen B. Wilson, through the Wheeler and Wilson Manufacturing Company, contributed his 1854 patent on the four-motion feeding mechanism;

3.   I.M. Singer & Co., the Singer/Clark partnership, contributed a number of patents, including those that Singer had acquired from others, such as the needle moving vertically above a horizontal work-plate (Bachelder patent), a continuous feeding device by belt or wheel (Bachelder patent), a yielding presser resting on the cloth (Bachelder patent), the spring or curved arm to hold the cloth by a yielding pressure (Morey and Johnson patent), and a most important monopoly patent that Singer had developed himself, the heart-shaped cam as applied to moving the needle bar (1851); all these patents held by the Singer Company.

4.   Finally, the Grover and Baker Sewing Machine Company contributed some of its patents, but its most valuable contribution was that its president, Orlando Potter, was the chief architect of the pool.

While there were twenty-four companies participating in the Combination, only four players held the most important patents: Howe, Wheeler & Wilson, Grover & Baker, and Singer. The consent of all four parties was required before any license could be granted. All manufacturers, even the Combination members, were required to have a license, and all were required to pay a fee of $15 per machine. Howe would receive his fee, now $5 per machine, and a small reserve was established for Combination expenses, primarily litigation. The balance was divided between the other Combination members. The advantage for other manufacturers was that they only had to pay one license fee for all of the necessary patents, rather than one for each patent. The advantages for the members of the Combination were significant. First, the amount of the fee was a significant component of the cost of production for non-members, as the members were, in effect, paying the fee to themselves. As production costs continued to be reduced with the introduction of machine tools, the relative burden of the fee increased. Second, any member of the Combination could deny a license to any applicant, particularly one who might represent serious competition in terms of product, distribution, or both.

Through this system of licensing fees, the Sewing Machine Combination created an effective monopoly of an industry that, hindered by the costs and energy devoted to litigation, had not yet been able to develop a product that satisfied the market need. Horace Greeley, in the *New York Daily Tribune*, noted that:

> The principal sale of sewing machines is to the poor needle-women, widows and orphans, those who by toiling day and night barely gain the bread for starving relatives and themselves. From each of these poor needle-women has this patentee drawn no less than five dollars; but more, and more still, the cost of making these machines may be set down as varying between five and twenty-five dollars. The *cheapest* sold by the parties to this most odious monopoly is *fifty* dollars. (Brandon, 1977)

In modern terms, the Sewing Machine Combination was acting in restraint of trade, but the Sherman Anti-Trust Act was not passed until 1890. Looking back, the impact on the composition of the sewing market was clear. The Sewing Machine Combination of 1857 created serious barriers of entry for anyone considering the manufacture of sewing machines. The three largest companies were assured of the dominant position in a market that was just beginning to grow and that they all believed had enormous potential. The fourth member, Howe, was less interested in manufacturing machines himself than in receiving his royalties. He was to collect approximately $2,000,000 of royalties over the life of the Combination.

While the Sewing Machine Combination wasn't in the strictest sense a monopoly of Singer, as it involved more than a single company, it was certainly an effective cartel that controlled the marketplace. Until the pool expired completely in 1877, the members had little incentive to reduce prices, as the licensing fees and ability to control market entry assured the three producing members very attractive margins on their machines. The retail prices charged by the members attracted increasing criticism in the press. They were accused of "suppression of competition, intimidation of competitors its threats of litigation, the prevention of the entry of new companies into the industry, and the general 'avaricious' behavior of the member firms." It was public knowledge that the cartel members were selling their machines in Europe at one-half the American price. In effect, although the price in the United States had dropped to approximately $65, the cost to manufacture was now less than $12 per machine. Singer would receive a total of $1,449,983 over the seven-year period ending in 1874 (Davies, 1976, p. 56). When the last of Singer's patents expired in 1877 (the 1850 Bachelder patent), Singer immediately dropped its prices to $30 for cash purchase ($40 for credit) and was still able to earn a $16 profit on each machine sold (Davies, 1976).

The success of the cartel's control of the market was evident when the last of the pool's patents expired in 1877. Competing companies were now free to enter the market and the market growth accelerated, with prices falling on average by 50 percent in the months that followed.

In moving to the monopoly model, Singer could enjoy the relative calm of technological product parity and exclusivity, while preparing for more active management in the development of its distribution channels and marketing innovations improvements. The only significant changes were in its core capabilities and partner network. The Patent Pools had the effect of eliminating competition from anyone other than the members of the Pool and limiting competition within the Pool to the existing technology. Edward Clark moved from being a legal advisor to an active general manager of the company, with Singer focusing exclusively on technology and sales.

The Critical Choice—Innovation versus Engineering

The end of the Patent Wars in 1857 meant that companies could now turn their attention toward sales of machines. Until then, manufacturers entered the market tentatively, if at all, because of the cost of participating in the patent wars. The environment of litigation and cross-litigation consumed large proportions of a company's resources. Despite the fact that a workable sewing machine, the first widely available consumer appliance, had finally been invented, the sewing machine had very a limited market. Within that market, the Singer machine was neither the best known nor the biggest seller. Wheeler and Wilson Manufacturing Company's machine was the most successful, and by 1856 it had become synonymous with the sewing machine. In 1852, the three largest manufacturers produced a total of only 3,198 machines. By 1858, that total had reached only 16,639 machines (Wheeler and Wilson made 7,978; Grover and Baker, 5,070; and I.M. Singer & Co., 3,591).

The commercial viability of a sewing machine for household use depended on the manufacturer's ability to overcome two fundamental obstacles; the weight of the machine and its cost of manufacture. Although Singer was the first to combine all of the elements of a successful sewing machine, it was not yet a practical machine for household use. First, the initial cost of producing Singer's machine was between $100 and $150, and we have seen that Howe's minimum profitable price was $300. The average annual income at the time was approximately $500. The purchase of a sewing machine for household use was roughly the equivalent to buying an automobile today. Second, these machines were made of cast iron for strength. The fifty-five-pound weight of the sewing machine, plus its cabinet and the foot treadle, meant that it took considerable effort just to transport it to the household, much less move it around once it was delivered. In the early years, Wheeler and Wilson enjoyed a considerable advantage in both machine weight and cost. The Wilson patents (granted in 1850, 1851, and 1852) for the rotary hook, a stationary circular bobbin, and the four-motion feed combined to produce a small and lightweight machine, weighing only six and one-half pounds. The relatively simpler and lighter design of the machine enabled the company to offer it to the public for $125, expensive for the average family but roughly the equivalent cost to manufacture the Singer machine. At this point, both companies were essentially offering machines for industrial use, Wheeler and Wilson for light fabrics and Singer for more general use (Davies, 1976).

The machines were large and heavy because they were designed to be sold primarily to commercial garment makers, not households. The high cost of manufacture made it virtually impossible to reduce retail prices as a marketing strategy to increase the size of the total market. The companies were caught in the dilemma of needing volume in order to reduce production costs, but they were unable to reduce prices in order to create that volume. Despite these constraints, the demand for sewing machines grew dramatically in 1859, with combined production of the three largest companies increasing by two and a half times, to 41,624 (Wheeler and Wilson made 21,306; Grover and Baker, 10,280; and I.M. Singer & Co., 10,953) (DePew, New York, p. 530). This growth had undoubtedly been helped by Singer's introduction of a machine specifically designed for household use.

The opportunity to reduce unit cost by using new manufacturing techniques had begun to arrive as part of the Industrial Revolution. The use of machine tools could reduce the amount of hand work necessary to manufacture workable machines. With the patent pool, two companies, Wheeler & Wilson and Willcox & Gibbs, chose to expand their manufacturing capacity using these new techniques in an effort to reduce their manufacturing costs and increase their share of a market that was beginning to grow rapidly. Singer chose another route, that of cultivating the consumer and expanding the overall market using innovative sales and marketing tools.

With the creation of the Sewing Machine Combination, Edward Clark could finally turn his attention to the sewing machine business. Burdened by lack of financial resources and a costly product to manufacture, Clark had to create non-cash ways of expanding the business. Singer was the inventive genius, with minimal interest in the business side (apart from his own income). Clark, although a lawyer, turned out to be an extremely innovative marketing executive, developing completely novel retail tools to expand the market.

Installment Selling

The financial barrier to sales was extreme, given that the price of $125 represented approximately 25 percent of the average annual family income. As the sewing machine was the first complex domestic appliance, the magnitude of the decision to purchase one was new to both manufacturer and customer alike. The typical household was more used to articles that could be made at home, such as linens and wooden implements, or articles that could be purchased inexpensively from a local shop or peddler, such as pots and pans. Mass production had not yet arrived, and complex articles, such as guns, were handmade and only acquired as a result of a perceived necessity. The price barrier for sewing machines limited the target market largely to professionals, who might employ dozens of seamstresses in a garment-making enterprise.

Clark reasoned that if a family could not afford to buy a machine at much more than a tenth of the current price, then he might be able to sell at that price, provided he sold ten times as many machines. The only financial limitation would be the cost of producing the first ten machines. Consequently, he devised a system of sales that required only a minimum of five dollars down, with the balance to be paid in monthly installments of three to five dollars. The payments would include interest, and the customer was encouraged to make a larger down payment, if possible. Agents were paid a commission to visit the customer each month in order to collect the payments, along with the opportunity to sell something else that the customer might need.

The system was dubbed the "hire-purchase plan," "hire" being the term at the time for renting. The system was an instant success and was copied by virtually all of the manufacturers. Installment sales of sewing machines remained a primary revenue and profit source for Singer throughout the nineteenth and twentieth centuries. Over time, the term "hire/purchase" was changed to "installment sales" or "credit sales" in most countries except Great Britain, where it is still used today. Anecdotally, the term was often derided (humorously) by the management of non-British countries as the "Higher Purchase" program.

Installment purchases had great appeal, as the sewing machine was viewed as a major labor-saving device, particularly in poorer families in which the woman's time could be completely consumed by the making and repair of garments for the family.

The Song of the Shirt[15]

For many purchases, however, it was easy to overestimate the ease of making their monthly payments when their family income was so small, and it was precisely these families who often fell behind in their payments and whose machines were repossessed. The sales agents could hardly send such machines back to Singer, and advertisements began to appear offering the used machines for sale. Agents developed a reputation for aggressiveness and egregious repossession cases, in which women who owed only one or two final payments, only to lose the machine, were often the subject of outraged opinion pieces in the journals.

Direct or Indirect Sales Organization?

Due to its shortness of working capital, Singer could not afford a large network of company agents with inventory. The solution that the company adopted was to create exclusive sales territories to be sold to aspiring entrepreneurs. The rights holders would purchase machines at a discount, resell them at the retail price, and profit from the difference. If the rights holder was aggressive, he could make a more than respectable income for himself. As the company was to later discover, the most effective tool for the sale of a sewing machine was the individual demonstration, but the agent couldn't demonstrate a machine he didn't have. By insisting that agents actually purchase the machines before they were sold, Singer deprived the sales reps of their most effective tool and the company faced the choice of either providing consignment inventory at little or no cost, or forgoing the sales that such inventory might produce. The inventory relationship was further aggravated by the fact that the limitations on production for inventory created long delays between the individual sale and actual delivery of the machine. Finally, the obligation to acquire the necessary inventory had the result of depressing the price that the company could expect to receive for the territories.

The discount structure necessary to motivate these dealers virtually precluded Singer from making a profit. With the retail price of $125, one might estimate the manufacturing cost to be on the order of $50 to $60. Dealers were initially sold the machine for $60, later raised to $70, barely enough to cover production costs, let alone the company's overhead and investments necessary to improve or expand manufacturing facilities. No sooner had the company begun selling exclusive sales territories than Clark realized that they had, in effect, turned over the fortunes of the company to individuals who were beyond their control. The sales approach, selling price, and individual sales effort devoted to the product were now in the hands of non-employees. Any development within a territory was contractually limited. His only alternative was to buy back the territories.

Thus, in 1856 the company began the process of repurchasing sales territories and creating a network of commissioned sales agents with non-exclusive territories. The process of choosing a sales agent was delicate. He (they were virtually always male) must know his territory intimately. He must have a complete familiarity with the sewing machine, both inside and out, in order to be able to demonstrate it with confidence and repair it with relative ease. It was crucial that the agent be loyal to the company, as it was not unusual for agents to represent more than one brand of machine without the company's knowledge. To cultivate this loyalty, the company often appointed relatives and friends to the more important agencies. Finally, the agent must be sufficiently extroverted to enjoy the canvassing experience, without being so aggressive that the prospective customer would be put off. Agents' commissions were 28 to 30 percent, compared to the 50 to 55 percent discounts previously given to dealers. The commission was reduced in 1859, when the price of a machine was reduced by one-half.

Trade-Ins

In 1857, Clark announced in the *Gazette* a:

> LIBERAL PLAN OF EXCHANGING SINGER'S NEWEST AND LATEST IMPROVED MACHINES FOR OLD OR UNIMPROVED SEWING MACHINES OF ANY KIND. The time has now arrived when we are compelled to say, frankly, that it is impossible to add improvements to the old Machines of our manufacture so as to make them equal, or anything like equal, to the new ones. THE PRICE WE PROPOSE TO ALLOW FOR OLD MACHINES, IN EXCHANGE FOR NEW ONES, IS FIFTY DOLLARS.

Throughout the history of the use of the sewing machine, the unavoidable fact has always been that, unless one does extensive and complicated decorative sewing, the basic features of the least expensive sewing machine are all that is required by the average household. Singer had seen, much to its regret, the ads for sale of repossessed machines, and they took no chances that trade-ins might compete with its new machines, particularly those of competitors. All of the old machines traded in were to be sent to New York, where they were to be destroyed.

Appeal to Women

Clark recognized that, notwithstanding the fact that the husband would pay for the machine, the actual customer was the woman of the house. He had to convince her that she needed a sewing machine; that she deserved a sewing machine; that the sewing machine would give her independence and signal to the world that she was at the forefront of the technology of the home.

Clark's approach could hardly be described as subtle, or lacking in hyperbole. But advertising was a relatively undeveloped sales tool in an environment where sales techniques could be described as brutal. As the company grew, it would fall to Frederick Bourne, the president of Singer at the beginning of the twentieth century, to understand the potential of advertising and the importance of establishing the brand as the cornerstone of the marketing effort.

In addition to the price barrier, which had been minimized by hire/purchase and trade-ins, there remained a significant psychological barrier. The middle class in the United States was rapidly changing. The Industrial Revolution had brought wealth and means to an entirely new generation, witness that of Isaac Singer himself. If the older, landed middle class considered such activities as sewing the family necessities to be inappropriate activities for the lady of the house, the newer middle class did not. After all, it was only a short time ago that

Women's Influence, c. 190[16]

such activity would have been judged not only appropriate, but essential to the good functioning of the household. The man was the primary, if not the sole, wage earner in the family, and it was difficult for him to see how a labor-saving device for his wife would benefit him. All he could see was the cost of such a machine. Sewing the family clothes was a proper and essential function of a wife.

Such roles were deeply imbedded in the new middle class, and Singer faced the considerable task of overcoming them. The solution Clark adopted was to direct its publicity directly at the women, not the men. Singer produced a booklet entitled *The Story of the Sewing Machine*, which carried on its cover the legendary phrase, "Singer the Universal Sewing Machine, Sold only by the Maker Directly to the Women of the Family" (Brandon, 1977). The first task was to convince women (and their husbands) that they were, in fact, capable of operating such a mechanically advanced device, that they would not find the machine so impenetrable that they might crumble in weeping despair at their own ignorance and lack of skill. From the very beginning, women were used by the company to demonstrate the machines at fairs and in store windows, as well as to teach prospective female clients how to operate the machine.

An early female employee, who joined the company in 1852, learned quickly how to operate the machine and spent her time demonstrating and teaching about the machine instead of selling. An 1853 advertisement pointed out that "we must not forget to call attention to the fact that this instrument is particularly calculated for female operatives. They should never allow it to be monopolized by men."

Opinion Leaders

The second task was to convince women that the use of a sewing machine was not only possible for them, but socially acceptable, as well. Practical household sewing had been traditionally associated with household labor, particularly among the lower classes. How was one to overcome the insecurities of the newly arriving members of the middle class, who sought to escape from everything that might identify it with its previous social station?

The solution Clark adopted was to promote the machine to members of the community whose opinions were respected and whose social position unquestioned, the wives of ministers. He published an offer:

To the Pastors of Churches and Ministers of the Gospel, of every denomination…We will sell to any minister of the gospel…, one sewing machine of our manufacture…, at one half the regular cash price…;

Happy Homes[17]

where a minister happens to have no family…, we will supply the one Machine on the same terms, for a sewing society connected with the church…. (Brandon, 1977)

Clark reasoned that by placing a Singer machine in a church, particularly in a church-based sewing club, he could create instant respectability, along with a group of potential customers who would like to have their own machines rather than share one at the club. Despite the local status that ministers and their wives enjoyed, most were closer to the working classes in terms of income, and they flocked to take advantage of the offer.

Female Independence

For the husbands of the period, female independence was something that had never occurred to them. The woman's role was exclusively in the home, tending to the family's needs and the husband's desires. The notion of "free time" for their wives was an oxymoron. What on earth could a woman do with such free time, which, incidentally, the husband must pay for by means of considerable effort on his part? Again, Clark created a booklet that appealed directly to the women:

> The great importance of the sewing machine is in its influence upon the home; in the countless hours it has added to women's leisure for rest and refinement; in the increase of time and opportunity for the early training of children, for lack of which so many pitiful wrecks are strewn along the shores of life; in the numberless avenues it has opened for women's employment; and in the comforts it has brought within the reach of all, which could formerly be attained only by the wealthy few. (Brandon, 1977)

Here was the definition itself of one's having arrived in the middle class: offering women a choice of daily activities, rather than obligations. Here, too, was an appeal to men, in the form of a hint at increased family income. If the purchase of a sewing machine resulted in the wife having enough time to consider a job outside of her daily tasks, it should at least cover the cost of the machine and, perhaps, provide for the acquisition of the trappings of the family's new position in the social hierarchy. In some advertisements, the appeal to female independence was quite direct; claiming that:

> The great popularity of the machines may be understood when the fact is known that any good female operator can earn with them ONE THOUSAND DOLLARS A YEAR. (Brandon, 1977)

After-Sales Service

Sales agents were required to visit credit customers each month to collect their regular payments. The company encouraged frequent contact with its client base, and follow-up demonstrations ensured that the woman not only knew how to use the machine, but was actually using it. As the customer's skill level increased, the agent could show her more advanced applications and decorative sewing. Despite the fact that the quality of the Singer machine was excellent, breakdowns did occur and repairs were sometimes necessary. Most repairs were simple enough to be accomplished during a home visit. More complicated problems had to be resolved in the agent's shop, but which necessitated yet another home visit.

Visits after the initial sale of the machine had two goals. The first was to build loyalty to the brand and instill in the client the habit of calling the agent for answers to any sewing questions she might have. The second was to create a new opportunity to sell something else. The agent would become in effect a traveling store, using the visit as an opportunity to sell attachments, sewing notions, and fabrics, and perhaps a newer generation of sewing machine. The satisfied client was also a prime source of referrals of new potential clients.

Clark's innovative sales and marketing techniques had the effect of not only creating new demand for sewing machines, but creating in the public mind the belief that the name Singer, not Wheeler and Wilson, was synonymous with sewing. The evolution of their sales during the decade following the creation of the patent pool tells the story.

	Wheeler and Wilson	I.M. Singer & Co.
1857	4,591	3,630
1860	25,102	13,000
1865*	39,157	26,340
1870	83,208	127,833

* U.S. Civil War (DePew, New York)

Wheeler and Wilson had used its technological advantage in manufacturing to satisfy the early rising demand for sewing machines. Singer created demand for its machines through creative marketing, and it satisfied that demand by building additional factories. It would eventually gain technological parity, but only with great effort to change old habits. Singer had no obligation to share these innovations with the other members of the Patent Pool, but their effectiveness of these changes was evident by their virtually universal adoption by competitors. By 1867, Singer's creative and aggressive marketing strategies had made it the largest sewing machine manufacturer in the world, with annual production of 40,000 machines and revenues of almost $2 million. By 1873, production had increased to almost 275,000 machines with revenues of $8.5 million.

With profit now assured by both direct sales and patent royalties, Singer could turn its attention to developing more effective channels of distribution.

The company began to open its own stores, both for sales and as a showplace to display and demonstrate its machines. Distribution was expanded initially through a network of non-exclusive dealers with exclusive territories. However, the difficulty of controlling margins, dedication to proprietary products, and the failure of the dealers to maximize Singer's market share in their territories, quickly led to a network of in-house agents and non-exclusive free agents. The company would rely on directly controlled sales of the Singer brand for the next century.

I.M. Singer & Co., New York Showroom[18]

Thinking Big—The First Multinational

The Singer Company has been called the first American conglomerate, but this is a mischaracterization of the company. A conglomerate is a company that does business in several different products or services as a means of diminishing the risk associated with any single business. In Singer's case, the company was and remained largely a single-product company until well after World War II. Rather, Clark's genius was his recognition from the very beginning that the immense potential of the sewing machine market was not uniquely American, but universal. The potential world market was so large that it could not economically be served by exporting sewing machines from the United States. At the same time that he was pursuing innovation in the United States, he began to consider the foreign markets. Successfully competing in that market would require an international sales and manufacturing organization, and the sooner Singer could develop one the better. Clark considered the potential of the international market an ideal means of supplying its factories with the production volume necessary to reduce its unit production cost to a level that would enable it to compete more effectively. In so doing, Clark created, if not the first, one of the first multinational companies

VERSAILLES, RUE DUPLESSIS, 15

in the United States, making an unusually early decision to expand its efforts to Europe. The market there was already more competitive than in the United States, as the patent pool limitations were difficult to enforce there without significant legal and administrative costs. In 1873, the Vienna Exhibition attracted fifty European manufacturers of sewing machines from virtually all of the developed countries of Western Europe.

By 1861 Singer was already selling more machines in Europe than in the United States, and by 1867 it had constructed a factory in Glasgow, Scotland. This facility was replaced in 1885 by the largest factory in Europe at Clydebank, a suburb of Glasgow, which would serve markets throughout the world until the late twentieth century. Singer had become the first multinational company with the world's first global brand.

In addition to the pure market size implications of doing business abroad, the overseas activity provided Singer with a hedge against unforeseen difficulties in its domestic market. Remittances from foreign entities enabled the company to ride out the Panic of 1873, a very deep nationwide six-year depression, which was in many ways similar to the modern dot-com bubble of 1997–2000, speculative overexpansion followed by a market collapse. The Panic of 1873 had the added stress of a series of traumatic events, beginning with an attempt by two wealthy speculators to corner the gold market in 1869. The attempt was quickly defeated by President Grant's decision to release government gold into the market, causing an unanticipated plunge in prices in the heavily leveraged market, eventually known as Black Friday, September 24, 1869. This was followed in rapid succession by the Chicago Fire of October 8–9, 1871 and, in a serious dry spell, simultaneous fires throughout Michigan and Wisconsin, severely hindering the rebuilding effort in Chicago. At the time, horses were still an integral part of the nation's transport system, and an outbreak of equine flu, along with a shortage of firewood to fuel the locomotives, crippled the nation's ability to move goods. The Coinage Act of 1873 shook public confidence as the country moved from a gold and silver standard to one of gold only. The government would no longer guarantee the purchase of silver at the statutory price and stopped minting silver dollars. Finally, in July 1873, Jay Cooke & Company, a major bank, found itself unable to market several million dollars of Northern Pacific Railway bonds, and the firm was forced to declare bankruptcy. Northern Pacific's construction was delayed and financed by another financier.

Even without the Panic of 1873, the Civil War placed extremely high demands on America's resources, both human and financial, with a corresponding decline in the domestic demand for sewing machines. It is somewhat surprising that any sewing machines were sold at all during this period, most being destined for customers outside the United States. The American Civil War had little or no effect on the economies of Europe, where business was flourishing. In fact, profits for Singer during that period were probably even higher than expected, because the value of the dollar was falling and remittances in foreign currencies were worth more in dollars. Finally, the creation of a worldwide manufacturing network would eventually allow Singer's factories to produce only one or two models in an expanded product line, taking advantage of the cost efficiencies that mass production could generate with extremely high production volumes.

From the very beginning, all of the principal sewing machine companies looked to foreign markets for growth. After failing to find funding in the United States, Elias Howe went to England, which had an old and successful fabric and garment industry. Two American companies displayed their machines at the 1851 Crystal Palace Exhibition in London. Both Singer, and Wheeler and Wilson showed at the same exhibition in 1853. Singer sought foreign patents as early as 1851, and it succeeded in England and France in 1854. The following year, Singer sold the French rights to a merchant and sent a machinist to help begin manufacturing. As he learned with the American organization, indirect distribution could be very costly due to the lack of control over non-employees. The new French manufacturer failed to provide any useful information about his production and sales. Even when he acknowledged sales, remittances were slow in coming. The Frenchman sold competing machines, and the two finally ended in litigation. This was to be Singer's first and last sale of patent rights to a non-exclusive independent businessman.

Next, the company sought foreign sales through the establishment of exclusive agencies in Europe and South America. This seems to have solved the problem of the agent selling competing machines, but it did little to establish any significant measure of control over the agents. In a first step toward direct distribution in 1861, the company hired salaried representatives to improve supervision. With the hiring of these representatives, Singer had finally taken the first step in creating a multinational organization. The added sales volume proved timely, as the outbreak of the Civil War diverted raw materials to the war effort, much as it has done in subsequent conflicts. Critical materials such as steel were scarce, and the local supply of needles declined. Singer's overseas trade gave it access to alternative sources of supply that were unavailable to other manufacturers, and by 1864 exports accounted for 40 percent of Singer's worldwide sales.

The success of the European efforts convinced Clark of the necessity to create a full-blown marketing organization as he had done in America. He dispatched two key employees, George Woodruff and George Neidlinger, to London and Hamburg as his new regional general agents. Woodruff had headed the Boston sales office, and Neidlinger was a mechanic from the New York factory. Both Woodruff and Neidlinger built their strategies on the same innovative sales and marketing tools that Clark had developed back home. In addition, Woodruff offered free sewing instruction and introduced the first illustrated catalogs in 1867. Still, the intense competition was such that even with the company's aggressive marketing program, sales in Britain were difficult to increase.

Woodruff's answer to this challenge was to take the sales effort out of the store and directly to the prospective customer's home. Britain had a relatively high and evenly distributed disposable income, a high level of urbanization, and compact geography, all of which lent itself to the creation of a productive door-to-door selling network. The success of the Singer door-to-door organization in Britain was such that Clark decided to adopt it as a model that would be used throughout Europe until well after World War II. Singer already had the experience of post-sales contact with the customer through delivery of the machines, collection of installment payments, machine repairs, and customer training. By focusing on pre-sale customer contact, Woodruff closed the loop that Clark had begun with the installment sale, an intimate connection with the customer that built enormous brand recognition and loyalty. It was logical to consider ways of contacting the pre-sale customer. The density of the urban population made it possible to minimize unproductive travel time in order to make profitable what was an inherently expensive channel of distribution. The expiration of the last of the Pool's patents in 1877 opened the market to the other competitors. By this time, the company had so developed its marketing and management capabilities that Singer had become the dominant player in the sewing machine market.

Life with Isaac

Clark's attempts to develop a marketing strategy based on appealing to women was not made easier by Singer's notoriously public private life. We left Mr. Singer's personal life in 1849, just before his invention of the last step necessary for the creation of a commercially viable household sewing machine, and just before his first encounter with Edward Clark. Singer's primary interest in the sewing machine was twofold. First was the notoriety associated with being an accomplished inventor. This desire had little to do with any success he might have achieved as a businessman, as from the very beginning of his partnership with Clark, he was quite content to let Clark concern himself with all of the business aspects of their endeavor. Rather, it was derived from the same need that had driven him to become an actor, a desire for public recognition. Second was the desire for great wealth. Singer led a very complicated personal life, one that required considerable resources to satisfactorily maintain, and it appeared that the sewing machine could be an extremely productive moneymaking product. Singer maintained a creative role with the company to the extent that it was necessary to retain a commercial edge over the competition and (peripherally) to renew his reputation as an inventing genius. So long as those two needs were satisfied, the business was Clark's to run.

In 1850, when Singer formed I.M. Singer & Co., the high cost of manufacturing a sewing machine limited the selling price and the consequent profit (or loss) of the company. Clark's marketing innovations lay ahead, and cash was certainly tight for the company and its founders. Nonetheless, even if they only made $2 on each of the 800 machines they sold in 1853, that would have constituted the equivalent of $44,000 in 2015 dollars, and that amount would grow exponentially as Clark created the volume necessary to reduce product cost.

In 1851, Singer and Mary Ann, who had just given birth, moved from the tenements of the lower East Side to the more acceptable East Fifth Street, near Fourth Avenue, before it became Madison Avenue, and in 1852 they moved again to 374 Fourth Avenue. As their income grew, they started to acquire the signs of wealth appropriate for his position, such as a grand piano and the carriages that he kept on Fifth Avenue. Catherine had been conveniently sequestered on Long Island, where she had apparently found a more appropriate replacement for Singer, although it was not yet apparent that Singer considered the relationship to be over. After twenty years and eight children by Singer, Mary Ann was now, for all practical purposes, Mrs. Singer.

In 1856, the Singers moved farther up Fourth Avenue, and in 1859, they bought Number 14 Fifth Avenue, just off of Washington Square, what was then the most desirable neighborhood in New York. Mary Ann had cards engraved, tutors and piano teachers were engaged for the children, and a coachman was hired to oversee the six carriages and ten horses they kept. Mary Ann became sufficiently well-known by the merchants so that she could incur bills of up to $200 without question, knowing that Singer would pay them. Despite all of the outward appearances of their new wealth, or perhaps because of them, the Singers remained estranged from New York Society. They were the "nouveau riche" and were not accepted by those of the traditional professions of law, banking, and politics, much less by those with inherited wealth. Clark's position as the descendant of an old, land-owning New York family and Ms. Clark's position as the daughter of the state attorney general, who had a clear opinion of where the Clarks stood in New York Society, virtually precluded any interaction between the two families. This was the time when the old landed gentry could not bring themselves to accept the brashness and audacity of these new captains of the Industrial Revolution. The Puritan ethic militated against self-promotion and ostentatious displays of wealth, and the families of the "old society" were determined to resist any invasion by the "new," which included Isaac Singer and his family. Singer flew in the face of such obstacles. He had been poor, and he had been rich. Rich was better and he was determined to enjoy it.

Singer had many children, and because none of the New York coach makers made a coach sufficiently large to carry his entire family, he designed one himself:

> At the back of the main body and attached thereto is a depressed coupe body... The coupe is provided with a middle door in the back, and with seats on each side, the space under one of the said seats being suitably arranged as a water-closet, and the other as a receptacle for baggage and &c. From the coupe openings are made...through the back of the main body to the spaces under the two back elevated seats, one for storing baggage, and the other for an extension of one of the side seats of the coupe to form a child's bed, or if desired both may be arranged for beds, or both for the reception of baggage &c.... By the arrangement and general construction of the main body and seats therein, I am enabled to obtain by a very slight increase of size ample room for nine, and if necessary ten persons, all so situated so that they can converse freely and none of whom, if limited to nine, will be required to ride backward: while in the coupe at the back, and in

communication therewith there will be ample room for children and servants and all the convenience of travel. (Brandon, 1977)

Singer received patent no. 25,920 for this vehicle, and he used it often, drawn by six, sometimes nine horses, three-abreast. When not traveling by his omnibus, Singer would amuse himself by driving through Broadway at great speed in a five-in-hand "unicorn team of three horses abreast and two leaders," which, not unreasonably, appalled Clark as the height of bad taste. Business was at a standstill, as most of the company's workers were fighting the Civil War, to which the company was expected to contribute. Singer's antics and public displays of wealth at the beginning of the War had succeeded in convincing the public that the company, including Clark, was rich, and the rich were assumed to be patriotic and obliged to give to the war effort. Singer's efforts in respect to the expected contributions did afford him a certain measure of acceptance he might not otherwise have attained.

In 1860, Isaac and Catherine, on Singer's request, were divorced. Singer sued on grounds of adultery, with his lawyer letting it be known to Catherine's that if she would consent to such a divorce, the sum of $10,000 would be forthcoming. As Singer had continued to pay her a stipend, which would risk disappearing should she not agree, she did so, and the divorce was granted. Why Singer wished such a divorce was puzzling. He had been married to Catherine for thirty years and the situation had permitted him freedom of action with other women without complaint. Mary Ann had pretty much accepted her situation and had little reason to seek a more legitimate relationship. The only person who might gain from such an arrangement was Edward Clark, ever concerned about the appearance of the company, as well as himself, in the eyes of New York Society, and it was, in fact, Clark who paid the $10,000. With Catherine out of the way, Mary Ann could legitimately hope that Singer would now formalize their relationship. When she so asked, he replied that he had no intention of marrying her, as that would make him her prisoner. That was how it was and how it would stay.

Once Singer's divorce from Catherine was settled, Mary Ann decamped to Philadelphia to join him. They then returned to Fifth Avenue at Singer's request, where they resumed life together, although certainly with a degree of stress that hadn't existed before. Their newly clarified partnership hit a new bump in the road in August of 1860. Mary Ann was driving along Fifth Avenue in her own carriage when who but Singer himself should pass in the opposite direction, accompanied by one Mary McGonigal, a companion of Singer's from the Philadelphia office. Mary Ann reacted with a fury sufficiently loud to make most of lower Fifth Avenue aware of the situation. When she returned home, Singer reacted with equal fury, and Mary Ann left home to stay with a friend. The next day, her rage not having subsided, Mary Ann had Singer arrested, accusing Singer of having beaten and choked her, and he was placed under orders to keep the peace for six months. The entire affair was fully covered by *Leslie's Weekly*, with a weekly readership of 500,000. Singer fled to Europe with Mary McGonigal's nineteen-year-old sister, Kate, and took up residence in Cornhill, near the company's office in London. Clark wrote to Singer, expressing his anger and frustration at the embarrassment and outrage he had brought on the company. Clark assumed that the source of the outrage was the rumors circulating about the previously unknown McGonigal sisters. The truth was actually worse than the rumors. Over the course of nine years, Singer had sired five children with Mary McGonigal. Singer had taken a house for her at Christopher Street in New York, where they lived under the name of Mathews, with the five children and Mary's sister Kate.

That wasn't all. Singer was supporting yet another family in lower Manhattan. In 1851, he had another daughter with Mary Eastwood Walters. They adopted Isaac's middle name, Merritt, as their family name and Singer took a house on West Twenty-Seventh Street for the Merritt family. The collective result of Singer's philandering was that by 1860, he had fathered and recognized eighteen children, sixteen of whom were still alive, and he was supporting them all in reasonable comfort. Since his arrival in New York in 1850, the birth dates of the children indicate that Singer had been supporting four families, only one of which was legitimate. There is little indication that any of these "wives" knew of the existence of any of the others prior to the catastrophic encounter of Mary Ann and Singer on Fifth Avenue. During all of this, the Civil War was going on and probably pushed the Singer antics further out of the news readers' minds than would have otherwise been the case. For the time being, however, the publicity around Singer's private life had been somewhat easy for Clark to control.

Now that, from Ed Clark's point of view, Singer's life was old news, it started up again. Mary Ann decided that their long public life together as man and wife, especially since his divorce from Catherine, had effectively established Mary Ann as Singer's common-law wife, and she sued him for adultery in all of its lurid detail. The paradox was that the documents presented painted Singer as a dark and brutal person, whereas the testimony in support of such a characterization came mostly from commercial enemies who had little to say as direct witnesses of his personal life. Those who could provide such personal testimony invariably noted that he apparently loved each of his families and took care of them economically. We now see why Singer needed a fortune to continue his lifestyle. Mary Ann won the case and was awarded $8,000 a year in alimony.

However Singer suggested a compromise, and the judgement was never executed. His proposal was to find her a suitable house in New York, which would pass to her children on her death, and the sum of fifty dollars a week in alimony. Against her lawyer's advice that this was generous, Mary Ann refused and continued the suit, with the result that the court said that she was free to marry, without prejudice. In June 1862, she traveled to Boston and, unbeknownst to the court, married one John E. Foster. In January 1863, Mary Ann had a bad fall and, fearing she would not live, disclosed her marriage to her daughter, who was living with her husband, a Singer Co. employee, in the house Singer had purchased for Mary Ann as part of the divorce agreement. Her husband disclosed Mary Ann's marriage, and all hell broke loose. Singer, now accepting in principle her previous claim that they were married, sued her for bigamy. After more claims and counterclaims, Mary Ann abandoned the suit.

Clark and Singer could never be characterized as close business collaborators. Each was highly protective of his own domain and considered the other to be, if not incompetent, at least significantly less skilled in their specialty. They had no personal affinity for each other, quite the contrary. In an effort to escape the increasing antipathy toward him in New York, Singer was spending more and more time out of the country. Clark found Singer's absences both convenient and frustrating. He was seldom present for any consultation on the myriad of technical problems that would arise in a complex manufacturing environment. On the other hand, Clark could spend much less time dealing with the public embarrassment and damage to the company's reputation as a consequence of Singer's behavior in New York. The situation finally reached a breaking point in June 1862. In a letter to Singer in London, Clark explained the impact that Singer's antics were having on the company. A copy of the complete letter appears in Appendix A, and shows how completely the relationship between the co-founders had disintegrated.

> I am in very low spirits today and although I regret to do so, I must inform you of the cause. You are out of the country. I heartily wish I was. The load here is getting very heavy for me to bear. On Saturday last, the same day you left New York, I sent down to the Chemical Bank a note for $3,000 to be discounted (cashed). Hopper had no doubt as to getting the accommodation, as our discounts at the bank were very small and money very plenty. On Monday the note was sent back to us not having been discounted. Hopper went to the bank and asked an explanation. The Cashier told him the Directors of the Bank had seen the publication about you in the Police Gazette and referred him to the President for further information. The President, Mr. Jones, said that the Directors had come to the conclusion that it was not reputable for the Bank to discount any notes for I.M. Singer…

Today Hopper went to the Bank again and was told by the President that the Bank positively would not discount any more papers for I.M. Singer. The only reason is the discredit of doing business with you on account of the disgraceful situation of your private affairs...

I hardly dare speak to any old friends when I meet them on the street. The firm of which I am the active manager has been publicly accused of keeping numerous agents in various cities to procure women for you to prostitute...

Now there is one remedy for a part of this mischief, and that ought to be applied as soon as it can conveniently be done. The name of Singer, as it now stands is a terrible weight upon the firm... Your interests as well as my own imperatively require that the name of Singer & Co. should be merged in that of a joint stock company...

Both you and I will at once make more money in consequence of the change. A new incorporated Company will have no bad name....

We shall be able to do much better I think in consequence of your having gone. I give it out that you have arranged your business affairs in this country and never mean to return to it.

Singer had lost interest in an active role in the company and agreed to retire to tend to his private life and fortune. Such was the relationship between the two men that Singer insisted that their partnership be dissolved and that neither would retain any active management of the company. The Singer Manufacturing Company was created, with Singer and Clark having equal ownership, and a president, Inslee A. Hopper, was named president. Hopper had been a low-level clerk with the company, and his appointment was nothing more than window dressing to satisfy Singer. Clark had effectively been the extraordinarily successful CEO of the company since the beginning, and with Singer's tacit consent, he would continue in that role without the title. Singer endured a brief period of social unacceptability in New York, after which he moved to France, then to England, where he died in 1875. It was not until Singer's death that Clark finally gained the title of president, which he retained until his own death in 1882.

Singer had made marginal improvements in the cost to manufacture the sewing machine, largely as a result of the dramatic increases in volume that flowed through its factories. However, Clark's innovations in the marketing and sales of the machines significantly lowered the cost of distribution, enabling it to compete effectively with the manufacturing cost reductions of the competition. Even with cost improvements in both manufacturing and distribution, the sewing machine remained an expensive product, beyond the reach of many prospective customers.

The introduction of installment selling and the acceptance of trade-ins, regardless of their origin, made the sewing machine "affordable," if not cheaper. Aside from taking advantage of the relatively lower labor cost in Britain, the creation of a manufacturing and sales capability there gave Singer the opportunity to actively compete in an enormously expanded potential market. The customer was now intimately tied to the company. The marketing strategy directed at female freedom and independence, coupled with the demonstrations, direct sale, installment credit, payment collection, after sales service, and follow-up sales pattern created an intense and, for its time, a unique company/customer relationship.

The Continuing Hunger for Volume—Mass Production

The enormous potential of the household sewing machine market was obvious to each of the four members of the patent pool. Howe had no interest in pursuing either the manufacture or the sale of the product so long as he was becoming very wealthy by merely collecting his fees. On the other hand, Wheeler & Wilson, Grover & Baker, and Singer were deeply interested in the market potential and faced critical strategic decisions about how best to compete. Not surprisingly, each was strongly influenced by the individual experience of their owners. Both Wheeler and Wilson, and Grover and Baker had been manufacturing sewing machines since the early 1850s and were strong advocates of the armory system. They both reasoned that the primary challenge in this rapidly growing industry would be the ability to manufacture in significant quantity to satisfy demand and increase their market share. Neither Singer nor Clark had any particular experience in nor taste for the manufacturing side of the business. Singer's primary interest and skill was technical creativity, and even that was limited given his active social life. Clark was a rationally reasoning lawyer who saw the challenge as one of making the total market grow as fast as possible without losing any market share. At the very least, the company could expect to enjoy a constant share of a rapidly growing market. If Clark could convince potential customers that Singer not only made the best sewing machines but make it easier in every way to own a Singer machine, the company might acquire an increasing market share in a rapidly growing market. From the beginning, Singer relied on the European method of manufacture, using traditional hand methods, largely subcontracted to third-party manufacturers. Over time, all three pool members would embrace their own particular notion of mass production, but they would be quite different in practice, timing, and effectiveness.

In many ways, the industrial river valleys of Connecticut were the crucible of the development of the American System and its application in a commercial environment. It was at the Springfield Armory where Hall's theory of parts interchangeability was proven. It was in Hartford where Colt built his arms factory. It was in New Haven where Whitney invented the cotton gin and pursued the principle of interchangeability in manufacturing. Bridgeport was the site of one of Singer's first major factories.

The Wheeler and Wilson Manufacturing Company

Nathaniel Wheeler grew up in this environment. Born in 1820 in Watertown, Connecticut, he learned manufacturing processes in his father's carriage business. Eventually he left to start his own business, fabricating small metal articles such as buttons and buckles, originally by hand, then slowly mechanizing the process. Allen Wilson was a young mechanic who, among other inventions, held the patent to the two-motion cloth-feeding mechanism for his own version of the sewing machine, which he was manufacturing in New York City. In 1850, Wheeler approached him and negotiated a contract to manufacture five hundred of the feed-mechanisms, convincing Wilson to move his manufacturing operations to Watertown, where Wheeler could oversee it. Much like Isaac Singer, Wilson was more interested in inventing than in manufacturing or selling. While in Watertown, he developed and patented a rotary hook and bobbin that would make a lock-stitch and, in 1854, he would patent the four-motion cloth feed, which would become a critical contribution to the patent pool and remains the basic cloth-feed principle used in sewing machines today. In 1851, Wilson formally joined Warren Wheeler's existing partnership, consisting of himself, Alanson Warren, and George Woodruff, to form Wheeler, Wilson, and Company. The partnership was later incorporated as the Wheeler and Wilson Manufacturing Company. Initially, Wilson oversaw the manufacture of the machines, which were then being built either individually or in small batches in the machine shop. Each machine was unique, and the extensive handwork almost certainly was critical in its relatively expensive selling price of $125. In 1855 Warren, the then company president, and Woodruff, the secretary and treasurer, left, and Wilson withdrew from active participation to concentrate on technical improvements.

Woodruff, who would eventually join Singer and rise to head its European marketing organization, was replaced by William H. Perry, a machinist who would completely change the manufacturing philosophy of the company. He had worked at the Colt Armory in Hartford, where his brother was an inside contractor. Perry moved to Wheeler and Wilson in 1855, and within a year had become secretary, treasurer, and superintendent of the factory. Wheeler and Wilson moved the manufacturing operations to Bridgeport in 1857, and there Perry would bring the American system of manufacturing to sewing machine fabrication. By 1859, production had increased to a level four times what it had been in 1857, and by 1864 the Bridgeport factory was producing 40,000 machines a year, almost double that of Singer. Wheeler and Wilson would continue to lead or match Singer in the rapidly growing sewing machine market for another five years, until the Singer marketing steamroller ran over them.

Sewing Machine Unit Production, 1853–1875

Year	Wheeler and Wilson	Singer	Willcox and Gibbs	All other
1853	799	810	n.a.	920
1860	25,102	13,000	n.a.	22,900
1865	39,157	26,340	n.a.	70,700
1870	83,208	127,833	28,890	272,839
1875	103,740	249,852	14,522	173,741

(Cooper, 1968) (Hounsell, 1984)

Perry focused relentlessly on quality and the use of the American System to increase manufacturing capacity to meet what appeared to be an almost boundless hunger for sewing machines. He surpassed his initial goal of 100,000 machines a year with over 120,000 in 1871, only to see Singer produce 180,000 machines, taking a lead it wouldn't relinquish until the end of the next century.

The Willcox and Gibbs Sewing Machine Company

Willcox and Gibbs was a partnership that in 1858 contracted with a company called Brown & Sharpe, in Providence, Rhode Island, to produce a sewing machine for it using the armory system of manufacture from the very beginning. Brown & Sharp had no experience in the fabrication of metal products, but rather they produced custom clocks, watches, and related watchmaker's tools. While James Willcox had designed and built a nearly perfect sewing machine prototype, he had no particular interest that the machine be manufactured using the American System, only that it be "got up right built" (Hounsell, 1984, p. 76). Notwithstanding Brown and Sharpe's lack of experience in the system, Wilcox and Gibbs were apparently impressed by its rapidly increasing reputation, and they set out from the very beginning to make sewing machines with the armory system of interchangeable parts.

Before even assembling a completed machine, Brown and Sharpe set out to design a model along with the special tools, jigs, fixtures, and gauges that characterized the armory system, and work on the first machine began in March 1858. The entire process took much longer than expected. The fabrication of the necessary special tools was especially complicated and expensive, costing ten times more than anticipated. The first machines required much the same hand machining as the traditional job shop manufacturing system. However, as the tools and jigs were refined with each batch of machines, the company began to approach the objective of parts interchangeability. The first fifty machines were finally completed in October 1858. By this time, Brown and Sharpe had become believers in the armory system and concluded that, using the present tools, they could manufacture five thousand machines a year and, with the addition of a few more lathes, they could double the capacity.

Although the Willcox & Gibbs's machine enjoyed popular acceptance, the annual sales never exceeded thirty-four thousand machines. Despite this relatively small market share, Brown & Sharpe was able to profitably manufacture sewing machines until the middle of the twentieth century. The company used its experience in sewing machine manufacture to begin designing and selling the same kinds of special tools for the manufacturers of other products, becoming a sort of training ground for mechanics and a testing laboratory for new tools and processes. A number of well-known mechanics worked for a time in the Brown & Sharpe shop, not the least of whom was Henry Leland, the eventual founder of the Cadillac Motor Car Company. Leland headed the sewing machine department from 1878 to 1890, and during his first year he introduced a piecework system that effectively tied pay to performance, resulting in a 47 percent reduction in labor cost. Unfortunately for Willcox & Gibbs, the dramatic improvements in their supplier's ability to manufacture sewing machines at low cost was not matched by an equally dramatic increase in market demand for the machine, and by 1890, Singer was manufacturing ten times as many machines per year as Brown & Sharpe.

The Singer Manufacturing Company

The conventional explanation for the rapid success of the Singer Manufacturing Company was its innovative marketing techniques and its ability to mass-produce. In fact, Singer was rather late to the mass-production party, not the leader as it is often described. The first manufacturer of Singer machines was Orson C. Phelps, one of Isaac Singer's early partners. Phelps was a scientific instrument maker, with neither the experience nor the equipment necessary to manufacture an appliance that weighed over 125 pounds. Phelps began to make sewing machines in much the same way he made instruments, one at a time. Phelps's primary skill was that of a craftsman. He would subcontract the fabrication of all of the necessary parts, and when they were delivered, in their inevitably rough form, he would have his mechanics fit them together in his shop, with all of the filing, grinding, and planning necessary to arrive at a working product. So long as demand for the machines was modest, this method of handmaking each machine sufficed. However, Singer and Clark were focused on creating maximum demand for their sewing machines, not a manufacturing facility. As they, particularly Clark, succeeded in developing the company's marketing strategies, including the claim that theirs was "much the best of the whole lot [on the market]" (Hounsell, 1984), the first element of the Singer marketing plan was to use women to demonstrate the machine, proving that it was, in fact, the best. Within a year, the need to have closer control over manufacturing led management to bring production to New York, with the result that Phelps essentially left the scene. Since neither Singer nor Clark had any experience or interest in the manufacturing process, they continued in New York with much the same job-shop system, only larger. An 1854 illustration of the factory floor shows a veritable army of workmen filing away at various parts held in vises, the European system on a larger scale. Where the other principal competitors, Wheeler & Wilson and Brown & Sharp, were quickly adopting the armory system, with piecework motivating improvements in both quality and productivity, Singer was focused exclusively on sales and marketing, its prime goals being, "1st to have the best machines and 2nd to let the public know it" (Hounsell, 1984). Quality was assured by having each machine "produced by hand at the bench" (Hounsell, 1984), with much the same pride in the time-consuming process as a traditional English shoemaker. Where the armory system was based on the belief that quality and uniformity of parts were inextricably linked, the European system relied on extensive hand-finishing by skilled workmen to be the key to quality.

Meanwhile, the combination of the pooling agreement, which essentially eliminated any technological advantage between competitors, and Clark's marketing innovations, which competitors were either slow or unable to duplicate, and the introduction in 1856 of a machine designed exclusively for household use, resulted in a dramatic growth in Singer's sales volume.

Year	Units	Growth
1853	810	
1858	3,594	344%
1863	21,000	484%
1868	59,629	183%
1873	232,444	290%

In 1858, in order to keep up with demand, Singer built a six-story factory in New York. By the time it was completed, the factory was already insufficient and the company built an additional five-story building to house the foundry. With the opening of the New York factories, Singer was becoming known as a significant manufacturer. However, unlike Wheeler and Wilson, Singer did not adopt the American system of manufacturing, and for the next fifteen years, increases in manufacturing capacity were accomplished largely by adding space and personnel for hand-finishing.

George Ross McKenzie

George Ross McKenzie[21]

George Ross McKenzie was born in Scotland and came to the United States in 1846. He joined I.M. Singer and Company as an apprentice cabinetmaker in 1851, working in the original New York workshop, located at that time over the New York, New Haven, and Hartford Railroad. As the company expanded its manufacturing capacity in the two new factories, opportunities for advancement for the ambitious young Scotsman expanded, as well, and by 1860 he had become the superintendent of the Mott Street plant. In 1854–1855, Clark had sent the machinist William F. Proctor to Paris to set up a factory there, and in 1863 Proctor returned home to become the first treasurer of the Singer Manufacturing Company. From the very beginning of the company, Edward Clark was essentially its chief executive officer, although he would not be permitted to hold the title of president until Isaac Singer died in 1875. We have seen that Clark's interests and skills were largely in marketing and sales innovation, and throughout the rest of his career he entrusted virtually all of the major manufacturing decisions to McKenzie, by then a vice president, and Proctor. Both men had come up through the manufacturing organization and were dedicated by virtue of their own work experience to the European method as practiced at Singer.

Singer's annual sales had grown from 3,594 machines in 1858 to 21,000 in 1863. As the volume grew, so did the problems of manufacturing quality. As quality problems increased, the number of complaints from the salesmen increased, as well, overloading the time and the ability of the field salesmen to cope with repairs, while focusing on sales of what was essentially a unique handmade machine. From a salesman's point of view, the simplest solution to a repair problem was to send the machine back to the factory, adding to the rapidly accumulating problems there caused by rising foreign demand. It was clear that Singer's entire manufacturing process was in doubt. The company took its first tentative step away from the European "bench-made" system toward the armory system by hiring Jerome Carter in 1862 and Lebbeus B. Miller in 1863. Carter was initially hired to improve the problem-plagued needle fabrication process, and Miller was hired to "design and supervise the construction of special tools for the production of interchangeable parts" (Hounsell, 1984, p. 92) for Singer sewing machines, what would become the arduous task of converting Singer's production processes to the American System. Over the course of the next two decades, he installed milling machines, adopted drop forging, constructed special machine tools, and introduced the system of inside contracting that characterized the armory system. It wasn't until the last decade of the nineteenth century, however, that the company developed a highly refined system of jigs, fixtures, and gauges necessary for a successful system of interchangeable parts.

The rapid growth of both the domestic and foreign markets, from 43,000 in 1867 to 87,000 in 1869, continually outstripped the company's manufacturing capacity, and the company decided to open a factory in the United Kingdom. The choice for the factory site was Glasgow, Scotland. It was chosen by McKenzie, a Scot, not for personal reasons, but because it offered such obvious advantages as an iron-smelting industry, cotton thread companies, an active ship-building and steamship business with worldwide trade and shipping connections, and a docile labor force that cost half that what it would cost in the United States. The company's natural preference at the time for the European system it was using in New York, allowed them to fabricate parts in America and ship them to Scotland for finishing and assembly, a process both time-consuming and expensive. Using this system, it initially took thirty-one men and boys to assemble thirty machines a week, a full man-week per machine (Hounsell, 1984). As changes that Lebbeus Miller was bringing to manufacturing in New York began working their way across the Atlantic, the Glasgow factories were producing 700 machines a week. Two years later, they were turning out 1,400 machines a week and were "the largest in the United Kingdom" (Hounsell, 1984).

While the opening of the Glasgow factories had taken a great deal of the pressure off of the New York facilities, domestic demand rapidly consumed the available capacity of 2,000 units per week. The directors decided to move manufacturing from New York City to Elizabeth, New Jersey, planning for a facility capable of producing 5,000 machines per week, while adding sufficient tooling in the interim to raise New York's capacity to 3,000 per week. The factory was completed in 1873 and was soon producing about 1,000 machines a day. Miller's improvements migrated to Scotland, and between 1868, when Miller was first appointed, and 1873, when the Elizabethport works opened, Singer's annual sales had grown from approximately 87,000 machines to over 232,000.

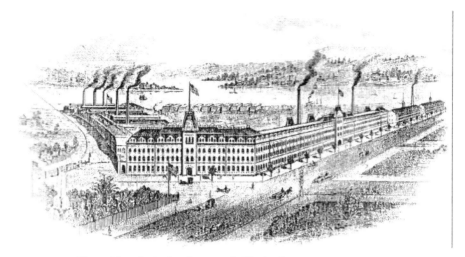

Singer Manufacturing Company's Elizabethport Factory, 1880[22]

Although he did not have any direct experience with the armory system, George McKenzie was an experienced plant manager, intensely focused on production cost. The Scottish factory represented a significant opportunity insomuch as labor costs in the United States were twice that of Scotland. The initial perception in the European market was that the machines made in Glasgow were of inferior quality, however. Eventually, the standardization and mechanization of production that Miller was emphasizing in the United States brought both factories to the same levels of quality.

Edward Clark had also created the basic sales organization at Singer, a series of branch offices in the primary markets, supervising a group of stores staffed with managers, demonstrators, salespersons, and mechanics. Inspired by the success of George Woodruff's system in the United Kingdom, Clark added a network of door-to-door canvassers to each branch. Exclusive agents were used in the adjacent secondary markets. When a secondary market grew to a sufficient size, a new branch office was opened to replace the agent. With the rapid growth of the company, the number of branch offices grew to cover all of the major cities in the United States, virtually all of the newly industrialized countries, and many developing countries. The organization became too broad to control centrally, and an additional level of regional management offices was opened in London and Hamburg. As this pattern repeated itself, the sales organization became very expensive, particularly the canvassers, who carried inventory around with them on their horses and in their carts. Clark had been the first to recognize that the demonstration was the essential ingredient to making the sale. The canvassers discovered an even easier way to make the sale, however: leaving the machine with the potential client after the demonstration as a "trial sample." The unsold inventory thus created was both expensive and clogged the order system, since the factory had to behave as if the sample had actually been sold, or else the canvasser would have nothing left to demonstrate.

In 1864, George Baldwin Woodruff became the general agent of the London office. Woodruff, who had previously worked for Wheeler and Wilson, had distinguished himself as the manager of Singer's New Haven and Boston offices. Woodruff built his marketing strategy for Britain on the same sales and marketing techniques that Clark had so successfully employed in the United States, with one significant addition: door-to-door selling, taking the sales effort out of the store and directly to the prospective customer's home. In 1880, after years of trial-and-error in Great Britain, Woodruff finally developed a set of rules and regulations that defined a "standard" field sales organization that could be transplanted outside Britain. The success of this canvasser method led Clark to adopt it as the standard model to be used throughout Europe. The critical element of Woodruff's system was the ability to monitor the daily efforts of each canvasser through the use of specific route assignments and systematic reports. McKenzie so admired this system that he adopted it for the United States and used it as a model for the company's expansion in Europe.

George Woodruff had been working in an advisory capacity since July 1882, and he left the firm permanently around the time of George McKenzie's retirement in 1889. He had, however, identified his successor, John Whittie, in 1882. Whittie, another Scot, had joined Singer in 1865, as a bookkeeper in Edinburgh. In 1876 he was transferred to London, and in 1878 he was promoted to assistant general manager. In 1892, he would become a victim of Frederick Bourne's plan to increase control over Singer's continental business, a presidential tendency that would recur from time to time well into the last half of the twentieth century, and in 1894, he would retire, burnt out and deteriorating physically at the age of forty-nine (Davies, 1976).

In 1878, following the end of the patent pool, Edward Clark was committed to writing his standard operating procedures for the most efficient organizational structure and the best operating procedures for the sale of sewing machines. Offices were to be organized by function:

—Headquarters

> —**Regional Central Office**: chief clerk, bookkeeper, lease (credit) account clerk, bills receivable clerk, shipping clerk, machinist, collector, traveler

> —**District Branch Office**: located in the largest towns with no less than 5,000 canvassing market size: manager, bookkeeper, mechanic, salesman, instructor

> —**Field Sales Personnel** (canvasser/collectors)* Note the focus on canvassing already in 1880

George Woodruff introduced a number of personnel management innovations to better control his canvassing organization in England:

- Compensation was to consist of a small fixed base plus commissions for sales—cash down—and collections.

- Territories were fixed and exclusive, with one route defined for each day of the week.

- Canvassers were to visit credit customers weekly to collect regular and late payments, and canvassers would use each collection visit to solicit new sales leads.

- Each office manager and salesperson was required to contribute to a "fidelity and guarantee fund," in the amount of one pound per year, "as a special assurance pool against dishonesty and embezzlement" (Davies, 1976).

George McKenzie had long admired Woodruff's field sales organization, and he was convinced that it should be adopted both in the United States and in the other countries of Europe. While the company was opening its own stores in the large central cities, these were largely for display and demonstration purposes. In its early years, Singer was primarily a door-to-door sales company. However, this final combination of retail stores for display and demonstration, door-to-door selling for customer education and service, and installment credit for affordability generated the enormous sales volume necessary for economic mass production.

The Continuing Hunger for Profit—Vertical Integration

Vertical integration occurs whenever a business firm does something for itself that it might otherwise have obtained on the market (Hovenkamp, March 2009, p. 1). Vertical integration can occur by means of three different legal structures. First, the firm can, without a change in its existing structure, simply begin doing something itself, rather than purchasing that product or service from a third party. Second, the firm might acquire a company that is vertically related, that produces the good or service the firm is currently purchasing on the market. The third method is contractual, in which the firm engages contractually with a vertically related firm, with each firm maintaining its own legal separation. A common example of such a relationship is franchising, which generally establishes the terms of an exclusive relationship between the two entities while maintaining separate ownership. In large multinational firms, management may create a series of vertically related legal entities for reasons other than vertical integration itself, such as tax minimization, union avoidance, or funding strategies through transfer pricing.

The incentive to integrate vertically derives from two sources: the desire to capture profit from as many of the levels from production of a product to its distribution to an eventual consumer, and the desire to have as much control as possible over one's sources of supply and distribution. The incentive can be directly economical, as the company considers the margins it loses each time it negotiates with its vendors or distributors. The incentive can be indirect, as the company considers the opportunity for cost of sales lost because a vendor failed to perform either on time or with acceptable quality.

Perversely, the decision to capture a production or distribution phase within a company does not necessarily eliminate the incentive to integrate vertically. It can merely transform the potential price/quality/delivery issues from outside the firm to inside. The sales manager will always tend to complain that his performance is, of course, dependent on his ability to have instantly available to him inventory of the right model with the best quality at an acceptable price. The factory manager who only assembles components manufactured elsewhere in the company is susceptible to delivery timing delays quality flaws that necessitate either rework or returns. And the component manufacturer is equally dependent on the vagaries of raw material availability.

From its very beginning, Singer displayed a strong tendency to vertical integration. Perhaps this derived from its unfortunate early experience with indirect sales organizations that management found difficult, if not impossible to control. Such integration could also have been a consequence of management's decision to build a business based on the marketing of the product, rather than its manufacture. Perhaps it was the result of the necessity to capture as much of the flow-through margin as possible in order to cover the high cost of bringing a sewing machine to market. Whatever the reasons, Singer began early on to manufacture as much of its own products as possible, rather than subcontract the manufacture to a third party, and it continued eventually to extend its direct control in phases over all of the components of production and distribution.

Phase One (1851): The Beginning

PRODUCTION: Sewing Machine Components: By the time Singer received the patent for his first machine on August 12, 1851, he had already formed a partnership with Orson C. Phelps, in whose shops Singer worked. It was natural then that Phelps would manufacture the machines for sale. By the end of that year, however, Singer had bought Phelps out and established I.M. Singer & Co., with its headquarters in New York. Phelps continued to manufacture the machine, although his scientific instrument-making shop was ill-equipped to manufacture the components for the 125-pound sewing machine. The result was that the original Singer &Company was essentially a sales and marketing firm, which subcontracted the manufacture of its product to Phelps, who in turn subcontracted the manufacture of the components to other suppliers and then assembled the finished machines.

DISTRIBUTION: Singer and Clark were both more interested in sales than manufacturing, and at this point Singer himself was the sales force.

Phase Two (1852–1853)

PRODUCTION: This two-tiered supply chain created inherent problems of both quality and delay in conflict with their publicly stated claim to have the best product on the market. However, it also presented the opportunity to capture the margin earned by Phelps for assembling the subcontracted parts. Within a year after Singer and Clark had formed the New York Company, they moved the assembly of sewing machines to a company facility on Center Street in New York. Initially, the New York factory employed essentially the same subcontracting system that Phelps did, functioning basically as an assembly plant rather than manufacturing itself.

DISTRIBUTION: In 1853 the company opened the first showroom/store at 458 Broadway in New York, employing its own demonstrators and salespersons. Singer himself was, by his own design, largely committed to improving the product technically, and Clark began to sign contracts with independent dealers for exclusive sales territories.

Phase Three (1854–1863)

PRODUCTION: The market demand for Singer sewing machines became so great that Singer could not keep up. Sales tripled between 1855–1856 and again between 1858–1859 with the introduction of the first household machine. The company continued to subcontract the manufacture of the working parts of the machine itself, while constructing its own foundry at Mott Street, New York, for the casting of the arms and beds. I.M. Singer & Co. was incorporated as the Singer Manufacturing Company, despite the fact that the actual manufacture of the parts was done elsewhere.

DISTRIBUTION: The independent dealer network presented the dual opportunities of capturing the dealer's margin and reasserting control over what had become uncontrollable anarchy in the sales organization. Clark repurchased sales territories from dealers and created the company's own door-to-door sales network.

Phase Four (1864–1881)

PRODUCTION: Gradually, the company expanded its own manufacturing capability at the Mott Street factory until by 1866 it had taken in house virtually all of the parts manufacture previously subcontracted. In 1869, the company opened its first overseas factory in Scotland and acquired the site for a much larger U.S. factory in Elizabethport, New Jersey. Still unable to keep up with market demand in the United States, Singer contracted with the Providence Tool Company for the manufacture of 27,000 separately branded sewing machines in an attempt to capitalize on the development of the low-end market that might diminish the image of the regular product line if sold under the Singer name. This same strategy would reappear later in the twentieth century as a means of stimulating total market growth once the company had captured a dominant market share. Begun in 1873, the Providence experience evolved into a joint venture called the Domestic Manufacturing Company until 1874, when it was terminated because of the factory's inability to deliver the quality that Singer required. By this time, the company had completed construction of the giant factory at Elizabethport, which by 1880 was producing all of the sewing machine components itself, from the arm and bed castings in its own foundry to the needles.

The integration of cabinet manufacture followed a different route. The earliest Singer machines were so heavy as to be largely limited to the garment industry. The introduction of the first household machines in the late 1850s necessitated the creation of a case to protect and carry it. For these machines, the company devised a packing box that, when opened, could double as a stand.

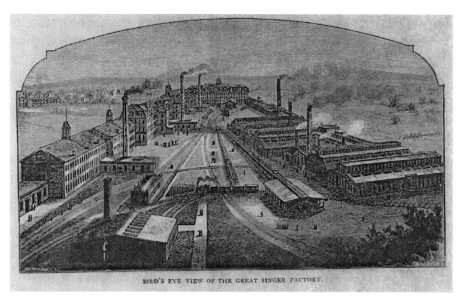

Bird's Eye View of the Great Singer Factory[23]

Singer Number One, 1858, in its original shipping crate, which was also used to provide foot power[24]

These boxes cum stands were manufactured in New York by a number of cabinetmakers. Among them, the firm of Francis X. Ross employed a young cabinetmaker, appropriately named Leighton Pine. In 1868 Pine, who had since joined Singer, convinced the company to open its own case manufacturing factory. At this time, the great hardwood forests of the United States still covered most of the Midwest, and the site chosen for the factory was South Bend, Indiana. The manufacturing of the cases quickly evolved into the production of hardwood cabinets and stands, some incorporating the use of veneers, in response to the Victorian tastes of the day.

Victorian cabinet, Singer automatic, showing the closed cabinet[25]

For three years, from 1868 to 1871, the veneers were supplied by companies in New York, after which the company switched to Midwestern suppliers. Finally, in 1881, the company opened its own veneer works in Cairo, Illinois (pronounced kay-ro).

DISTRIBUTION: The success of the British system of combining canvassers and collectors in the United States led Clark to replicate the system in the United States.

Phase Five (1882–1958)

PRODUCTION: As worldwide demand continued to grow through the first half of the twentieth century, the company would continue to expand its manufacturing network, opening major manufacturing facilities in Floridsdorf, Austria (1882); Montreal, Canada (1882); Podolsk, Russia (1902/05); Wittenberge, Prussia (1904); Bridgeport, Connecticut (1907); Bonnieres, France (1933/35); Monza, Italy (1933/34); Anderson, South Carolina (1950); Campinas, Brazil (1955); Utsunomiya, Japan (1956); Karlsruhe, Germany (1958); and Queratero, Mexico. Singer also acquired its principal competitor, Wheeler and Wilson, in 1905, and the company that made its electric motors (Diehl) in 1918. Additional cabinet factories were opened in Canada (St. Johns, 1906) and France (Alencon). The St. Johns factory offered an example of the lengths to which the company would go to vertically integrate its manufacturing processes. In 1923, Singer acquired five hundred square miles of hardwood forest in Quebec, the Thurso Woodlands, to supply the factory. It then constructed a mill at the railway used to ship the milled wood to the factory. To complete the circuit, in 1925 Singer constructed the Thurso and Nation Valley Railway to transport the cut logs to the mill. Although this extreme of vertical integration was only possible by the proximity of hardwood forests, which were very soon to disappear, everything in the manufacturing and distribution process in North America, from the trees to the collection of the customers' installment payments, was now an integrated component of the Singer system.

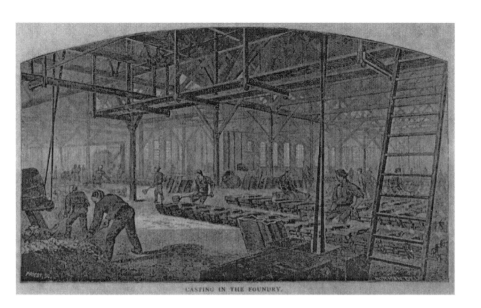

CASTING IN THE FOUNDRY.

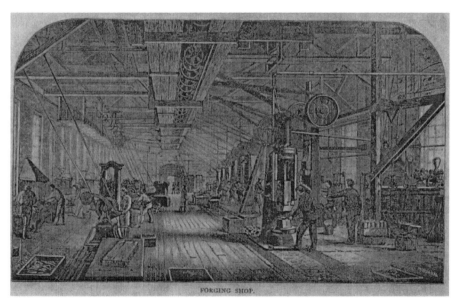

FORGING SHOP.

BRASS FURNACE.

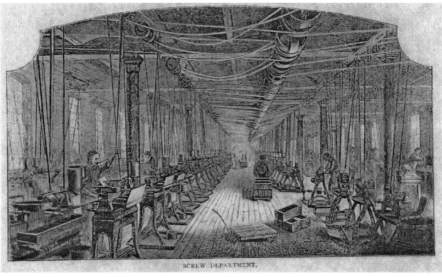

SCREW DEPARTMENT.

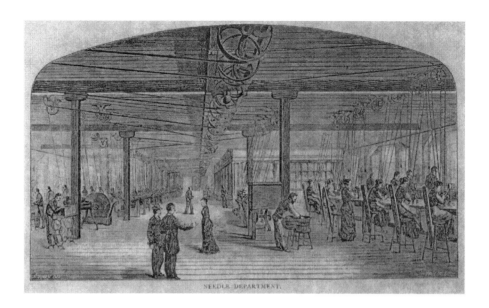

NEEDLE DEPARTMENT.

ASSEMBLING ROOM.

JAPANNING FURNACES.

POLISHING ROOM.

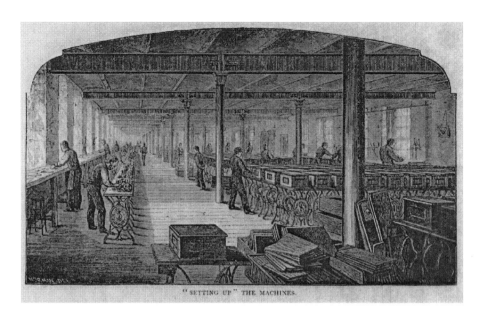

"SETTING UP" THE MACHINES.

TESTING THE MACHINES.

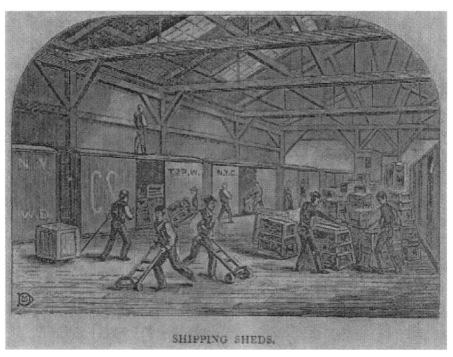

SHIPPING SHEDS.

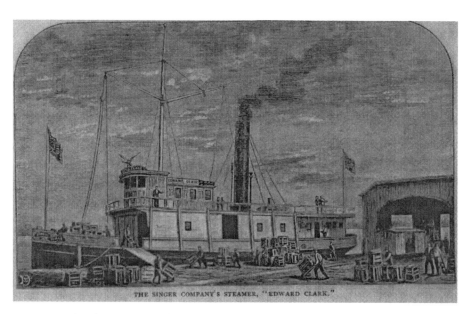

The Singer Company's steamer "Edward Clark," Elizabethport, 1880[30]

Notwithstanding the complete vertical integration of Singer's manufacturing and distribution systems, there remained an additional opportunity to maximize the flow-through margin earned on sewing machines. In countries where Singer did not manufacture, governments saw an opportunity to impose substantial duties on imported sewing machines, creating both a new potential revenue stream and an opportunity for less efficient local manufacturers to produce competing machines. Singer's reaction to this was to open local plants for the assembly of sets of parts shipped from the primary factories. This had the dual advantage of minimizing the duties, typically determined as a function of the value added at the port of entry, and using lower cost local labor for the assembly of the machines, minimizing the cost advantage of local competition. This strategy was particularly effective in combating the sales of other "foreign" importers who did not have the local sales volume to justify the construction of a local assembly plant. Finally, the locally assembled machine built further on the fiction that Singer was a local company.

The Core Model for the Singer Manufacturing Company was now complete. Isaac Singer, Edward Clark, and George McKenzie had pooled their individual talents to create a business model that, with relatively minor improvements, would serve the company until the Japanese sewing machine invasion following World War II.

The Final Components of the Singer Core Business Model

Unequaled product design and distribution capabilities: Through the development of its own patents and the strategic acquisition of others, the company produced the first truly household sewing machine. The Patent Pool had frozen further competitive product improvements, as any advances would be shared with other members of the pool. Singer was thus able to concentrate on designing, but not incorporating, technical improvements in anticipation of the end of the Patent Pool in 1877. Innovative marketing techniques created a significant discernible difference between Singer and the competition. An extensive proprietary international sales network, coupled with an equally strong overseas manufacturing capability, permitted strong market development, both domestic and foreign, while carefully controlling retail prices and flow-through margins.

An improbable but highly effective partnership: Isaac Singer was a talented inventor with an ego that rendered him incapable of admitting to any technical inferiority in his product. He was self-motivated in the extreme, both by the desire for wealth and an inability to concede fault or control over his product's development. His "take no prisoners" attitude toward business made it difficult for him to deal with in a partnership, much less a large and growing corporate organization. Edward Clark was a highly skilled lawyer who carefully protected the company's interests, but he also had exceptional innovative talents in marketing and sales management. Clark could admit his own lack of interest in the actual production of sewing machines, but nevertheless he foresaw the need to develop sophisticated a worldwide manufacturing organization, one that could satisfy the extraordinary demand that he had created for their product while maintaining high quality and technological superiority, all at the lowest possible cost. George McKenzie's primary skills were in manufacturing organization and management. He had been with the company since its earliest days, advancing step by step to senior management. McKenzie's interest and skill in manufacturing was the equal of Clark's in marketing, and he oversaw the construction of two of the largest manufacturing facilities in the world at Clydebank, Scotland, and Elizabethport, New Jersey.

An invaluable contract with the customer: The rationale that makes the business mutually beneficial for both the company and its customers had not changed from the very beginning. It was the opportunity to mechanize a task that had consumed enormous amounts of labor, both industrially and in the household. The challenge was how to make the device affordable, easy to use, and reliable. While the sewing machine was initially directed at the professional and industrial trades, the market for which, although substantial, was limited relative to the potential of household use. Singer had introduced the first machine dedicated to household use.

Market domination: With the patent pools, Singer had essentially neutralized any potential technical advantages by the competition. It used that period of parity to develop an image of technical superiority and affordability through the introduction of a succession of marketing innovations that quickly became standard operating procedure for the retail sales of consumer appliances. By the time the patent pools expired, Singer had created a market demand for its sewing machines that had grown from 25 percent of the market when the Patent Pool was created, to almost 50 percent when it ended, twice that of the nearest competitor.

A practically infinite target market: The worldwide demand for the sewing machine quickly expanded beyond the United States, potentially to the entire world. Singer responded by opening branch sales offices in the 1850s in Europe and South America, followed by branches or exclusive agents on all of the continents by 1883.

Tightly controlled distribution channels: The Company initially used an independent sales organization based on exclusive territories. The inability to control the agent's activities, particularly their selling of competitive machines, led Singer quickly to convert to a direct sales organization combining stores and door-to-door salesmen in England and in the United States. The same pattern would be followed elsewhere overseas, using independent agents only where demand was insufficient to justify the cost of a direct organization.

A continuing customer relationship: The links between the company and the customer were extremely close, especially in the door-to-door organization. Demonstrations, collections, and service calls provided frequent opportunities to create customer loyalty and the demand for follow-on sales of related products.

The lowest manufacturing cost structure: The cost of the retail organization was high, but it was more than covered by the contribution of the installment credit business. Manufacturing costs were initially higher than the competition, but the sheer force of the unit volume generated by Clark's marketing innovations, coupled with the gradual adoption of mass production methods at the factory, brought unit production costs below those of the competition.

Revenues and profit: The combination was a total flow-through margin that gave Singer a virtually insurmountable advantage over the competition. Following its acquisition of Wheeler and Wilson, the Singer Manufacturing Company would reach an estimated 90 percent of the world market for sewing machines by the end of the century. In 1882, the year Edward Clark passed away, the Singer sold over 600,000 sewing machines and its estimated profits were $3,800,000 ($92 million in 2014 dollars).

Although it was called the Singer Manufacturing Company, it remained essentially a partnership, as there were only two shareholders. It was a money machine, creating wealth for the Singer and Clark families beyond their wildest dreams. They would become two of the first great fortunes in America that were neither linked to land ownership nor inherited. It was almost inevitable that those fortunes would become a mixed blessing. While alive, both partners focused on increasing the symbols of their wealth, mimicking the lifestyles of the wealthy families who had gone before. At the time of their deaths, Singer in 1875 and Clark in 1882, neither founder had a family member interested in running the company. Their descendants were accustomed to an easy life of extravagance and leisure, and both partners had left estates more than sufficient to provide for such a life for as far as the eye could see. Singer's estate of $15 million ($273 million in 2014 dollars) would be split among his twenty-four acknowledged children, both legitimate and illegitimate, and their mothers, with the exception of Mary Ann, who had sued Singer for adultery. Clark's estate of $50 million ($1.2 billion in 2014 dollars) was left to his sole surviving son, Alfred. Both of the estates consisted largely of each's 40 percent ownership of the Singer Manufacturing Company, the value of which had more than doubled in the seven years following Singer's death. The estimated current values of those estates almost certainly understates the eventual value to the descendants, as they reflect only the impact of inflation and not any of the intervening growth in the value of the company itself over the ensuing century.

In any case, both families found themselves with fortunes beyond their abilities to spend on themselves, although several made valiant efforts.

CHAPTER THREE:

The Legacies of Singer and Clark

At the end of the nineteenth century, the strongest believer in a philanthropic obligation of the wealthy was Andrew Carnegie, who put forth the rationale for this belief in an 1889 essay titled "The Gospel of Wealth." In it he contends that the Industrial Revolution had created great disparities of wealth and that it was "…the proper administration of wealth that the ties of brotherhood may still bind together the rich and poor in harmonious relationship." He believed that there were only three ways of disposing of surplus wealth; leaving it to the descendants; bequeathing it for a public purpose; or administering it in one's lifetime. The first he equated to the vanities and privilege of the European monarchies and their evident failure to improve society. The second he equated to an abdication of responsibility to ensure that the legacy be put to the beneficial purpose desired. The third he found to be the only mode with the potential to alleviate the "temporary" unequal distribution of wealth. He believed that, "The man who dies thus rich dies disgraced."

Such belief was much discussed at the end of the 19th century, but had not yet reached broad consensus during Singer and Clark's lifetimes. The difference in how each treated the disposition of his fortune reflected either, in the case of Singer no relevant reference points whatsoever or, in the case of Clark the Puritan New England tradition. As successive generations of these two families moved into the twentieth century, it is interesting to consider how, in each case, their feelings concerning the responsibilities of wealth evolved.

Prior to the industrial revolution and the creation of a middle class in the United States, the relationship between the wealthy and the poor followed that of the European countries from which the new Americans had emigrated. Ownership of the land and the ability to pass it from one generation to the next was the defining socio-economic characteristic. To the extent that the gentry might feel a need to favor the people who worked their farms, it was more likely to have found its origin in a desire to preserve the existing serfdom structure than any sense of altruism. The Singers and the Clarks were for their time two of the wealthiest families in the World, having amassed wealth beyond their ability to spend within their lifetimes. Each had to deal, consciously or not, with the question of how that wealth would be used once they were gone. Someone also once said that "There is no such thing as a purely altruistic act." It was clear at the end of the nineteenth century, however, that either through a desire to create the best public image for one's self, or to counter some sense of guilt associated with the distance between the wealthy and the poor, the notion of philanthropy became the means by which the families of great wealth unburdened themselves.

The Very Extensive Family of Isaac Singer[31]

Upon his retirement and return to Europe, Singer had met an Englishwoman there named Pamela Lockwood, who had married a Frenchman, Louis Boyer. Pamela ran a pension in Paris, where Singer apparently called on her, but he soon transferred his attention to Pamela's daughter, Isabella Eugenie Boyer Summerville. This story has several variations, depending on which family is relating it. In any case, Pamela urged her daughter to do the best that she could, and Singer was soon traveling with Isabella on both sides of the Atlantic. Isabella had been living in America after her marriage to a Mr. Summerville, but she and Isaac installed themselves in Singer's Fifth Avenue house. Isabella, now pregnant, obtained a divorce from Mr. Summerville, Singer obtained a renunciation from Mary Ann, and in June 1863, they were married. He was fifty-two years old and she twenty-two. A striking woman, Isabella was rumored to have been Bartholdi's model for the Statue of Liberty.

Isabella Singer[32]

Singer thought that he was through with both Catherine and Mary Ann, was ready to settle down with a pretty young woman, and was about to become a father for the nineteenth (known) time. All was good, except that Catherine now reopened her case, claiming that at the time of their divorce Singer had falsified his wealth. Singer engaged his and Catherine's son, William, asking that he testify on Singer's behalf. William, wishing to remain independent, refused, and Singer became violently angry. The two became estranged and never spoke again.

Singer's waning interest in the company had been accompanied by a waning interest in the United States. He discovered in 1864 what many businessmen of the twentieth century had found, that when the dollar was no longer linked to gold, floating currencies provide some interesting opportunities (and risks). In 1860, he expressed his opinion that overseas agencies were a waste of time.

> My belief is that if we had never had anything to do with foreign countries and had attended more strictly to that of our own, we should be much better off today. Now I should like to know in past (?) I want Mr. Hooper to send me the exact account of profit and loss of the business outside of the one (in the) United States of America. Our country—what will become of our country. I am satisfied that the feelings of the English are with the south and are only waiting for our government to (do) something which they may construe into an overt act to lend aid to the South. (WSHS, June 1, 1861 letter from Singer to Clark)

By the end of the Civil War in 1864, the Pound Sterling was worth thirteen to fourteen U.S. dollars. A machine sold in the United States, if one could find a customer with any money, was worth much less than one sold in Great Britain. The reverse was also true. The company had to provide him with twelve to thirteen U.S. dollars for each dollar he wished to spend in England, and he wished to spend a lot. In order to continue his accustomed lifestyle, he was draining the company's resources. Clark reasoned that his partner's lifestyle could well contribute to a short life expectancy, and there was a good chance that his will, had he drawn one, could be as complicated as his life, with many of its elements contested by some of his twenty-something known heirs.

By this time, Singer and Clark were no longer the sole shareholders in the company. They had sold shares to four officers, at which time the ownership of a certain number of shares became a requirement to become an officer. Twenty-three other employees were given the opportunity to purchase shares, and twelve took up the offer, for which the company accepted personal notes. Within two years, dividends had returned the cost of those shares and from then on it was all profit.

Singer now had few worries to distract him from his distractions. He had enviable income, a more or less stable personal life, all had been disclosed to his young wife, and the family was comfortably installed in the Fifth Avenue house. But comfort was not to be. Isabella, possibly feeling that New York Society still had no place for Singer, expressed a desire to make a complete break with the city and move. The choice of Yonkers, New York, might appear surprising to the modern reader, but in 1864 Yonkers was a suburban town on the Hudson River with superb air and enchanting views across the river. They first moved to a house where they could live comfortably while Isaac focused on the real project. He purchased several hundred acres on the edge of town and set out to build what was to become known as "The Castle." The house on Fifth Avenue was fashionable, but that was all. It was convenient for work, but now he had no further work responsibilities. It was convenient for their relatively small social life, but that had always tended to be around family or a few close friends, never a destination for the higher reaches of New York Society. Yonkers would be different. It would be magisterial, a destination that New York could not ignore.

When it was finished, great plans were made for an unforgettable house-warming party. A newspaper reported that "hundreds were invited. Few went" (Brandon, 1977). Singer had always been more interested in his own pleasure than the reputation that that behavior had created in Manhattan. Now that reputation had followed him. While his lifestyle was still the subject of conversation in New York, it would not be the subject of conversation in Yonkers. Singer and his family were completely isolated.

Isaac and Isabella stuck it out for two years before moving to Paris. In 1866, the Castle was closed up and rented to a wealthy New York hat manufacturer. In Paris they settled in on the Boulevard Malsherbes, a respectable but undistinguished address, and by 1870, they had three more children to join the two who had been born in New York. In 1870, the Franco-Prussian War broke out and the family decamped again, this time to London, where they first settled at Brown's Hotel, then, in response to Isabella's delicate health, to Torquay on the Devon coast. At first they resided at the Victoria and Albert Hotel, but this proved inappropriate for a large and occasionally boisterous family. Besides, Singer thought they should have something more appropriate for their "stature." He commissioned a local architect to build him a fitting successor to the Castle, and to announce that he was an American, he named it after the American Indian word for "home," the "Wigwam." In acquiring a suitable amount of land, Singer had acquired the large property already for sale, plus, with one exception, about twenty other cottages, gardens, and other open lands. He wished to have an unobstructed view of the sea, and he was every architect's nightmare, on the site every day, criticizing what had been built and having it torn down to begin again, offering suggestions that couldn't be realized and making endless changes at the drop of a hat. Cost was of no consequence. A particularly Singer architectural innovation was the construction of an arena next to the house. It would have a removable circular floor, perhaps inspired by the courtyard for the white stallions of the Vienna court, so that it

Oldway (the "Wigwam"[33]

could be used to exercise horses, have parties for the children, and host performances by a company of artists Singer intended to form so that he might return to his original love of acting.

The parties at the Wigwam were appropriately lavish, with invitations to all of the better-class folk of the district. He would distribute lavish gifts to some of the belles of the ball, if they attracted his still-roving eye. Nonetheless, his scandalous behavior in America followed him to Torquay and the source of his wealth was unacceptable to the landed gentry of Devon. He continued to throw his lavish balls, inviting primarily the tradesmen of the region, who were unlikely to have any knowledge of his past, much less to care, as he was a generous and entertaining neighbor.

Isaac Singer died on July, 23, 1875, at age 63, without ever seeing the Wigwam completed. Singer left detailed instructions for his funeral, certainly the most elaborate ever seen by the two thousand people of Torquay who attended.

> "After the mourning coaches (reported the local paper) came Mr. Singer's carriage, with blinds drawn, and drawn by two splendid bay horses. This was followed by carriages containing the men and women servants employed at Oldway (the estate), and behind them walked four deep, about 50 men who worked on the estate. Large numbers of private and tradesmen's carriages closed the procession. The funeral slowly wended its way towards Torquay, along the road to which a large number of persons had assembled. By the time the cortege reached the Strand the private carriages had nearly doubled in number; all along the route men, women and children of all stations of life lined the footpaths. The principal establishments at Torquay and Paignton were partially closed, flags lowered to half mast, and at the latter town, the church bell was tolled. The funeral procession was nearly three-quarters of a mile long, and contained between seventy and eighty carriages. The planned mausoleum at Paignton cemetery took up too much room so it was built at Torquay cemetery instead."

Singer left an estate estimated at fifteen million dollars (approximately $273 million in 2015 dollars). Most of this consisted of Singer company stock, of which he owned forty percent. In his will, Singer made a few small bequests, then had the remainder divided into sixty equal parts of $250,000, which were distributed to each member of his extended family. (Singer would admit to siring twenty-four legitimate and illegitimate children.)

- Isabella received four parts. Of the children Singer had with Isabella:

  Adam Mortimer received six parts,

  Winnaretta received five parts,

  Washington received six parts,

  Paris received six parts,

  Isabelle Blanche received five parts,

  Franklin received six parts,

- His daughter Violetta received nothing, on the grounds that Singer had arranged for the employment at the company of her husband, William Proctor, through which he had built his own fortune.

- William and Lillian, his first legitimate children, received only $500 and $10,000 respectively, due to their support of their mother in her 1863 countersuit.

- Mary Ann received nothing and, alone among the legatees, contested the will.

  Attempts at settlement between Isabella, the primary legatee, and Mary Ann failed, and the trial fulfilled everyone's worst nightmares with the full disclosure of Isaac Singer's complicated personal life. Only the lawyers and the newspapers profited from the month-long testimony of Mary Ann and her supporting witnesses. The judge finally found that Mary Ann's claim to be Mrs. Singer was "undoubtedly without foundation," and that Isabella was the legitimate widow. Journalists debated the result, with Singer receiving considerable support for taking responsibility for his extended family in his will. Mary Ann appealed the decision but lost.

Postmortem

In 1879, Isabella returned to Paris where, as a good-looking, young, and wealthy widow, she was asked to be Bartholdi's model for the Statue of Liberty. She received much notice among the community of appropriate suitors and went on to marry Victor Reubsaet, a Belgian musician rumored to have been a "friend" of Isabella's before her marriage to Singer. Reubsaet had inherited the title of Viscount d'Estemburgh from an uncle, followed by another title when an additional uncle died, allowing Victor to become the Vatican Duke of Camposelice. Isabella was now a duchess. Out of fear that the duke would waste his new wife's fortune, as well as their own, Isabella's boys were advised, upon reaching the age of sixteen, to run away and become wards of the court, thus protecting their shares of the estate. This naturally created serious strife within the family, as Victor considered their shares to be part of the "family fortune," to be drawn upon as needed by Isabella and himself. The conflict was resolved when the duke finally accepted the fait accompli, but not without some lingering bitterness. Victor, the duke of Camposelice, died in 1887, and Isabella went on to enjoy eventual social, if not familial, acceptance by Parisian society. Isabella's children went on to varying degrees of social and financial success.

Adam Mortimer Singer made England his permanent home, becoming Sir Mortimer and, in 1921, the high sheriff of Berkshire.

In 1887, just prior to Singer's death, Winnaretta Singer had married a presumably wealthy prince, Louis de Scey-Montbeliard. As it turned out, the prince had little more than his title. His family continually asked her for money, and apparently both his title and his wealth had been fabricated. By 1889, she so regretted the marriage that she sued for divorce. Winnaretta went on to become a patron of the arts, as both a painter and a musician herself. In 1893, she would marry Prince Edmond de Polignac, a talented composer, art collector, and literary figure, a member of the set so avidly documented by Marcel Proust. Prince Polignac, considerably older than Winnaretta, died in 1903, and as the Princess de Polignac, Winnaretta went on to create the Foundation Singer-Polignac, for the purpose of supporting the arts, letters, and sciences. In 1928, she endowed the foundation with a gift of 300,000 francs, and upon her death in 1945 she left it her grand house on the Avenue Georges Mandel, which the foundation occupies to this day. At the same time, the foundation received an additional anonymous gift from the Royal Trust Company of Montreal "in memory of Winnaretta Singer, princess Edmond de Polignac." The esteem in which Winnaretta was held by the French was such that one of the first board members of the foundation was Raymond Poincare, past president of France. This gift to France appears to have been the first overt act of significant philanthropy by any member of the extended Singer family.

Washington Singer also remained in England, where, in 1924, he became the sheriff of Wiltshire. He was particularly interested in horse racing, and his most tangible gift to the public is now the Washington Singer Stakes run every year at Newbury.

Paris Singer, the son most after his father's heart, was also inclined toward the arts. He combined this taste with an apparently inherited taste for beautiful women in a much publicized liaison with the dancer Isadora Duncan. Aside from Isadora's ability to interpret social and artistic theories, she was a communist, which created certain problems for their relationship. Following the birth of their son, Patrick, she considered marriage but rejected it as a contradiction to her life as an artist. She consented, however, to a trial life together at the Wigwam in Torquay, which Paris had acquired by buying his brothers' interests. Paris had it renovated to resemble Versailles and the Petit Trianon, but to no avail. She refused to marry him, as she could not get beyond the fact of his wealth. Paris would go on to finance the building of the new resort of Palm Beach, Florida, before losing much of his fortune in the crash of 1929.

Isabelle Blanche Singer became engaged to Duke Decazes, the young son of a government minister, whose title had apparently also been manufactured. Nonetheless, Isabelle became the second "duchess" of the Singer family, but unfortunately she died suddenly in 1896, at the age of only twenty-seven.

Franklin Morse Singer would go on to pursue his abiding interest in sailing.

The Clark Family's Love of Real Estate and the Arts[34]

By the time Ed Clark met Isaac Singer, he and Caroline Jordan already had a complete family of four children: Ambrose (1836), Edward (1838), Julia (1841), and Alfred (1844). Unlike Singer, Clark was already a member of the emerging upper-middle-class establishment. His father, Nathan, owned a nationally known successful business, the Athens Pottery Works, was a senior warden in the Episcopal Church, and was well respected in the community. Nathan helped build the local church and was well-known for his generous giving to charity. He was free from ostentation and forever conscious of the needs of his community. Edward, tutored in Latin at home, was a voracious reader, and at the age of fifteen, one of the first men to enroll at Williams College. It being well before the existence of bar exams, Edward apprenticed at the firm of Ambrose L. Jordan, and in 1835 he married the boss's daughter. Three years later, he moved with his stepfather's firm to New York, where it became known as the most prestigious law firm in the city.

In his first encounter with Singer in 1849, Clark resolved for him the question of the title of Singer's latest invention, the sewing machine, and when in

1851 Elias Howe initiated litigation against him, Singer turned naturally to the lawyer who had solved his most recent legal problem. By this time, Caroline Clark had formed a strong opinion of this "nasty brute," and she urged Edward to have nothing further to do with Singer. Edward, however, saw right away the potential for Singer's invention to make them both rich, and the partnership, while never close, was well established.

Caroline Clark died in 1874, a year before her loathed Isaac Singer. Following Singer's death, Clark looked after the well-being of Isabella Singer and her children and began to consider the condition and eventual disposition of his own estate. His eldest son, Ambrose, never married or had children. His second eldest son, Edward Lorraine, had died in 1869 at the age of thirty-nine. His daughter, Julia, had survived for only two months after her birth in 1841. That left only Clark's youngest son, Alfred, who had married and started a family. Alfred and his wife would eventually have four children, two of whom would establish, for better or worse, the family's somewhat unique philanthropic reputation in the twentieth century.

Central Park West construction, c.1890[35]

After Singer's death, Clark returned to guiding the company to success upon success, generating a degree of wealth that would far surpass that of Singer at his death. In 1877, continually searching for opportunities to leverage his wealth even further, Clark invested in real estate. First he purchased a parcel on the west side of Seventh Avenue, between Fifty-fifth and Fifty-sixth streets. On it, he had built the Van Corlear, a luxury apartment building designed to appeal to those with a propensity toward French culture. Each apartment had two thousand square feet and was designed to feel like a private house. The second parcel was located on Central Park West, at the corner of Seventy-second Street. At the time, the site was so far removed from any neighborhood considered desirable that it became known as "Clark's folly." A friend likened it to building in the distant Dakota, the territory that would later be admitted to the Union as two states. Clark immediately adopted the name and began construction.

He would not see it finished, as he died in 1882, two years before its completion. As we know today, the building that stood all alone on the crest of a hill overlooking

The Dakota, c.1895[36]

Central Park would become the legendary home of John Lennon and Lauren Bacall, among other notables.

Edward and Caroline had also begun to travel. They decamped three times to a rented home in France and spent a winter in Italy. During those trips they began an art collection, and, in 1869, they built a stone mansion, called "Fernleigh," near Cooperstown, New York. His father-in-law had begun practicing law there, and it was to become a lifelong anchor for the family.

Fernleigh was more than sufficient to display the trophies of their travels. This was an ostentation quite different from the explosive brashness of Singer. Clark

"Fernleigh" c.1890[37]

felt he was bringing the best of continental European style to America, setting a family pattern of spending money with panache and no self-consciousness, a tradition that his grandsons would eagerly follow. Five years later, Clark acquired an additional five hundred acres near the town, on which he constructed a Swiss chalet "picknicking" house. This was followed, two years after Caroline's death, by a sixty-five-foot castle that rose out of Lake Otsego, New York, and resembled an eleventh- or twelfth-century French chateau. The construction of Kingfisher Tower, as it was known, brought both an appreciation of European culture as well as employment to Cooperstown during a period of widespread unemployment.

As both of Clark's eldest sons predeceased him, Edward in 1869 and Ambrose in 1880, Alfred Corning Clark became Clark's sole surviving heir. Edward Clark had never been entirely at ease with the notion that Alfred might end up managing the family's as well as the company's affairs, and he had left his real estate portfolio to his grandsons: Edward Severing Clark, Robert Sterling Clark, Frederick Ambrose Clark, and Stephen Carlton Clark. The block that

"Kingfisher Tower"[38]

included the Dakota went to Edward, and each of the other three sons received a city block or its equivalent on the west side of Manhattan. In addition to the real estate, Clark left an estate of fifty million dollars ($1.2 billion in 2015 dollars), a sum sufficient to sustain the family, their real estate, their collections, and their philanthropy through the twentieth century. Edward Clark had straddled two worlds, the upper strata of New York society, with its Puritan notions of acceptable behavior, and an association with someone universally regarded as the most uncouth heathen in the city. Clark's exclusive focus on building his personal fortune permitted him to ignore the pleas of Caroline to dissociate himself from Singer. He single-mindedly pursued his goal and left his grandsons with the notion of the importance of control, along with sufficient bravery to take risks. Sterling and Stephen applied those principles in spades. Fifty years later, their bank accounts permitted them to take risks that , arguably, altered the culture of the United States.

Alfred Corning Clark lacked the traits necessary to manage the family wealth with the same fervor as his father. Initially, he wanted little to do with the Singer Manufacturing Company, and he escaped the family pressures by moving to Milan. While there, he inherited five hundred thousand dollars from his grandmother, which gave him independence from his demanding father, and there he experienced what he described as the happiest period of his life, engrossed in art and companionship. Without an occupation and relieved of the need to make money, he was famously generous and a quintessential business and family man with four sons, interested in both philanthropy and the arts, but with one less conventional trait: his attraction toward other men. While never overtly stated, there is ample evidence to suggest that Alfred was homosexual and that he led a passionate existence among a community of the arts on the other side of the Atlantic. He began a relationship with a Norwegian tenor, Lorentz Severin Skougaard, which lasted nineteen years. Alfred was able to maintain his double life by doing what was expected of him. He married, had children, and conducted his life in New York as a respected father and businessman. At the same time, he would depart for an annual summer visit to Norway, where he would see his friend and his friend's family. He became the music critic for the *New York Times* and installed Skougaard, who lived just down the block from Alfred and his family, as his assistant.

Edward Clark had nurtured the hope that his eldest son, Ambrose, would assume responsibility for the family upon his death, and since Alfred had little desire to assume that role, he begged his father to convey his share of the family fortune to Ambrose. To Alfred's surprise, his father agreed and sent Ambrose to Italy to sign the necessary papers. Once in Milan, Ambrose became ill and within a week was dead. When Edward Clark died two years later, Alfred had no choice but to assume many of his father's roles. He continued with his male companion for three more years, until the singer suddenly died. His sons, Sterling and Stephen, were particularly influenced by Alfred's nineteen-year relationship with Skougaard, described by one writer as "Clark's lifelong male companion."

Following the singer's death, Alfred engaged George Grey Bernard, a young and handsome but struggling American sculptor living in Paris, to carve a muscular nude memorial to commemorate his companion. Alfred eventually turned the destitute artist into his "kept boy," taking him to New York, where, with Alfred's assistance, he helped create the Cloisters Museum. Alfred's sons maintained a friendly relationship with each other, and as Alfred nurtured their appreciation for the wonders of European art, they began collecting it.

Alfred devoted himself more and more to philanthropy, becoming a trustee of Williams College in 1882, although for a time, he was obliged to concern himself with the management of the New York real estate holdings. Earlier, Alfred had become friends with Frederick Bourne, a young man he had encountered as a member of the Mendelssohn Glee Club, an all-male singing society that Alfred had joined in his youth. Impressed by Bourne's industriousness, Alfred recommended him to his father, who made him the construction manager of the Dakota, which he successfully managed to completion, and in 1889, after his father's death, Alfred had Bourne appointed president of Singer, effectively recusing himself completely from the business. From the time of the tenor's death and Alfred's meeting Bernard, Alfred's life was consumed by an ever-growing appreciation of art and an ever-decreasing interest in the affairs of the Clark estate. He had become "an eccentric, warm-hearted, conflicted father…(who)…was inevitably a major determinant in the lives of Stephen and Sterling Clark and their brothers. Their public veneers, their sympathies, and their intense rages had their origins in the truly unusual nature of their childhoods, which seemed so orderly on the surface and were so full of surprises underneath" (Weber, 2007).

One of the traits of the relatively unknown in Alfred was his compulsion to use his inheritance for the benefit of others, well beyond mere kindness or generosity. He particularly sought young men under duress, perhaps reflecting the lifelong pressure his father had placed on him. A notable example was a piano prodigy named Josef Hoffmann, who, at age eleven, made his debut at the Metropolitan Opera House in New York. The effect of his performance was electric, and he was immediately put on tour, giving fifty-two concerts within two months. Alfred felt that this fragile boy was being used as a circus performer, and he approached the boy's father and offered him five hundred dollars if his son would leave the stage and not return before he was eighteen. The father accepted Alfred's offer and immediately departed with his son for Berlin, where the boy studied, as the only private pupil, with the famous Russian composer and pianist Anton Rubinstein. At age eighteen, the boy returned to the stage, where he went on to have a spectacular career.

By 1893, Alfred was regarded as one of the most generous people in New York. That year, the World's Columbian Exposition in Chicago had a major loan exhibition. Alfred kept art in both his vast apartment at the Dakota and in the family house on Twenty-Second Street. Aside from a Corot, three Millets, and two by Delacroix, Alfred also lent a work by Jean-Leon Gerome, depicting a young naked boy, as seen from behind, with an immense snake curled around his body. Here were all of Alfred's tastes made manifest, not just his sexual preferences, but his craving for other worlds, for the exotic, for the confrontation with danger, for ruggedness. Having entered the kingdom of beautiful art, rich music, and strong young men, Alfred Corning Clark was "beyond the point of wearing a mask" (Weber, 2007).

When Alfred died of pneumonia in 1896, his fortune surpassed that of J.P. Morgan, who died seventeen years later. All of the Singer shares were in a trust to be divided equally among his widow and four sons. Elizabeth Scriven Clark, Alfred's widow, had weathered a complicated life, but she was of great character with strongly held values. Shortly after Alfred's death, she built one of the most spectacular mansions ever seen in Manhattan. It was designed by Ernest Flagg, the Paris-trained architect who had designed the Singer building on lower Broadway, then under construction. Built on a bend in Riverside Drive at Eighty-Ninth Street, it seemed more of a country estate than a city townhouse, and it was far removed from the Clark residential history at the Dakota and in lower Manhattan. Alfred's widow, Elizabeth, was about to make a name for herself.

Elizabeth Scriven Clark's residence at Ninety-Ninth Street and Riverside Drive, c.1905[39]

A major crisis facing New York at the beginning of the twentieth century was the shortage of decent housing for the tenement dwellers of lower Manhattan. The legislature could neither destroy nor improve their "slaughter-houses." A group of wealthy capitalists formed the Association for Improving the Condition of the Poor, banded together, and formed the Suburban Homes Corporation, which raised one million dollars by subscription to build homes. Mrs. Clark was the first person to support the effort in any significant way. She bought a tenth of the stock of the new company to erect new tenements on nineteen lots west of Tenth Avenue, which housed nearly four hundred recently arrived families of Italian immigrants.

In 1902, Elizabeth married the Episcopal bishop of New York, Henry Codman Potter. The bishop had gotten to know Mrs. Clark especially well when she laid the cornerstone of the Alfred Corning Clark Memorial Church on East Thirty-first Street, on which Elizabeth had spent about one hundred thousand dollars. Elizabeth immediately became associated with charitable giving on a grand scale. At the time, the bishop was occupied with the Cathedral of St. John the Divine, whose construction he had initiated. When he died only six years after marrying Elizabeth, she again paid for a church in her husband's memory, the St. James Chapel at the Cathedral. By now, the Clarks had altered the city of New York in visible ways. The palatial mansion on Riverside Drive had become an instant landmark.

The Singer building on lower Broadway was for a time the tallest building in the world. Frederick Bourne, now the president of the Singer Manufacturing Company, had acquired additional land for a loft building at Broadway and Prince Streets, also to be designed by Ernest Flagg. Dissatisfied with the current style of Manhattan skyscrapers, Flagg convinced Bourne to acquire more land to accommodate a new style of construction, with the building set back from the street to allow more light to find the surrounding sidewalk, a style that eventually found its way into the setback requirements of today's New York construction code.

The Singer Building, 149 Broadway, c.1910[40]

In many ways, the Clarks most lasting legacy was yet to come. With the deaths of Alfred Corning and Elizabeth Scriven Clark, their four sons became some of the richest people in the world, and they continued the philanthropic tradition instilled in them by Edward Clark and reinforced by their mother. The Clark brothers were comfortable with their wealth, and they accepted the responsibilities that came with it, the obligation to be generous to those less fortunate. Each followed that tradition in his own unique way, but with a competitive ferocity that only someone with limitless resources could match.

Robert Sterling Clark and Stephen Carleton Clark[41]

Sterling had spent the winters in New York City and the summers at the family's Cooperstown estate, Fernleigh. At twenty-one, he suddenly found himself in one of the Upper West Side's most spectacular mansions. He studied engineering at Yale, followed by a tour in the U.S. Army during the Spanish-American War and the Boxer Rebellion. He returned to the United States to work for the War Department in Washington, where he continued another family tradition of extravagant entertaining. Impatient for further adventure, Sterling returned to China in 1905 as part of a research expedition, where he indulged a newfound passion for the artistic representation of beauty. Returning from the expedition, he decided to move to France, where he bought himself an imposing house in one of the most desirable neighborhoods in Paris. There, he devoted himself to amassing an art collection that even his father could never have imagined.

Sterling Clark's house at 4 rue Cimerosa, c.1910[42]

In the aftermath of their mother's death, the sons attempted to behave responsibly, working together to maintain the various aspects of the family's wealth. It was with the division of the family art collection that the first signs of discord arose. Prior to departing for his foreign adventures, Sterling had shown little interest in his parents' collections, particularly furniture and paintings. While he was away, Stephen, now a lawyer, had overseen the distribution of those objects among the brothers. Sterling, now interested in the collection, resented his brother's assumption of authority and objected, expressing his opinion that many of the rarer objects would find a more appropriate home in his new Paris home. It was from that point that relations between the two brothers went downhill and competition for the art began. They both felt that it was the art, not the wealth that had become the defining force in their lives, and each set out to become something more valuable. Stephen saw himself as the keeper of the family flame in New York and Cooperstown, while Sterling was the gadabout, impressing "tout Paris." Stephen persisted in giving Sterling advice on how he should conduct his life, which only irritated Sterling all the more. Despite the mounting stress, the brothers remained for the most part cordial and sincerely interested in one another's lives.

The conflict over the distribution of the family's objects, however, continued without resolution, and Sterling, having been absent for the division, found himself without any paintings for his Paris mansion. He resolved to remedy this situation by becoming one of the most aggressive collectors in the most prestigious galleries of Paris, London, and New York. Merely collecting art was not enough to satisfy Sterling. The collection had to be displayed to the public, an act that would respond to both the family tradition of giving to the public and his need to define his own existence. What emerged was the idea of a museum, initially to be built in Cooperstown. Stephen disagreed, suggesting that

New York would be a more appropriate setting, as there it would represent the entire Clark family. Sterling expressed his belief that the city was now the subject of a foreign invasion of the type he would rather not encourage, whereas in Cooperstown the audience would be more "American." Without agreeing on the site, the two brothers agreed on the concept and set about, with the help of George Bernard, the sculptor their father had befriended, to assemble an appropriate collection. Initially they concentrated on Gothic tapestries and remnants of cathedrals, many of which turned out to be fakes. Bernard found the arrangement to be extremely satisfying, as the commissions he received on each purchase allowed him to settle debts and begin a more comfortable life. Sterling even went so far as to propose that Bernard be given the assignment of decorating the new museum. That relationship came apart when the brothers realized that the generous commission rate they had agreed upon when the purchases were modest had become very substantial as the value of the collection grew and they reduced the rate. Bernard reciprocated by threatening to hire a lawyer, and the relationship was saved only by the intervention of a friend who acted as intermediary. The relationship was reestablished but with a somewhat diminished role for Bernard, as Sterling began to trust his own taste and proceeded to grow his collection on his own. Stephen continued to collect, with Bernard's help, while Sterling offered him advice on what to collect and the foolishness of allowing Bernard to influence him. At this point the relationship between the brothers was more one of friendly needling than unpleasant conflict. Sterling continued collecting, with an eye, appetite, and pocketbook that allowed him to acquire more and more important works, filling his Paris house with Whistlers, Rodins, and nine museum-quality paintings from the elegant Colnaghi Gallery in London.

Sterling's collecting continued during the First World War, and in 1917 he resumed his military service and was appointed a liaison officer with the French army. In full uniform, he made the rounds of the London and Paris galleries, acquiring paintings by Gainsborough, Goya, Corot, Degas, and Claude Lorrain. His tastes were eclectic and, depending on the moment, ranged from the Renaissance to seventeenth-century Holland to Winslow Homer's rural America. At his core, however, he was a devoted and adoring Francophile. He loved everything French, especially a former actress from the Comedie Francais named Francine Clary. Francine was everything the Clark family feared her to be, the sort of woman Singer might have married, but not a Clark. Although they married in 1919, Francine had been living with Sterling since 1910. That same year Sterling would acquire, in a single day, drawings by Perugino, Durer, Rembrandt, Rubens, and Watteau. His marriage seemed to temper his appetite for collecting the Old Masters, and he began to focus on paintings that were more recent and less expensive. Sterling preferred art closer to his own time and disdained modernism. It never occurred to him to collect the likes of Picasso and Mondrian.

Red House Farm[43]

In 1921, despite his family's coldness toward Francine, Sterling decided they should return to New York. They took an apartment on Park Avenue and had constructed a house in Cooperstown, which they called Red House Farm. In New York, Sterling and Stephen sometimes toured the galleries together. Sterling was always quick to decide, while Stephen usually wished to consult his wife about how a piece would fit in their house. Sterling disdained what he thought to be Stephen's lack of decisiveness, and he was often snide about his brother's judgment. Meanwhile, Stephen's wife, Susan, had become concerned that Sterling was burning his way through his share of the family fortune and might soon be depending on his brother for support. The trusts that Alfred had created determined that so long as Sterling remained childless, the bulk of his fortune would go to Stephen and Susan's children. As Sterling diminished his wealth, there would be less and less available for Susan's children. At the same time, Sterling believed more and more that his brother was managing the family's affairs with the Singer Manufacturing Company in a way that favored his own family at the expense of the others. Whether or not this was true, the mutual mistrust grew to the point that, in the spring of 1923, the relationship snapped. At a meeting in the office that managed the family's affairs, Stephen accused Sterling of sneaking around behind his back. Sterling hit Stephen in the mouth. Sterling struck back, and the two ended up on the floor. The two brothers withdrew whatever accounts each controlled individually, and it was the beginning of a lifelong schism.

Stephen Clark's townhouse at 46 East Seventieth Street in New York, constructed 1911[44]

While Sterling had been collecting with a vengeance in Europe, Stephen had been conducting his own version of philanthropy in New York. As the only brother with a "profession," he was more attuned to the management of nonprofit institutions than collecting. He graduated from Yale in 1903, and after attending the Harvard Law School, he returned to New York, where he could better manage the family affairs while completing his law degree at Columbia. It wasn't until 1920 that Stephen bought his first French painting. He occasionally bought art but, unlike his brother, treated it more as a sideline.

Stephen's primary philanthropic efforts extended beyond the institutions devoted to the fine arts. He became a dedicated board member of the Metropolitan Museum of Art, but he also founded the Baseball Hall of Fame in Cooperstown. In his own reserved way, he was more adventurous than his brother, acquiring art that others found curious, such as paintings by Van Gogh and Picasso, and he supported the creation of the Museum of Modern Art, then one of the most revolutionary institutions in the world. Founded by a group of wealthy New York patrons, the most active of whom was Abby Rockefeller, the Modern began to assemble a collection of the premier modernists of the day. Once incorporated, the museum needed a larger board of trustees, and the first person they turned to was Stephen Clark. Those members who had visited the Clark house had been struck by seeing there at least eight paintings by Matisse, for which the surroundings had been especially modified. The only others in this country who had shown such interest were the Cone sisters, of Baltimore, and Alfred Barnes, of Philadelphia. Stephen resisted becoming a trustee until the Museum's opening exhibition, not yet convinced that it could display the full magnitude of modern art. That show consisted of 125 paintings by the early masters of modern art, such as Gaugin, Cezanne, Seurat, and van Gogh, and it convinced Stephen that the new museum was worthy of his attention. He was appointed chair of the building committee and set out to better facilities for the collection, to which he had begun to donate some of his own paintings. Stephen Clark's increasing generosity was not limited to donations of works to the Modern. He began to contribute what were considered inelegant paintings of the "Ashcan School" to his alma mater, in particular two paintings by George Luks. In 1932, Clark was elected to the board of the Metropolitan Museum of Art, and there, too, he became a contributor.

Fenimore House[45]

Stephen's brother Edward died the following year, leaving him his mansion Fenimore House, later to become the headquarters for The New York State Historical Association, the Dakota, his collections of art and antiques, Fenimore Farm, and the bulk of his cash and investments. Sterling was, of course, appalled that Rino, as he was called by the family, had not given it all to charity, rather than to Stephen. Edward Severin Clark had supported the work of Dr. Mary Imogene Bassett, a physician who had devoted her life to the sick and unfortunate of Cooperstown. She became a friend of Edward Clark, who, upon hearing that she wished to have a laboratory, built her not only a laboratory but a 100-bed hospital. The hospital opened in 1922, with Dr. Bassett as chief of staff. However, Mary died suddenly the same year, and by 1925 the hospital had become too large for the village and closed. Stephen was contacted about his brother's hospital by Dr. Henry Cooper, a physician at New York Presbyterian Hospital and a descendant of the founder of Cooperstown. With Stephen's aid, the hospital reopened in 1927, and it continues to serve the community to this day. In 1947, again with Stephen Clark's help, the hospital established a formal link with

Columbia University's College of Physicians and Surgeons, one feature of which is to provide a number of scholarships to medical students at Columbia as a means of eventually attracting graduates to serve in the community.

Mary Imogene Bassett Hospital, c.1940[46]

In 1937, looking for an opportunity to change the town's fortunes, Stephen founded the Baseball Hall of Fame, subsequently renamed the National Baseball Hall of Fame and Museum, in Cooperstown, which he supported liberally for the rest of his life. He also funded the transformation of Rino's dairy barn into the Farmer's Museum and became a supporter of the state historical society, to which he also gave magnanimously. In New York, he donated three fifteenth-century marble capitals needed to complete one of the structures of the Cloisters, which was then under construction.

Farmer's Museum (Fenimore Farm), c.1925[47]

Meanwhile, Sterling Clark continued to collect classic works, and was rumored to be funding travel to Europe for the creation of an army of insurgents to install a fascist leader in America. Stephen Clark continued to acquire modern paintings for his collection, lending them and sometimes donating them to museums. Both brothers were building larger and larger collections of more and more expensive paintings. Of particular note was *The Night Café* by Vincent van Gogh, which Stephen acquired in 1933. Now considered a masterpiece, this painting was one of the most daring of its time. Eventually donated to the Yale University Art Gallery, it would eventually be worth more than the total of the estate that Alfred had left his four sons (excluding inflation).

Sterling's bitterness at losing his attempt to contest the family trusts infected virtually every aspect of his life, including both his collecting and his marriage. By the 1930s, he had turned his wrath on the public institutions, believing that Roosevelt was swindling the country and the modernists were violating all that was good and truthful in the art of painting. This culminated with an article in the *New York Times*, reporting that Sterling was accused by one General Smedley D. Butler of being a part of a plot by Wall Street interests to overthrow President Roosevelt and establish a fascist dictatorship backed by a private army of 500,000 ex-soldiers. Other rumors ensued, and the affair became the subject of hearings before the House of Representatives Committee on Un-American Activities, headed by Representative John W. McCormack. The brouhaha between Sterling and Butler played out in public hearings before the House committee, lasting from April 1934 until February 1935, with a report concluding that "…there was evidence showing that certain persons had made an attempt to establish a fascist government in this country. There is no question that these attempts were discussed, were planned, and might have been placed in execution when and if the financial backers deemed it expedient" (Weber, p. 204). The scandal would rise briefly again in 1964, when the then Speaker of the House, John W. McCormack, mentioned the plot in a speech at the Democratic National Convention.

In Cooperstown, the brothers battled over buying and selling various parcels of land, with the public following each feud with entertained interest. Sterling complained increasingly about the fraction of his income going to the government, but that didn't stop him from buying artwork so fast at the Parisian Durand-Ruel Gallery that he had to store fifty paintings there, not even bothering to ship them to the United States. Through the Depression and its aftermath, he continued to buy masters, slowing down only slightly for World War II.

By 1945, when he finally stopped buying in volume, Sterling decided that it was time to decide on an appropriate venue for the public display of his collection after he was gone. He bought three adjacent buildings at the intersection of Park Avenue and Seventy-Second Street, with the intention of tearing them down, to be replaced by the Robert Sterling Clark Collection. In 1950 he changed his mind and sold the buildings and sought a better location for the museum. While visiting Williamston, Massachusetts, in 1949, he decided that the small New England town was a more appropriate setting for his masterpieces, and it was there that he decided to build his museum. In 1955, Sterling supervised the completion, at a cost of three million dollars, of the Sterling and Francine Clark Art Institute in Williamstown, Massachusetts, the home of his grandfather's alma mater, Williams College. The Institute contained thirty-nine Renoirs, seven Winslow Homers, and masterpieces by Goya, Turner, Sargent, Della Francesca, and Courbet, to be seen free of charge. Sterling loved North Adams, an adjacent town. There he was seldom identified and could pursue a secret passion for cars as an auto mechanic at Vic & Paul's Motor Sales, a dealer of imported cars from England. Robert Sterling Clark died in December 1956, at the age of seventy-nine. His collection remains at the Clark Institute in Williamstown and is still available for public viewing.

In 1937, Stephen Clark was the primary defender of a new building for the Museum of Modern Art on Fifty-Third Street in Manhattan. The style was considered out of place at best and enraged most if not all of his Yale classmates. Nonetheless, Stephen persevered, and in May 1939, two days before the opening of the new museum, the board held its meeting in the penthouse of the new facility. Nelson Rockefeller was named president, and Stephen Carlton Clark was elected chairman of the board. Clark went on, with Abby Rockefeller's support, to rule the Modern with an iron hand until 1959, when a trustee involved in a fund-raising drive for the museum told Stephen that, at David Rockefeller's request, he had put him down for a million dollars. Stephen had a precise code about how one solicited donations from the rich; the arrogance of this request violated that code, and he ended his support of the Modern. A friend attributed the split to Sterling's dislike of homosexuals, in particular the flamboyance of Philip Johnson, then on the Modern's staff. This friend apparently had no idea homosexuality might be a loaded subject to a son of Alfred Corning Clark.

Stephen Carlton Clark died in September 1960, at the age of seventy-eight, and he was buried in Cooperstown. In his will, he left five million dollars to Bassett Hospital, two to the New York State Historical Association, a million to Yale, five hundred thousand to the Metropolitan, and the same to his son-in-law. His daughter, Anne, received his Rembrandt. The Museum of Modern Art was not mentioned in the will, which Stephen had had rewritten after David Rockefeller presumed that he was giving a million dollars in his donation. During the last decade of his life, Stephen became devoted to the Yale Art Gallery and had given it a number of his more important Picassos and Matisses. Stephen felt that at Yale his paintings would receive outsized attention compared to the Modern, and it would be only a short trip away. In the end, Stephen gave sixty-one of his most important paintings to Yale, with the knowledge that they would be welcome. Anne received the Rembrandt, which she then gave to a foundation she had created for "the Aid of Education, Social Justice, and Human Service." The Foundation sold it at auction for $25 million.

Edward Severin Clark had apparently suffered from polio as a child, along with some vague mental infirmity. He spent most of his life at the family's Fenimore Farm on Otsego Lake. He never married or had children. He died in 1933 at the age of sixty-three and was buried in Cooperstown. He limited his charitable activities to local causes, giving the town its first motorized fire engine, building the Otsega Hotel, giving the town a second Alfred Corning Clark gymnasium, and, above all, supporting the Bassett hospital.

Frederick Ambrose Clark died in 1964 at the age of eighty-three. Ambrose was the family bon vivant, most at home in the saddle or with a glass of champagne in his hand. He lived the highest and longest of the brothers. After being obliged to leave Columbia College at the end of his sophomore year, he passed his time foxhunting, racing steeplechase horses, driving his carriage, collecting sports art, and being charming. He married the daughter of the president of the Manhattan Life Insurance Company, a kindred spirit with her own inheritance of thirty million dollars. Ambrose was an aggressive sports rider and he suffered enough from sports accidents that he was obliged to retire from those activities in 1930. He and his wife continued to enjoy horses, however, and they kept stables at their estates in Cooperstown; Westbury, Long Island; Aiken, South Carolina; and Melton Mowbray in England, where he went foxhunting with the Prince of Wales. Although they had a house in New York, Ambrose and his wife pretty much avoided the urban world. Ambrose inherited some of his parents' paintings, but his interest in art was limited to sports paintings. His only discernible charitable act was to auction off for charity his wife's horses after she died. Although publicly childless, he and his wife had a daughter who was mentally disabled. She lived to the age of thirty-two, with the mental age of a six-year-old and a prodigious ability to play the piano.

Postmortem

There is little evidence in his behavior that Isaac Singer had reflected at all on how he or any of his descendants might use his fortune, other than to satisfy a need for dominance, public exhibition, and the desires of the flesh. If his forbears had instilled any altruistic motivation in him, it was hidden well below the surface. At every stage in amassing his fortune, his first instinct was to use it to control, to take pleasure, and to be notorious. Of his extensive family, only his daughter

Willametta felt any need to give to the community. Whether this came from her husband or her internally developed abiding interest in the arts was difficult to determine, but in creating the Fondation Singer-Polignac, she was the only member of the Singer family willing to publicly share her good fortune with the disadvantaged. The forbears of Isaac Singer had lived in a social structure in which one never expected to share in any way the fruits of one's labor for other than for subsistence and pleasure. As far as they were concerned, that was the way it was, and it was unlikely to ever change. If one was fortunate, by hook or by crook, the winnings were to be kept. In the America of the Industrial Revolution, wealth creation became available to all, and there was not yet any universally perceived need to share it.

The Clark family had quite a different outlook. Although Edward Clark had profited from the commercial success of his father, which had lifted him up a step on the socioeconomic ladder the family had grown up with in Europe, he had also assimilated the Puritan values of his ancestors, who had arrived as the first immigrants. The notion that they had been blessed was an integral part of their legacy. Wealth was not to be given away to the indigent, who were unable to make their way, but should be shared with those whose lack of success was due to their situation, not their efforts. Nathan Clark believed that sharing the wealth of one's efforts was not only the natural instinct of those who were successful, but it was their felt need rather than an obligation. The form that tithing would take was for each individual to decide according to the needs of the times. The members of the Clark family satisfied this obligation in a peculiar way, one that responded to each one's desire to give to the larger good, but in a way that satisfied their egoistic need for recognition for their charitable acts. In this sense, the Clarks and the Singers were not that far apart. Once their basic needs of food and shelter were satisfied, they turned to a need for recognition and self-fulfillment. They chose ways to give back that were far removed from any notion of responding to the basic needs of the less fortunate. They focused their wealth on their own need to be acknowledged for their success, even if, in the case of the Clarks, that success descended from their forbears rather than having been earned by themselves. They were not so different, the Singers and the Clarks, in that their primary need was acknowledgment of their success, whatever its source, and the satisfaction of that need surpassed everything else.

CHAPTER FOUR

Perfecting the Business Model

FREDERICK G. BOURNE • *Popular 1899-1905*

Frederick G. Bourn[48]

The Singer story is full of surprises, but none as unlikely as Frederick Bourne's rise to Singer's presidency. Bourne was born in Boston in 1851, the son of Reverend George Washington Bourne of Massachusetts and Harriett Gilbert of Portsmouth, Maine. He was educated in the public schools of New York, and at the early age of fourteen, he was already destined for a life in business, taking a position with the Atlantic Submarine Wrecking Company. By all accounts, Bourne was nothing special, a moderate success in a very mundane career, but he was about to have a life-altering encounter with Alfred Corning Clark, the son of Edward C. Clark, the president of the Singer Manufacturing Company.

There are two versions of how that encounter occurred. One has Alfred observing Bourne's work as a clerk in the Mercantile Library. The most cited version is based on their shared interest in music. Edward's son was keenly interested in singing and, in 1867, was a founding member of the Mendelssohn Glee Club, the oldest non-university glee club in America. Frederick Bourne was equally interested in singing, and the two sang together at both the Mendelssohn Glee Club and the choir at the Old Trinity Church, best known today for being adjacent to the site of the World Trade Center collapse in September 2001. Their strong shared interest quickly evolved into a close personal relationship. The nature of their relationship has been suggested by biographers of Alfred Clark to have been a homosexual one. However, this might be tempered by the fact that Bourne married in 1875 and had a total of nine children.

In any case, Bourne's encounter with Clark was fortuitous, as in 1880, Alfred recommended to his father that he engage Bourne as construction manager on the Dakota, the spectacular apartment building that Clark was having constructed at the corner of Seventy-second Street and what was to become Central Park West.

Following his father's death in 1882, Alfred apparently engineered Bourne's appointment as the manager of his father's estate. In 1883, Bourne joined the Singer Manufacturing Company and in 1885 was made its secretary. If Alfred Clark had any interest in working for the Singer Company before his father's death, that ambition died with his father. As the Singer family's only interest in the company was the regularity of its dividends and Alfred had no desire to run the company he had inherited, in 1889 he appointed Bourne the president of Singer. At the age of thirty-eight, Bourne was the first of the second generation of executives who had not been related to the company's founding pioneers. Frederick Bourne would also be the only president in the first century of the company's existence who did not die in office. (Inslee Hopper was never in reality the president; Clark was.)

Bourne's presidency was notable for two achievements: his commitment to overseas market expansion and the importance of the sales and marketing functions in an international company whose organization had developed along technical rather than functional lines. Clark and Isaac Singer had concentrated on their belief that the secret to the successful marketing of the sewing machine was the technical superiority of the product, and they had created a brand synonymous with quality in the public eye. Aside from Clark, the senior managers had mostly technical backgrounds and were focused on the problems of satisfying the virtually universal demand for the product with machines of superior quality in ever-increasing quantities. Headquarters activities were largely informal and unorganized, relying more on the personal relationships common in many ways to today's start-ups, where product development and production drive the business model. Functional responsibilities were loosely defined in what could be described as a "club-room atmosphere" (Davies, 1976). Collective decisions were more the rule, rather than consideration of proposals made by functional specialists typical of today's organizations. While Isaac Singer had been a technical genius, the primary characteristic of the inventing process in the Industrial Revolution was trial and error. It had taken almost a century of such trial and error to create the first successfully functioning household sewing machine, and the organization of the Singer Manufacturing Company had developed along similar trial-and-error lines. It must have seemed a natural way of organizing behavior in the constant race to stay ahead of competitors eager to copy every feature as it was introduced in a new machine.

Door-to-door installment selling had proven to be the most effective way to bring the product to the customers' door, but Bourne felt that further successful expansion of the company's business, particularly outside the United States, would be significantly enhanced if the Singer name could be firmly established as a global brand. He strongly believed in the use of advertising to create such a global brand and made Singer one of the first manufacturers of a home appliance to establish a creative and effective stand-alone advertising department.

Singer's Greatest Asset—Its Globally Recognized Brand

In 1891, Bourne established a separate advertising department to provide the sales organization with calendars, posters, and leaflets for each class of sewing machines. The department designed the large letter *S*, which would become the unique and uniform identification of the Singer shops throughout the world. Even the shade of red used in the *S* was unique, and it would eventually be trade-marked as "Singer Red."

In 1891, the company introduced the "nation" cards. Initially created as a set of twelve colored reproductions of women in their national costumes, they were expanded to a set of thirty-six. Ever conscious of an opportunity to combine publicity with revenue generation, the first card was issued free to the public, while one could buy the entire set for twenty-five cents. The public collected them while the salesmen had a useful device for developing their sales messages. The cards were well received, and encouraged by their success, Bourne had thousands made up for distribution at the World's Columbian Exposition, to be held in Chicago to celebrate the 400th anniversary of Columbus's voyage to America. (The complete set appears on the Singer website.)

The rationale for spending scarce resources on marketing has always been somewhat of a chicken-and-egg situation. Some argue that it was the creation of high-volume mass production that lowered product cost sufficiently to support a significant marketing function. Others counter by contending that it was the development of mass-marketing techniques that generated the volumes necessary to achieve mass-production efficiencies. In any case, from the very beginning, the dynamics of the Singer Company were demand pulled, rather than production pushed. It was the desire of the customer to own a machine that drove sales. It was the responsibility of the company to make that ownership possible through a combination of high-quality, low-cost, and affordable payment terms. As other competitors emulated Singer, producing quality products at competing prices and offering similar payment terms, the company's expansion depended on its ability to create products that were discernably different and uniquely attractive to the public. By creating an in-house advertising department to support the sales organization, Bourne was refocusing attention

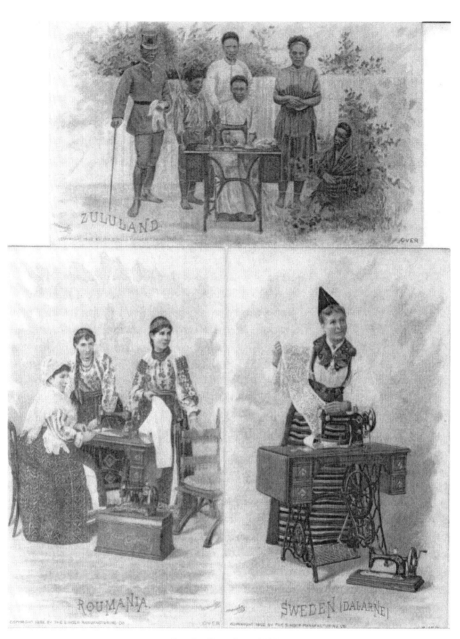

"Nation" cards, c.1892[49]

on the Clark strategy that had served the company so well until then and would continue to be the essential ingredient of the core business model for most of the coming century.

The Columbian Exposition cards proved so successful that, on the occasion of the 1901 Pan American Exposition, the company created a new series of collectible cards entitled Singer Souvenirs, with views of various tourist destinations in the United States. The cards were issued in packets, each containing up to ten postcard-sized views of a destination, such as New York City, Yosemite Valley, Niagara Falls, or the South. These were displayed at stores in the subject destination, to be purchased as souvenirs to be sent to a family member or friend. (The packet for the South contained memories best forgotten.)

In his study of Singer's international marketing strategies, Godley noted that "...the importance of marketing is wholly proportionate to the importance of brands. Without a brand the incentive to develop the marketing function is absent." He further defines a brand as "...a complex bundling of dedicated market support services (such as advertising, demonstration and after-sales service)." He finally adds that "when marketing is successful it adds enormous value to the, by comparison, relatively straightforward manufacturing function" (Godley A., 2009).

A major issue of brand during Bourne's presidency was the question of whether or not Singer had an exclusive right to the use of its own name. Today we are used to brands such as Kleenex, Xerox, or Cuisinart becoming generic labels for an entire family of competing products. However much we might use these names verbally to refer to any of the individual products in that family, their use in print, especially by competing manufacturers, is highly controlled by an extensive system of trademark laws and regulations. In 1894, the question of Singer's legal right to its own name, both at home and abroad, came before the United States Supreme Court in the form of a case in which an Illinois firm had advertised its sewing machines as "Improved Singer" machines. The importance to Bourne of the singular importance of the Singer brand was clearly reflected in the instructions he gave to the attorney representing Singer in the case:

> This name is of so much importance to the Company today that we could continue our business (and) maintain its prestige (even) if our entire product of machines was not covered by the Patent Office. Our machines are of no value to the public until we make them so, our reputation as producers being of the most value, the ownership of patented articles being secondary. This statement may be limited to our family trade. As an example, we bring out a new machine tomorrow for family trade, we call

"Singer Souvenir" cards, c.1901[50]

it a Singer Machine; through our organization it is before the public, the guarantee to the purchaser that that is the Singer Machine, the latest Singer Machine, the Best Singer Machine that the Company has to offer at the present time, is of more value to us than if it was covered by letters patent. The fact that it is made by this Company is what gives it a reputation and nothing else.

Singer's position as the market leader with a global brand of the self-claimed highest quality gave it a distinct advantage as it entered the overseas markets. While its combination of stores and door-to-door canvassers was very expensive, the sales network blanketed a country in such a way as to create high barriers of entry for any company wishing to compete with it. The network cost, however, pushed the company toward the high end of the product line, where its reputation for quality and the continuous introduction of technically sophisticated new features allowed the company to set the prices for the industry in a given country. Competitors soon realized that the primary tool they had for competing with Singer was price, rather than any particular advantage in product design and features. By the same token, Singer had no interest in price competition, as the reputation of its products and the ease of purchase for the customers allowed it to set the price at whatever level was necessary to cover the manufacturing cost and its selling and administrative expenses and still yield an acceptable profit. No matter what price Singer set for its machines, the competition would always price just below, content with a somewhat smaller profit in a market that Singer had created and supported with national advertising and virtually universal distribution coverage. Gross margins for Singer in the European markets often exceeded 60 percent of the net sales price, with market shares approaching or even exceeding 65 percent. The tendency for the competition to price just below Singer continued well into the post-WWII environment, particularly in Europe, where high-end machines were in particular demand. The effect was not unlike the phenomenon seen in higher education in the United States at the end of the twentieth century, when colleges with less-renowned reputations than the Ivy League schools discovered that they could set their tuition costs just below the elite schools without suffering any decline in demand.

Godley concluded that, beyond quality and price, the most important components of Singer's global retailing strategy were demonstration and after-sales service. The canvasser network was the critical means of initiating the marketing strategy, and the collection of installment payments was essential to its completion. The purchase of an expensive and complicated mechanical home appliance, particularly in the nineteenth century, was a source of great uncertainty, even anxiety, for the purchaser that could be substantially reduced by the initial demonstration and the knowledge that the agent would be available for follow-up visits for additional demonstrations if necessary (as well as for collection of payments and sales of sewing accessories).

Local or Foreign?

From the very beginning of the Singer Company, Edward Clark had focused on the potential for expansion outside the United States, with the belief that an understanding of the local culture was the key to the successful implementation of the core model in foreign countries. The most straightforward way to acquire that knowledge was to staff each operation with local nationals as senior management. By the time of Clark's death in 1882, Singer's sales of sewing machines outside the United States represented 35 percent of its total unit sales (210,803 foreign units out of 603,292 total units) (Godley, p. 22; Wisconsin Historical Society). During his seven years as president after Clark, George Ross McKenzie continued Singer's overseas expansion, opening branch offices in China, Japan, Malaya, Chile, Peru, and South Africa. He had overseen the construction of the huge factory at Kilbowie, Scotland (later to be renamed Clydebank), the cabinet factory in Cairo, Illinois, and a sewing machine factory in Montreal, Canada. At the time of McKenzie's retirement in 1889, the company was selling almost 700,000 sewing machines per year, of which approximately 45 percent were sold outside the United States (301,944 foreign units out of 692,764 total units) (Godley, 2009; Wisconsin Historical Society).

Frederick Bourne continued to use the basic Clark sales model of stores and canvassers as the company continued to expand rapidly, both in the United States and overseas. However, he concluded that it had become increasingly difficult, not to say impossible, to manage all of the details centrally, and he began to modify the organization according to product line and target customer. He carried out the first product line–oriented decentralization of the company, splitting the overseas organization into household and industrial machine divisions. In 1891 he separated business in the United States into a Manufacturing Trade Department (industrial sewing) and a Family Trade Department (household sewing). A new company, the Singer Sewing Machine Company, was formed to take over most of the U.S. sales operations, leaving the Singer Manufacturing Company with the U.S. manufacturing operations.

Finally, the rise of protectionism, in the form of tariffs in both the United States and in Europe, forced the company to modify its legal structure in ways that not only addressed the apparent problems of the tariffs themselves, but had the serendipitous result of creating an environment that reinforced the existing effort to create companies viewed as "local" by each country's population. This also gave the company an extremely valuable tool for managing its foreign tax liabilities and foreign currency exposure.

In 1890, Congress passed what was known as the "McKinley Tariff," named after Senator (later President) William McKinley of Ohio. The law, partially motivated by a desire to encourage the purchase of American-made products, established an across-the-board tariff of 48.9 percent, the highest in American history, on all imports. The McKinley Tariff was a major contributor to the Panic of 1893, which marked the further downturn of a major economic depression that had begun in 1873 and lasted almost to the end of the century. Strong economic expansion following the Civil War had led to overbuilding of the railroads, speculation in commodities, particularly silver, coincident with a series of droughts that had crippled Midwestern farmers. Investors chased the railroad stocks, much as they chased dot-com companies and housing at the beginning of the twenty-first century. The first victim was the Philadelphia and Reading Railroad, which overextended itself and went bankrupt. Eventually the Northern Pacific, Union Pacific, and Atchison, Topeka, & Santa Fe Railroads would all go bankrupt. Bank depositors, fearing a crash, ran to withdraw their savings from the banks. Credit dried up and the stock market plunged. Over five hundred banks failed, and unemployment rose to almost 20 percent.

Sewing machine manufacturers feared that the McKinley Tariff would cause Europeans to build branch plants in the United States, much as Singer had done in Europe. The McKinley Tariff lasted only four years and was replaced by a more acceptable, yet still high tariff of 35 percent on most sewing machines and 25 percent on needles. While Bourne claimed that the impact of the tariffs on the Singer Company was minimal, due to the fact that it imported little from its European factories, he was very concerned that the actions of Congress could trigger tariff retaliation by the Europeans that could have a serious impact on the company's ability to import machines from Europe, especially the machines that were manufactured in Scotland and destined for the United States. Should a tariff war spread more generally, say between countries in Europe, the impact on Singer would be dramatic. The company had always maintained strict confidentiality concerning its internal workings. There was no need to release any financial or operational information to the public. Any filing requested by a government agency, American or otherwise, was traditionally kept to the absolute minimum necessary to satisfy the letter of the law. Secrecy was not limited to external communications. Internal reports concerning financial results, production quantities, wholesale and export prices, or taxes paid were limited to senior management, and even then only on a "need to know" basis.

As Bourne had feared, the protectionism that had developed in the United States soon found its counterpart in Europe in the form of a change in the French tax law regarding dividends of foreign corporations. In Europe, confronted with efforts by many of the European governments to tax local agencies of U.S. corporations, Bourne began to create what would become a series of national legal corporations for France, Italy, and the other countries. First was the Singer Company Nahmaschinen Aktiengesellschaft in Germany (1895), followed by Kompanija Singer in Russia (1897). In Great Britain, the United States sales and manufacturing organizational split was duplicated with the formation of the Singer Sewing Machine Company, Ltd., and the Singer Manufacturing Company, Ltd.

Historically, Clark had exerted strong control over the organization by appointing loyal assistants to the senior overseas management positions. Even through most of the twentieth century, manufacturing executives for virtually all of the sewing machine factories around the world would invariably come from either the Elizabethport or Clydebank factories. Bourne's decision to change the sales organization by creating local legal entities would have a major impact on the company's further development in the twentieth century.

Although Bourne served as president for seventeen years, a rather brief tenure by Singer standards, it was more than enough to permit him to retire at age fifty-four. The capacity of the Singer Manufacturing Company to create wealth had been understood in principle by Clark, but the magnitude of that success must have surprised even him. Clark's wise generosity in making available 20 percent of the company's common stock for purchase by key employees would make Frederick Bourne a very wealthy man. By the time Bourne was appointed president, the company was earning between three and eight million dollars a year, with virtually all of it being paid out in dividends. If we assume that Bourne's share of the ownership was 10 percent, he would have been receiving between three and eight hundred thousand dollars per year on top of his salary…and at that time there was no income tax. This was the equivalent of between eight and twenty-two million in 2014 dollars. If this seems large, remember that Singer and Clark were earning four times these amounts.

Bourne had considerable outside, and very expensive, interests. Chief among them was sailing, and he was for many years the commodore of the New York Yacht Club. In addition to his apartment, which occupied the entire first floor of the Dakota in New York City, he owned Indian Neck Hall, a two-thousand-acre estate in Oakdale, New York, part of an exclusive South Side sportsman's Club on the south shore of Long Island; a three-hundred-seventy-five-acre farm near Montauk, New York, which he kept undeveloped as a hunting preserve; an apartment on Jekyll Island, Georgia; and Dark Island, a seven-acre island in

Indian Neck Hall, 1897[51]

the Thousand Islands of the St. Lawrence River, which became known as the "Singer Castle," where he kept the Maritime Museum archives (Forde, Frederick G. Bourne, n.d.).

"Singer Castle" 1905[52]

When Bourne died in 1920, he left an estate of $43 million ($502 million in 2014 dollars), within which his real estate holdings were valued at only $1.4 million. It was the largest estate ever filed in Suffolk County, to be exceeded, however, by that of William K. Vanderbilt, which was being probated at the same time. Bourne had started with little and died with a fortune, consisting largely of Singer stock. Although Singer and Clark had been the sole owners of the company's stock at its creation, they soon decided that the loyalty they required could be best assured by granting certain key executives shares. Eventually they reduced their holdings to 80 percent, still sufficient for royal lifestyles, while the remaining 20 percent permitted the succeeding presidents to live, if not quite up to the standards of the Singers and Clarks, more than adequately.

CHAPTER FIVE

Steady As She Goes

SIR DOUGLAS ALEXANDER • President 1905-1949

Douglas Alexander[53]

Douglas Alexander was probably the best remembered of the Singer presidents. He served longer than the combined total years of all of his predecessors. (Edward Clark did not carry the title until 1876.) As long service was typical of the senior management in both the United States and abroad, the company folklore concerning "Sir Douglas" was firmly etched into the institutional memory well into the last half of the twentieth century.

Alexander was born in England on July 4, 1864, at Halifax, Yorkshire, England. His father, Andrew, was a Canadian horticulturist and botanist, and Douglas was but a boy when his parents settled in Hamilton, Ontario. He was educated at the Hamilton College Institute and passed the bar in 1886. In 1891, he joined Singer as a correspondent (a private secretary) in the office of Frederick G. Bourne, then secretary of the company. By 1896, at the age of thirty-two, Alexander had been appointed second vice president and a member of the board. A year later, he was appointed vice president in charge of North American operations. In 1905 Bourne retired, and the following year Alexander was named president of the Singer Manufacturing Company. In 1906, he would preside over the dedication ceremonies of the most visible symbol of the company's success, the new Singer Building at 149 Broadway in New York. At the time, it would be the tallest skyscraper in the city, rising well above the surrounding buildings at City Hall Plaza. Although that distinction would be short-lived in the race to build the tallest structure in New York, it was nonetheless a dramatic achievement for a company barely fifty years old and that made only a relatively inexpensive household appliance. Alexander would serve as president of both companies until his death in 1949.

At the beginning of his tenure, he surely saw a bright future for the company. The core business model was in place, and his mission was to extend it throughout the world, to keep the ship steady and pointed in the right direction. Unfortunately he encountered a storm roughly once each decade during his term as president. Appointed in 1905, he was almost immediately confronted with the Panic of 1907, when a sudden 50-percent drop in the stock market caused vast numbers of people to withdraw money from the banks, triggering a liquidity crisis. The relative commercial peace that followed collapsed with the 1914–1918 World War and the Russian Revolution. The Russians expropriated Singer's huge factory just outside of Moscow, which at the time was producing over one million sewing machines a year. The Roaring Twenties ended with the stock market crash and the start of the Great Depression, which, in turn, ended with the beginning of World War II.

Jacques Ehrsam, the general manager of Singer's French company, remembered Douglas Alexander with affection. Ehrsam's grandfather, Adolphe, had been the first general manager of Singer, France, having been appointed to head Singer's first incorporated overseas subsidiary in 1888. He served in that capacity until 1924, when he was succeeded by his son, Maurice, the father of Jacques Ehrsam. At the end of World War II, the young Ehrsam was considering two possible careers, public service or employment at Singer. The weight of his family's tradition pushed him toward Singer, and his father sent him to the United States to begin his grooming as Maurice's successor. Jacques Ehrsam would succeed his father in 1961 and would serve in that position until the consolidation of the company in 1983. He was to be hosted in America by none other than Sir Douglas Alexander, Singer's president. Alexander had an apartment in New York at Number 1 West Seventy-second Street, in what had apparently become a sort of residence club for Singer presidents—the Dakota. His preferred residence, however, was Edgehill Farm, his estate in Stamford, Connecticut. Here, in his own words, is Jacques Ehrsam's description of that encounter at both the Singer Building and Edgehill:

> I was welcomed to New York by Mr. Myslik (the vice president responsible for Europe), who told me that I would be staying at the home of the worldwide president of Singer, Sir Douglas Alexander, a great honor, and that he would take me each night to Stamford, where he lived.
>
> The Singer building had been for some time the tallest in New York and it was magisterial, with an immense store on the ground floor which also sold fabrics. It also had a training center, where I was given the assignment to create a man's coat and suit. I don't think my suit was likely to be worn, but the director of the center proclaimed it "original."
>
> On the day of my arrival, a young man came to look for me at 4:00 to lead me to Sir Douglas, who was waiting in his office. This young man took me to the top of the building, knocked on a door, and it opened into the world of the president's office which made me think of Jules Verne's

"Twenty Thousand Leagues Under the Sea," especially when Captain Nemo looked out on the deep sea through an enormous window.

Singer building7[54]

Sir Douglas resembled God, as pictured in our first children's books; a handsome white beard, beautiful bearing, white hair, allure of a great man; an office which faced the river, a grand river filled with sea-going vessels. "Delighted to receive you, Jacques. You are the latest in a long-respected family. I very much liked it when your father stayed with me and you have a strong resemblance to him. You know my daughter Elisabeth, who tends to my house as she tends to the apartment I have in your building on the Avenue de l'Opera. She will explain our household routines to you. Go retrieve your suitcase and I will find you in the car waiting for me out front."

At that moment a strange scene took place. I heard four whistles sound from a boat which was passing before us in the Hudson. Sir Douglas got up, walked to the window, and saluted. "You are witnessing a tradition. My predecessor, Isaac Singer, had created a large factory on the port at Bridgeport (certainly Elizabethport, not Bridgeport, which was in Connecticut) and each time a boat loaded with sewing machines left to deliver these machines around the world, it sounded four whistles, and Isaac would stand and salute. I want to continue that tradition, but let us now go down to the car which is waiting for us in a no-parking zone."

The car which awaited us was a magnificent Lincoln Zephyr. Sir Douglas had me sit in the back with him and I again thanked him for the honor of inviting me to his home in Stamford. "Jacques, I do it because of my friendship with your father and because your family has contributed so much to the success of Singer in France and North Africa. What's more, my daughter Elisabeth likes to meet my loyal colleagues from around the world, a group of which I hope you will be a part one day.

"Begin by telling me about you, as up to now I know only that you had an interesting life during the last war, that you succeeded in your Singer training in Paris and that you play golf. In an hour you will see at my home a nine hole golf course and we will play every morning, weather permitting."

"But I don't have any golf equipment."

"Don't worry. None of my guests come with equipment. We've predicted that and you will have a complete set of clubs every morning at 8:00."

Stamford was an impressive property, managed by the only daughter of Sir Douglas, a widower—a charming welcome by Elisabeth, a sumptuous bedroom.

At 6:00 p.m., "A game of Boules in a half hour." I was never very good at Boules, not completely without ability, but naturally beaten.

Aperitif at 7:30 and dinner at 8:00…. During the modest dinner, Elisabeth brought me up about the customs of the household. "My father plays the organ every morning at 6:00 a.m., which wakes everyone, but leaves you plenty of time to prepare for breakfast at 7:00 a.m. After breakfast and golf, the car will take you to the office. Be on time, because my father is as accurate as a Swiss watch." At golf, I was beaten by Sir Douglas' precision. He drove less far, but his approaches and putting were remarkable.

During the drive in the car, the president asked me many questions, and I permitted myself but one, "You knew Isaac Singer. How did you come to meet him and what was he like?"

"I met him once by chance because, as his name implies, he was an excellent Singer and I shared that passion…. We both belonged to the same group of amateur singers and that's how I came to know him." (Here Alexander's memory conflates Singer and Bourne, as Alexander would have been only eleven years old when Singer died in 1875, and it was Bourne, not Singer, who sang with the New York glee club. He further shows deterioration of memory as he says that he is the one who recommended Clark to Singer, when that had, in fact, occurred thirteen years before Alexander was born. This conversation would have taken place within a year or two of Alexander's death in 1949, at the age of eighty-five.)

(Ehrsam) When I returned after twenty-two months, Sir Douglas received me and asked if I was satisfied with my training and if I understood the importance of good organization to the company. I could but agree.

That same evening, I found myself in a "Constellation" (the first post-war transatlantic commercial aircraft) flying to Paris, taking notes in order to remember everything said by Sir Douglas, who had been knighted by the Queen of England for his services during the war. (Recounted in an interview with Jacques Ehrsam, June 3, 2012, and later transcribed by him.)

The business model developed by Clark and McKenzie and refined by Bourne (the Core Model) was in place. Alexander was intimately familiar with the operating details of the company, and he had, for its time, a sophisticated reporting system at hand to control its far reaches. Douglas Alexander undoubtedly saw his primary mission to be that of taking this enormously successful business model and extending it as far as possible around the world. The development of Singer during the presidency of Bourne had been so successful that the company had reached the practical limit to its growth, with sales at a ceiling of approximately one million machines per year. However, Douglas Alexander proved to be more than up to the challenge. During the first decade of his presidency, sales increased to three million machines per year, new factories were opened at St. Johns, Quebec, Wittenberge, Prussia, Truman, Arkansas, Stanhope, New Jersey, and the Old Wheeler and Wilson plant in Bridgeport, Connecticut (absorbed in 1907). National sales companies were formed in France (1907) and Belgium (1908) (Davies, 1976). By 1912, Singer was the seventh largest firm in the world by capitalization (Godley A., 2009), had an 80 percent share of the world market for sewing machines, and was paying $60 million in annual dividends (*Business*, Gloomy Singer, September 28, 1936).

In 1913, the company formed a new holding company, the International Securities Company (IESCo), which acquired from the Singer Manufacturing Company (SMCo) the shares of all of the overseas subsidiaries. SMCo received royalties on all machines manufactured or assembled by its subsidiaries, and a profit (transfer price markup) on the prices that each sales organization paid for the machines shipped to them. This was largely the formalization of the organization and processes practiced by McKenzie's predecessors. His personal objective was to create a sense of community throughout the organization, whether domestic or foreign. Alexander's work ethic was legendary within the company, and he would travel to Europe at least twice a year, even during the First World War.

Alexander recognized early on that the successful marketing of a sophisticated consumer product, particularly in a foreign country, was highly dependent on an understanding of local culture, and no one understood their country's culture better than a national who had been given the responsibility of running and staffing the company. The introduction of such alien sales techniques as installment selling was much more likely to succeed when implemented by someone completely accepted by the local community who could overcome the natural apprehensive of all things "foreign." The presence of a local company selling a product recognized as locally made was considerably easier than selling a product identified as "Made in the USA." The major national markets in Europe were the United Kingdom, France, Germany, and Italy. (Russia joined the "Big Four" in 1895.) These companies were staffed and managed by nationals, and Singer would eventually locate a sewing machine factory in each of them to manufacture with pride a sophisticated product made "locally." Each factory would produce but a few models in the entire product line, becoming the worldwide supplier to the countries that had local demand for them. The image of the company in the eyes of the local consumers and, not incidentally, the local governments was certainly enhanced as the company became known as not only a manufacturer and seller of sewing machines, but an *exporter* of them. The strength of the brand thus developed was such that, even in a country such as France in the late twentieth century, if one asked a Frenchman the national origin of "La Compagnie Singer," the response would be that it was a French company, of course, as it had existed there since 1882.

Alexander undertook international expansion with a vengeance. In 1888, La Compagnie Singer had been formed in France, and the Sewing Machine Company acquired the business of Adcock and Company in Spain. In 1908, La Compagnie Singer was incorporated in Belgium, and in 1915 the Singer Manufacturing Company transferred its business in Turkey to the Singer Sewing Machine Company. In 1919, the Singer Sewing Machine Company was registered in Czechoslovakia, and in 1920 the Compagnie des Machines a Coudre Singer was incorporated in Switzerland. The Singer Sewing Machine Company replaced Bourne and Company in Bulgaria in 1926, Yugoslavia in 1929, and Greece and Romania in 1939. A new company, Singer Maatschapppij, was formed in 1935 to carry on the business in the Netherlands. During World War I, the Singer factories in Great Britain, Canada, and the United States engaged in important work in the munitions program. In recognition of the exceptional efforts of both the Alexander and the Clydebank factory, he was made a baronet by King George V in 1921. He would proudly carry the appellation "Sir Douglas Alexander" for the rest of his life.

By the time of the Revolution, Singer's Russian sales volume had become larger than that of the United States. By 1918, the huge factory at Podolsk, outside Moscow, was producing over one million sewing machines a year, largely for domestic consumption, a level not reached in the United States until after World

War II. When peace came following the war, the entire Russian organization had been expropriated during the Revolution, a loss of nearly one-third of Singer's prewar worldwide sales. Alexander undertook an ambitious program to rebuild the company's profits, returning them to their prewar level by the end of the decade. Despite the depression, the company continued to expand its manufacturing capability, beginning construction on new factories in Monza, Italy, and Bonnieres, France, in 1934, and in 1940, an electric motor factory for Diehl in Finderne, New Jersey, and an additional woodworking plant in Pickens, South Carolina.

Singer and the World Wars

Alexander's response to turmoil was always to tighten the belt and find other ways of keeping the ship afloat. Singer's multicultural understanding, its ability to adapt to the changing environments as they affected its core business model served it well during the catastrophes of both WWI and WWII. During the first war, Singer plants in Britain, Canada, and the United States diverted production from sewing machines to munitions. During the second war, Singer's factory in Wittenberge, Germany, was converted to war production by the Germans. Then, following the armistice, the factory was confiscated by the Russians in East Germany, dismantled, and sent back to modernize the Russian factory at Podolsk. This was the same ex-Singer factory that had been expropriated during the Russian Revolution at a cost to Singer of $106,000,000 ($1.65 billion in 2014 dollars).

The Singer factories on the allied side were once again diverted to the war effort. The company helped the rapid conversion of the textile industry to the production of the clothing and shelter needed to support the military forces. The Bridgeport factory produced automatic arms and gun parts. A new plant was built in New Jersey for the manufacture of classified instruments—believed to be bomb sights and related mechanisms.

Despite the turmoil throughout Alexandre's tenure as president, the company remained profitable in every year. Many a CEO would envy this record.

$millions		$millions		$millions		$millions	
Year	Profit	Year	Profit	Year	Profit	Year	Profit
1905	$ 8.6	1916	$ 7.4	1927	$25.6	1938	$ 9.5
1906	$ 8.9	1917	$ 1.3	1928	$24.0	193	$ 3.1
1907	$ 8.9	1918	$ 5.8	1929	$24.7	1940	$ 8.8
1908	$ 9.6	1919	$ 3.0	1930	$19.9	1941	n.a.
1909	$14.7	1920	$ 2.5	1931	$ 4.1	1942	$12.8
1910	$14.4	1921	$11.9	1932	$ 2.4	1943	$13.6
1911	$14.7	1922	$21.6	1933	$10.8	1944	$13.9
1912	$16.9	1923	$18.2	1934	$13.8	1945	$14.3
1913	$16.1	1924	$27.8	1935	$16.3	1946	$15.2
1914	$11.2	1925	$22.2	1936	$15.1	1947	$13.7
1915	$ 9.0	1926	$25.0	1937	$14.3	1948	$15.2

Sir Douglas Alexander's career effectively ended with the reopening of the offices that had been closed by the war. The aftermath of the war would bring changes in the nature of the market for sewing machines that no one in the company could have contemplated. He died at the age of eighty-five on May 22, 1949, having worked for the Singer Sewing Machine Company for fifty-eight years, forty-four years as the company's president.

CHAPTER SIX

The End of Market Domination

Milton Lightner[55]

Milton Lightner was born in Detroit, Michigan, in 1890. Graduating from the University of Michigan in 1910 and Harvard Law School in 1913, he joined the New York law firm of Carter, Ledyard, & Milburn. In 1916, he joined the National Guard, serving in the Texas border towns as part of the force sent to repel the raids of the legendary Pancho Villa. During World War I he served as a captain in the Quartermaster Corps, handling shipments from New York to the front in Europe. After the war, he became a partner in in the New York law firm of Verplanck, Prince, Burlingame, & Lightner. One of the firm's clients was the Singer Manufacturing Company. Douglas Alexander convinced Lightner to join the company in 1927 as a director and vice president of the company's marketing and distribution subsidiary. He would serve the company for thirty-one years, concentrating largely on Singer's domestic sewing business, where he was identified with the development of the company's educational programs. Following Douglas Alexander's death in 1949, Lightner was appointed president. He would quickly discover that he had reached the pinnacle of his career with exquisitely poor timing. He would be the last shepherd of Singer's traditional business model, the source of such enormous wealth for Isaac Singer, Stephen Clark, their heirs, and a succession of Singer presidents.

On the Defensive: (With Friends Like This...)

It has been virtually an article of faith in United States economic history that no sooner had the United States defeated Japan and signed the armistice ending World War II than the Japanese undertook a second invasion, that of conquering this country by copying our successful products and technologies for manufacture in Japan with cheap labor then exporting them to the United States for sale at a fraction of the price of competing U.S. products. There was a vision of hordes of Japanese businessmen swarming over the United States buying samples or taking pictures of anything suited to their labor force and mass production facilities. In fact, the Japanese did not undertake this effort on their own, but were aided in significant ways by the United States government.

Prior to World War II, the Japanese sewing machine industry was largely domestic. Trade to and from Japan was controlled by the large Japanese trading companies (the Zaibatsu), who, with the complicity of the authoritarian government, operated without serious competition behind a wall of protectionist tariffs. The U.S. government reacted in kind, as did Europe, with the result that there was little or no competition in or from Japan in the major sewing machine markets of the West prior to 1946.

Following the armistice ending the war, the United States undertook a policy of reconstruction aid to the countries whose industries had been decimated in the battle. In Europe, this aid took the form of the Marshall Plan. In Japan, General Douglas MacArthur was appointed the Supreme Commander of the Allied Powers (SCAP), effectively the viceroy of occupied Japan, to undertake the effort there. Although the Marshall Plan did not originally include Japan as a candidate for economic reconstruction, the policies contained in the Plan were soon extended to Japan. In 1946, the Zaibatsu were dissolved under a law for the "Elimination of Excessive Concentrations of Economic Power" (Miwa, 1991, p. 2), protective barriers in the United States were lowered, and MacArthur's staff began to look for specific industries that could be quickly rebuilt. During the war, Singer had halted production of sewing machines and become a major producer of war material, as did the White Sewing Machine Company of Cleveland, Ohio. White had acquired the Domestic Sewing Machine Company in 1926, and by the beginning of the war had become the sole supplier of sewing machines to Sears Roebuck and Company under the Kenmore brand. The Kenmore machines disappeared from the Sears catalog during the war and would not reappear until 1948, by which time the nature of the sewing machine market had changed dramatically.

MacArthur's staff could hardly have found a better candidate for rehabilitation as an exporter of small technical appliances than the sewing machine industry. The very nature of the machine was such that the parts and subassemblies were easily copied and could be manufactured in different locations. There was a large surplus of both skilled machinists and machine shops that had been idled by the end of the war. The Japanese government had instituted a policy of subsidizing imported machine tools needed for expansion, at up to 50 percent of their cost. Finally, the United States had the only economy with sufficient purchasing power after the war to be able to afford imported goods. It was the most logical and virtually the only market able to support high volume imports. The results were dramatic.

Japanese Sewing Machine Exports

Year	Units	% Change
1935	12,301	-
1936	40,924	233
1937	53,133	30
1938	104,204	96
1939	132,997	28
1940	154,402	16
1941	142,317	(8)
1942	51,129	(64)
1943	25,783	(50)
1944	16,047	(38)
1945	2,150	(87)
1946	36,912	616
1947	133,949	263
1948	165,726	24
1949	274,468	65
1950	493 038	80
1951	1,030,289	109
1952	1,260,293	22
1953	1,318,059	5 (Miwa, 1991)

By 1953, eight years after the end of the war, Japan exported almost nine times as many sewing machines as it had in its best year prior to the war, virtually all of them destined for the United States. By 1954, two of the four remaining sewing machine manufacturers in the United States, New Home and National, had gone out of business, and only Singer and White remained. With the arrival of the Japanese, White formed a joint venture with Pfaff, a German manufacturer, only to have Sears replace the German-American machine with Japanese imports by 1958.

In 1951, the Singer Sewing Machine Company celebrated its 100th anniversary. At its celebratory banquet, Milton Lightner noted that "the strain of the second world conflict was even greater than that of the first, but in the past five years the recovery of our organization has steadily proceeded…. The ravages of war have been overcome" (Singer, Company, 1951). In fact, the third world war, the war of the sewing machines, had just begun. For the first time ever, the Japanese manufacturers were selling more sewing machines in the United States than Singer.

Although the creation of the first commercially viable sewing machine had ten essential components for simple sewing in a straight line, the modern sewing machine incorporated three additional complex elements that could vary, depending on the intended application of the machine. These were: a needle that carries a thread that is designed to reciprocate in a vertical direction; a loop-taking element that operates with the needle to form stitches; and a feeding mechanism designed to feed the work between the needle and the loop-taker. All three elements may be operated using an electric motor, a foot treadle, or a hand crank, with the operator controlling the speed. The amplitude of the feeding mechanism may be altered to increase or decrease the length of the stitches, and the direction of the feed may be reversed to feed the work away from or toward the operator. The conventional name for such a machine is a straight-stitch machine, and it is typically used for the simplest task of joining two pieces of material. A zigzag machine differs from a straight-stitch machine in that the needle reciprocates not only in a vertical direction but may be shifted back and forth laterally as the work is fed into the machine so as to create stitches that follow a zigzag pattern, rather than a straight one. By varying either or both the amplitude of the lateral movements of the needle and the speed with which the work is fed into the machine, the pattern of the zigzag stitch can be varied.

To complicate matters further, an additional mechanism could be added that could cause the needle's lateral movements to begin in the left, middle, or right sides of the stitch. Such machines could also be provided with a removable cam that caused the machine to vary these elements of the stitch in such a way as to create an ornamental pattern, which itself could be repeated in any desired length. In addition to all of its zigzag capabilities, such a machine might also be operated as a conventional straight-stitch machine. Zigzag machines had been in use since the nineteenth century, but their primary use was industrial, in the manufacture of clothing. Prior to World War II, Singer sold and had patented (Wisconsin Historical Society) a general zigzag machine that it had sold for many years to the needle trades industry. This machine, like most machines sold at the time, had a cam for determining the lateral movement, but lacked a means for automatically adjusting the feeding movement. None of these machines had ever been sold for household use, and such use was practically nonexistent prior to World War II.

One of the first, if not the first, zigzag machines designed for household use was made in Singer's German factory from 1934 to the beginning of the war, after which the manufacture was moved to Scotland, where it continued to be manufactured until about 1952 (Wisconsin Historical Society). These machines could not produce any pattern other than a zigzag stitch, and they were sold only outside the territorial limits of the United States. Up until 1950, neither Singer nor any of its competitors imported any substantial numbers of these machines. Following the war, however, the demographics of the market for sewing machines began to change. American women had participated in the war effort, leaving home to work in factories, either to directly support manufacturers of war materials or to replace the men in less critical industries, but they were now serving in the armed forces. After the war, many of these women stayed in the factories. They were now used to the workplace, and they welcomed the opportunity for additional family income. Others soon left the home to work in white-collar jobs as the postwar expansion created increasing demand for clerical as well as professional and technical employment.

Publicly Owned but Privately Controlled

Milton Lightner was the last president of Singer to manage it paternalistically, as if it was still a family company. The Core Model had withstood the challenges of two world wars, the Russian Revolution, the Great Depression, and most importantly, the competition. The company had prospered and paid enormous dividends to its few shareholders. However, it was still a very closely held, single-product company. Although the shares were traded publicly, they were not listed on any exchange, as the company had never sought nor needed to raise any additional capital. The shares were only traded between individuals connected in some way with the company or friends who had been stockholders for decades. Initially, all of the common stock had been held by Isaac Singer and Stephen Clark. Over time, shares were granted to very senior trusted employees, and with the death of the company's founders and these employees, their holdings were passed down to successive generations. Stephen C. Clark, grandson of the company's founder, Edward Cabot Clark, served on the board of the company from 1905 until his death in 1960. There was little incentive to sell the stock, as the cash distributed as dividends each year was more than sufficient to support even the most extravagant spendthrift, Isaac Singer. However, Singer died in 1875, before he could waste his entire fortune, leaving an estate of $14 million ($298 million in 2014 dollars), and his descendants had lived comfortably ever since. When Edward Clark's grandson died in 1960, he left an estate of $11.7 million ($92 million in 2014 dollars), a priceless art collection, which was shared by Yale University and the Metropolitan Museum of New York, and extensive real estate holdings, including the Dakota, then a residential hotel (rental apartment building) on Central Park West.

The environment for the sale of sewing machines was changing very rapidly for Singer. The Japanese were not only exporting their own branded machines, but they were making private-label machines for American companies to sell, most notably Sears, Roebuck & Co. Lightner's efforts to save the company by promoting sewing education through classes, remained focused on the preservation of a single product. While women in the domestic (U.S.) market were moving away from sewing and into the workplace, such was not the case overseas. In countries such as England and France, where every family was still visited by a Singer salesman at least once a year, by tradition, the sewing machine was virtually always the most important and traditional wedding gift. Given the economic hardship of the war in Europe and its immediate aftermath, a sewing machine was often the most important contributor to household savings or income. In the non-electrified countries of the third world, the Singer treadle machine was still a household necessity. But that was about to end. Cultural change in the United States inexorably found its way to Europe and beyond. Whether it be due to popular culture, the sudden availability of wide choices of inexpensive, ready-to-wear clothing, or women seeking both economic gain and fulfillment beyond the home, the market for sewing machines was becoming increasingly constrained. In order to grow, the company would have to consistently attract a larger share of a diminishing market. As if these problems were not enough for Lightner, the company was becoming an attractive target for a takeover. In 1951, the first year for which the company's accounting statements became available to the general (non-stockholding) public, the till-then suspected attractiveness of the company as a potential acquisition became publicly obvious. The company had earnings of almost $19 million on sales of $308 million, with $202 million of assets and no debt. To grow and remain independent, the company decided it must look beyond the sewing machine.

CHAPTER SEVEN

The Conglomerate Temptation[56]

Conglomerate: A combination of two or more corporations engaged in entirely different businesses together in one corporate structure, usually involving a parent company and several (or many) subsidiaries. Often, a conglomerate is a multi-industry company and multinational.

Despite the collective relief and joy that the United States experienced with the end of World War II, the underlying mood in the country was one of uncertainty. The economy had never fully recovered from the Great Depression. The war had provided an extraordinary boost in industrial activity, pulling virtually all sectors to full capacity, but what would happen when this artificial stimulus disappeared? Would the country fall back into a depression? How could the strong demand related to the war in Europe be replaced by an equally strong domestic demand? What would support the tens of thousands of soldiers and sailors as they returned home? The experience following World War I had been catastrophic. Economists noted that GNP had fallen by almost 25 percent and now predicted an equivalent or even worse decline. Although by the beginning of the war, the economy had doubled in the ten years since the beginning of the depression, it was still below the level of 1929. The GNP had doubled during the war years, but this was all war-related. What could replace it? Unemployment, at 14.6 percent in 1940 had, for all practical purposes, vanished. Yet, there were 11 million servicemen about to return home, and many of the 11 million women who had entered the workforce to replace them wished to stay on their jobs. There was a genuine fear that if the returning servicemen couldn't find jobs, they could quickly become depressed, despondent, and easily radicalized.

But this time there was no postwar depression. Consumer demand, which had been pent up for the better part of two decades, soared. There was no problem of industrial capacity. Businessmen had tooled up for the war, and it was now a question of which industries could shift from war to consumer products. By 1948, the economy had absorbed all of the veterans, and unemployment was at only 3.8 percent. Inflation was modest and manageable, while corporate profits soared. Postwar pessimism quickly vanished as the country began an unprecedented period of prosperity. A brief economic slump following the defeat of Thomas Dewey for the presidency was short-lived, as the North Korean invasion of South Korea added a war economy stimulus to an already stable industrial base. The country needed a prolonged period of political support and stability if it was to prosper, and it came in the form of General Dwight Eisenhower. This outwardly gentle father figure was exactly what the country needed to instill the confidence and stability to move forward. Businessmen were optimistic. Interest rates were low and stable, and the dollar had become the king of currencies around the world. The stock market was strong, and it was easy to raise money for expansion. Growth was the order of the day, and the hunger for growth would lead to a new generation of businessmen, developing business models never before seen.

Initially, conglomerates were born from the conviction that if a company could diversify by conducting business in more than one market and that market had a natural business cycle different from the original business, the resulting company could tamper some of the effects of business cycles on its activity, reducing risk. By the same token, if the acquisition was of interest because of its profit potential, the acquiring company could minimize the risk of acquiring the target company simply by virtue of its own business cycle. Carried to the extreme, if one did business in enough markets with different cycles, one could theoretically eliminate the effects of an economic downturn except when everything went south at the same time, i.e., in a recession.

It didn't take long for acquisition-minded companies to discover that in an environment that rewards growth, one could grow through acquisition relatively pain-free by financing the acquisitions through the issuance of stock, and so long as the stock market continued upward everyone could win without any outlay of cash. In some cases, the gain in value of the stock issued to the seller was even non-taxable. In effect, the market rewarded growth where none had really occurred. This process was far more interesting to some CEOs than the hard work necessary to create true internal growth. The merger activity associated with the new conglomerates reached its peak between 1965 and 1975, when the Federal Trade Commission reported that 80 percent of the mergers that took place during that period were conglomerate mergers (Gaughan, 2007, p. 40).

The conglomerate era can perhaps be better understood by tracing brief histories of some of the best-known players: Royal Little, of Textron; Charles (Tex) Thornton, of Litton Industries; James Ling, of LTV; Charles Bluhdorn, of Gulf and Western; and Harold Geneen, of ITT. There were many others, of course. As the phenomenon grew, it attracted many aspiring conglomerators, some more successful than others, some copiers and some innovators, each convinced that he had a unique business model. The definition of what constituted a conglomerate evolved over time, with little consensus on a distinct philosophy or business model.

Royal Little was not really a conglomerator in the sense that the name came to be known in the 1960s. But in many ways he was the precursor to the conglomerate movement. While he had no clear-cut guiding business strategy, he would develop one over time that seemed less designed to support a distinct strategy than to justify what Textron had become. Little was more of a "turnaround" specialist, who sought to grow his company by acquiring companies with weak management at very low prices, sometimes for cash, more often by printing paper with the company's name on it. He discovered and developed many of the tools of the conglomerate trade that the next generation of aspiring CEOs would use with much success as the movement exploded.

Little had also become a student of the tax laws. He discovered many of the now well-known techniques of conglomerate strategy. He learned that a company with excess profits could acquire one with excess losses (called tax loss carry-forwards), combine them, and often completely eliminate the acquiring company's tax liability for several years. He learned that although a target company might have significant losses, it could be acquired with a bank loan. Then, certain parts of the company could be sold, raising enough cash to pay off the bank loan (the leveraged buyout). As he trolled the marketplace for potential acquisitions, he became more and more interested in the acquisition process, rather than whether or not the target company would fit into his goal of dominating the textile industry.

For Royal Little, becoming the first conglomerator had been a sometimes painful learning process. He learned how to use financial and fiscal tools to maximize acquisition leverage, and he learned that careful diversification could reduce the risk of the business cycle. As is often the case with strategies gone wrong, Little had gotten the cart before the horse, the strategy before the objectives, and the easiest way to correct that in his mind was to rewrite the history, to create objectives that fit the strategy. Nevertheless, Little's list of after-the-fact guidelines was prescient in the sense that it became a virtual model for the construction of a conglomerate and would find its way, in one form or another, in the strategic announcements of subsequent hopefuls.

The Litton Conglomerate's Objectives (Sobel, 1984)

Our basic concept of unrelated diversification at the time was to accomplish these objectives:

1. Eliminate the effect of business cycles on the parent company by having many divisions in unrelated fields.

2. Eliminate any Justice Department monopoly problems by avoiding acquisitions in related businesses.

3. Eliminate single industry's temptation to over expand at the wrong time. Finance the growth of only those divisions which show the greatest return on capital at risk. Rather than over-expand any division, use surplus funds to buttress another business.

4. Confine acquisitions to leading companies in a relatively small industry. Never buy a small company in the $5 to $10 billion industry.

5. Having made a complete analysis of all major manufacturing companies' return on net worth and found that only about twenty-five earned over 20 percent on common stock equity, I set that rate of return in 1953 as Textron's goal for the future.

Tex Thornton. While Royal Little discovered how to acquire companies by using their own assets as collateral for the purchase price—the leveraged buyout—Tex Thornton discovered how to acquire companies using paper—his own company's stock. The objective in both cases was to create growth, as it was growth in both revenues and earnings that beguiled Wall Street. Neither Little nor Thornton exhibited much interest in creating real value by managing a successful company manufacturing and selling real products.

Thornton found an acquisition vehicle in Litton Industries. He was able to convince Lehman Brothers to underwrite an issue of bonds, convertible preferred stock, and common stock to acquire Litton Industries. The issue was successful; however, by the time Thornton had paid Charles Litton, the owner, and covered the commissions and expenses of the issue, there was little left to operate the company, much less acquire others. As a consequence, Thornton's subsequent acquisition activities were confined to mergers with other small electronics companies, essentially growing the company, both vertically and horizontally, into a significant but not yet giant military electronics firm. Thornton spent his time promoting the image of Litton as a new breed of company with a revolutionary business management model.

Growth within the military electronics industry had limits, however, and Thornton's ambitions chafed at those limits. His efforts at building the company's image had succeeded in lifting the value of Litton's common stock over fivefold within two years and, more importantly, its price/earnings ratio to a level more characteristic of the exciting new company Thornton claimed it to be. Litton's earnings were growing about as fast as could be hoped in a military market in a postwar world. If Litton was to grow rapidly through acquisition, it would have to move outside of its traditional business, and it would have to move quickly while its price/earnings ratio was high. Thornton's goal was rapid growth, and growth through acquisitions fit his strategy better, and considerably easier, than the slog of internal development. The solution he adopted was to use Litton's high P/E ratio to generate rapidly growing earnings per share by acquiring companies with significantly lower P/E ratios. Everyone was happy. The acquirer could report earnings growth without spending any cash. The acquired company owners received more than market value for their company. The investment bankers earned serious commissions and would eagerly look for new acquisition candidates…and the lawyers were kept very busy.

During the next five years, Thornton approached over fifty companies in an effort to expand his newly named Industrial Systems and Equipment Group. Most companies were not interested in Thornton's paper transactions, and only five agreed to be acquired. Undaunted, Thornton began acquiring totally unrelated companies in such industries as Atherton Microwaves, Stouffer Foods, American Book Company, and Fitchburg Paper. By 1967, acquisitions were coming in at the rate of one every three weeks.

James Ling. LTV was founded by James Ling in 1947, the product of Ling's acquisition of Temco Aircraft in 1960 and Chance Vought, an aerospace firm. Ling was more interested in companies as financial entities rather operating companies producing goods or services. In 1947, Ling had founded Ling Electric Company, and by the mid-1950s, the company had grown to two million dollars a year in revenues. Ling, however, had become more interested in the wheeling and dealing of the Texas business environment than electrical contracting. In particular, he discovered that he could raise money for expansion by recapitalizing his company, selling new shares to investors, and using the proceeds for growth. He also discovered that investor interest in electronics was far greater than for electrical contracting, and the higher multiples of earnings that investors would pay for a glamour stock became, in his mind, a road map for growth. He purchased L.M. Electronics, renamed it Ling Electronics, and folded it under his newly created holding company, Ling Electric. With low interest rates, Ling went on an acquisition binge, buying almost any unrelated company so long as its rate of earnings exceeded the interest on the incremental debt required to make the acquisition. He was more interested in, and skilled at, making earnings grow through financial manipulation than improved productivity. In 1960, Ling made a hostile tender offer to acquire Chance Vought, the largest defense contractor in Dallas, with sales of over $250 million. Ling recognized that the problems at the company were caused by overdependence on military contracts, and he vowed to never again be dependent on a single market, product, or technology. Ling had defined what it meant to be a conglomerator. In the process of spinning off companies to reduce the company's debt, Ling made another important discovery— that often the individual parts of a company are worth more as independent entities than they are as part of a larger organization, that the so-called synergy that was held out as one of the rationales for conglomerate acquisitions was not always the case. In fact the reverse was often the case.

By 1969, LTV had acquired thirty-three companies with combined sales of $2.7 billion selling fifteen thousand different products and services, with such well-known brands as Wilson & Co. (Wilson Meats, Wilson Sporting Goods, and Wilson Pharmaceutical and Chemical) and Greatamerica Corporation (Braniff Airways, National Car Rental, Franklin Life, First Western Bank & Trust Company, and Stonewall Insurance).

Gulf & Western Industries was founded in 1958 by the renaming of a company called Michigan Plating & Stamping, an underperforming automotive parts manufacturer located in Grand Rapids, Michigan. Charles Bluhdorn was born in Vienna and came to the United States in 1942 from England, where his family had relocated prior to WWII. The automotive industry was thriving, as were its parts suppliers, and Bluhdorn managed to find what perhaps was the only company that wasn't thriving—Michigan Plating & Stamping. Bluhdorn bought MP&S with money borrowed from two friends who, like Bluhdorn, saw the company more as a vehicle for expansion than an interesting opportunity in and of itself.

Bluhdorn and his new partners quickly discovered that the actual management of the business was less interesting and exciting than the acquisition of the company itself. They hired new management to run MP&S and set out to find other companies in the auto parts business that they could acquire. From 1959 on G&W acquired companies with a vengeance, at a rate of one every two or three months. During this period of exceptional growth, Bluhdorn quickly learned the importance of maintaining earnings growth in order to leverage G&W's stock as a vehicle for future acquisitions. A valuable tool for improving earnings was the incorporation of onetime events into the reported net income of the company as if they were part of ongoing operations, rather than exceptional items. These might include sales of fixed assets, changes in the method of valuing inventories, changes reserved for doubtful accounts receivable, changes in the dates for ending accounting periods, and gains on securities transactions that had nothing to do with G&W's core business. While Bluhdorn did not invent "creative accounting," he certainly used it whenever he could.

Not all of Bluhdorn's acquisition proposals were successful. But he discovered that if the target company was properly valued, he could have his cake and eat it, too. In pursuing an acquisition, Bluhdorn would acquire a position in the target company's common stock on the open market, say 5 percent of the outstanding stock. He would then make a public tender offer to acquire the stock of a company at a price greater than the current price but still below what he considered the true value of the company. The tender offer would typically push up the price of the stock. If the offer succeeded, Bluhdorn had acquired the company at a bargain price, which would boost earnings. If it failed, he would sell his common stock on the open market at a profit due to the increase in price that the acquisition activity had created (Greenmail). This gain on the stock sale would be reported as net income for G&W, as if it was a normal part of the ongoing business. Bluhdorn was increasingly willing to let his managers concern themselves with operations while he became increasingly fascinated by and an expert at mergers and acquisitions. He would pursue growth through the process of the acquisitions, rather than focus on managing internal growth. He would perfect the strategic use of the process as his primary activity and in so doing would develop, assemble, or refine many of the more commonly used tools of M&A.

- Using other peoples' money rather than his own, whether borrowed from banks (leveraged buyouts), borrowed from investors (private equity) to borrowed from shareholders by issuing stock (dilution)

- Creative accounting (reporting non-operating items as normal operations)

- Hostile takeover offers (greenmail)

Harold Geneen. ITT was founded in 1920 as International Telephone & Telegraph (IT&T), and it became one of the best-known conglomerates of the 1960s under the direction of Harold Geneen, generally recognized as one of the great, if not the greatest businessmen of the times, the first who defined conglomeration with a set of management principles and techniques that formed a consistent management philosophy that could be replicated and studied by the management institutes and business schools of the time. He exhibited a "take no prisoners" style of management that drew harsh, sometimes negative criticism from the business community and could strike fear within the ITT organization itself, displaying the characteristics for which he would become well-known, an aggressive and hard-driving personality, and a visceral intolerance for ineptitude and poor performance.

Geneen introduced the infamous performance review meetings that he had created at Raytheon. One former ITT operating manager described these meetings as ITT stress tests. Geneen would leave New York with all of his analysts in a chartered Boeing 707 and begin a round-the-world tour of the overseas operating units. The reviews would always begin at 8:00 a.m. Eastern Standard Time, in a hotel or local headquarters conference room that had all of the windows blacked out so as not to disturb those on NY time. The managers from that part of the world would be seated in a semicircle facing Geneen and his analysts. They would each be permitted to have two assistants seated behind them. With this format, the inquisition would begin. The managers would be asked a series of questions about their operations, explaining the details of one performance report or another and explaining any variances from their approved plan. If a manager failed to respond with the expected degree of understanding and clarity, he would be asked another question. If he failed a second time, there was a good chance that he would be asked to leave and he would be replaced by one of the two men behind him, who would then submit to the same line of questioning. (This first-hand account was recounted with only the slightest feeling of exaggeration.) Managers were exceedingly well paid, but also exceedingly stressed. Internally it was called the "management by fear" model.

Concerned by his company's single business exposure to the vagaries of the business cycle, he embarked on a search for acquisition targets that not only strengthened ITT's domestic business and reduced its dependence on the international, he came to regard diversification as a viable strategy to reduce risk. By transforming ITT into a conglomerate, he could achieve the growth he had promised while minimizing the attendant risk.

The titans of conglomeration were pioneers of the movement, preaching diversification to minimize risk and maximize return, developing the now-familiar transaction models of pooling of interests (issuing stock), leveraged buyouts, hostile takeovers, stock manipulation, and borrowing from the shareholders (dilution). The atmosphere of the 1960s was one of high competition in the search for acquisition candidates. Entrepreneurs who had started or inherited family companies in small niche markets suddenly found themselves courted by the "conglomerators," often the subject of bidding wars between prospective acquirers.

CHAPTER EIGHT

A New Singer[57]

Donald P. Kircher[58]

Donald P. Kircher, an engineer's son, was born in St. Paul, Minnesota, in 1915. He attended the University of Minnesota in Minneapolis, where he graduated in 1936, followed by the Columbia University Law School, graduating in 1939. Following graduation from law school, Kircher joined the Wall Street firm of Winthrop, Stimson, Putnam, & Roberts (Winthrop, Stimson), a major firm that had enjoyed a long relationship with the Singer Company. At the time, Winthrop, Stimson was involved in what would become famous as the McKesson & Robbins scandal, a major fraud that resulted in significant reforms at both the SEC and the American Institute of Accountants. The work that Kircher did on the company's restructuring in this case earned him considerable notoriety, which did not go unnoticed at the Singer Manufacturing Company, where Winthrop, Stimson was also general outside counsel.

In December 1941, Kircher left the firm to enlist in the U.S. Army. He was sent to Europe, where he served with distinction as a tank commander in General George Patton's Sixth Armored Division. He was twice wounded and was awarded a Silver Star with Oak Leaf Clusters, a Bronze Star, and a Purple Heart with Oak Leaf Clusters, Chevalier, Order of Leopold and Croix de Guerre (Belgium). Kircher much admired Patton and his leadership skills, certain aspects of which he would eventually incorporate into his own management style at Singer. After the war ended, Kircher rejoined the law firm.

In 1948, Don Kircher was asked by Lightner to join the Singer Manufacturing Company as his assistant, initially working on special projects, as do most assistants to presidents. It seems clear in retrospect that he was brought in as an agent for change, probably on Lightner's initiative. The composition of the board of directors at the time was typical of the traditional Singer way of doing business. Its six members consisted of Lightner, the company treasurer, the manager for Europe, the heads of manufacturing and R&D, and Stephen C. Clark, the grandson of the co-founder of the company. All were at or near retirement. This was not a group likely to change the direction of the company in any significant way. Before he could begin to make any substantive changes, however, Kircher had to constitute his own reformist team and gain full control of policy-making.

Within two years, Kircher was appointed assistant vice president in the legal affairs office. Also appointed assistant vice president was Donald G. Robbins, who would become an important and loyal ally of Kircher's throughout his term running the company. Interestingly, in the spring or summer of 1952, the Singer Manufacturing Company published its first annual report of 1951 operations for general release. Up to this point, the company had released little information about its results. The annual report was referred to in the news as having been "distributed to the shareholders" at the annual meeting. This 1951 annual report was certainly a spare document by today's standards, consisting of a half-page textual presentation of the key financial numbers, such as Revenues (here called "gross income"), income before taxes, net income, earnings per share, and dividends. These were presented without any qualitative explanations of changes from one year to the next, but merely as fait accompli and signed by the president, Mr. Lightner. The second page contained a list of the six directors and thirteen officers of the company. The remaining pages were devoted to the audited financial statements and the audit firm's notes. It is probably fair to assume that Kircher was a significant force behind the general release of what had heretofore been considered virtually private information.

In July 1952, Donald P. Kircher was made a full vice president. The annual report for that year followed the same format as the prior year, with little in the way of additional explanation or clarification of the 1952 results. By1953, however, Kircher's hand was apparent in a much-changed annual report. Following the usual recitation of the numbers in textual format, there followed a page and a half of qualitative information about what had happened in the past year and what one might expect in the year to come. There was a final paragraph announcing changes in the roster of directors (unchanged) and officers, followed by President Lightner's signature. The following year, the analysis of results was expanded from two pages to three and a new tabular format was introduced. Most importantly, the board of directors was expanded from six to eight members and both Don Kircher and Don Robbins, although still an assistant vice presidents, were elected to the board. Finally, the 1957 annual report announced the successful completion of Donald P. Kircher's consolidation of power and the first step in his implementation of the strategy he increasingly considered vital to the company's survival.

Effective January 1, 1958 Donald P. Kircher is elected President of The Singer Manufacturing Company. Milton C. Lightner is elected to the newly created post of Chairman of the Board of Directors, making Kircher both president and Chief Executive Officer. Mr. Lightner, as Chairman, will continue to exercise supervision over the Company's general policies.

In February 1958, barely one month after becoming president, Kircher made his first acquisition. The Company purchased for $2.45 million, Haller, Raymond, and Brown, Inc. (HRB), a research organization located in State College, Pennsylvania. HRB had about 350 engineers, scientists, and support personnel doing research for the military in electronic and mechanical engineering, applied physics, and weapons systems integration. This would be Singer's first step away from total dependence on the sewing machine for survival.

Donald Kircher's efforts to remake Singer into a fast-growing, highly profitable conglomerate, insulated from the major uncertainties of the business cycle, can be better understood by examining four relatively distinct time periods in his tenure: First (1958–1960), prepare the stakeholders for change in the organizational structure and corporate culture. Kircher's staff seemed uniformly to agree that acquisitions was the best strategy, but the present course of acquisitions was a strategy without objectives. To reverse this, by developing objectives that would define the targeted acquisitions, represented a radical change of the strategic business model. Second (1961–1963), develop an appropriate set of objectives in order to guide the first acquisitions. Move from a functional organization, with sales, manufacturing, and research as the principal operating units directed from the top, to a profit-center organization with managers responsible for everything affecting their products, from raw material acquisition to post-sale collections. Third (1964–1968), refine the business model with final definitions of the primary business operating groups with a major acquisition in the target industry. Fourth (1969–1974), develop the primary business groups, both internally and through additional acquisitions in the target industry along with a new strategy for the sewing machine business appropriate for the company's new mission.

If there was one symbol of the heritage of the Singer Manufacturing Company in New York City, it was the Singer Building at 149 Broadway. In 1896, Frederick Bourne commissioned the Paris-trained architect Ernest Flagg to design a Beaux-Arts tower at Broadway and Liberty Streets in Manhattan to serve as the new Singer worldwide headquarters. Completed in 1908, the building had forty-one stories, a bulbous mansard roof, and a giant lantern at its peak, and with a tower rising to 612 feet it was the tallest building in the city until it was surpassed in 1909 by the 700-foot-tall Metropolitan Life Tower on East Twenty-Third Street facing what is now Madison Square Park. Flagg was an outspoken opponent of the trend of building skyscrapers to the edge of the property line, believing that such construction inhibited the view of what he felt should be beautiful structures and would eventually deprive New Yorkers from sunlight as they wandered through the darkly shadowed canyons. The result was an architectural icon that stood as a permanent and highly visible reminder of the company's success.

On November 6, 1961, Donald P. Kircher announced that the building was inefficient and unsuitable for Singer's executive offices and that they would move uptown to new offices in Rockefeller Center. Flagg had designed the Singer building to occupy only one-quarter of the building site, with the result that its footprint was only sixty-five feet square and yielded only 4,200 square feet of space on each floor, approximately 172,000 square feet in total. The building that eventually replaced it, One Liberty Plaza, would have over two million square feet. In deciding to leave the most visible symbol of the company's past (aside from the red S), Kircher had announced to the world that the "old Singer" of the past was behind him and that he was leading the company into a new, modern era. Demolished in 1967, it was the tallest building ever brought down in New York City until September 11, 2001.

Don Kircher was not a tall man, probably around five feet eight, but he appeared taller than his actual physical height, holding himself erect with the military bearing he had acquired while serving as a tank commander in the 6th Armored Division under General George Patton. Although he had been prevented from becoming an officer as a result of General MacArthur's decision not to let business leaders become officers, he likely felt MacArthur's decision should not apply to him, and he carried himself as if he were an officer long after he left the army. One in-house rumor had it that he had gone so far as to have shortened the front legs on his office chairs in order to oblige their occupants to always sit at attention, lest they slide to the floor. This was almost certainly fanciful, but it fit perfectly the image he was creating for himself.

Kircher was fond of quotes, especially those in Latin. He would launch one in the middle of someone's presentation with a statement rather than a question, often with the pontificate air of an intellectual display. Few of his colleagues had the self-confidence to puncture his balloon from time to time, but there were a few who weren't terrified of him and would take the chance, but certainly never in public. On one occasion in a small meeting in his office, Kircher chose to quote a poem, citing the author by name. A brave colleague present noted that Kircher had the reference wrong; it was by a different author. They argued back and forth peacefully, but without a resolution, and finally they agreed to a two-dollar bet for whoever could be proven correct. Kircher probably assumed that the subject was over and forgotten, but the colleague didn't and produced the evidence. Kircher had lost the bet and admitted his error with grace, albeit in private, and no mention was made of the bet. Not satisfied with the state of the wager, the colleague sought an appropriate reminder and acquired a stuffed crow from a friend in advertising, which he then placed in the silver swivel-top soup tureen on Kircher's dining table. Kircher opened it and had to laugh (and pay the two dollars). Few of the senior executives would have been sure enough in their relationship with Kircher to try this, but notwithstanding his increasing remoteness, he still retained a sense of humor with a few close colleagues.

Kircher professed a strong belief in delegation as the core of his management philosophy. He was convinced that he delegated freely and gave managers the authority to get on with the expected results, but if a significant operational decision went wrong, he would interrogate the responsible manager, asking why he hadn't been brought into the loop. Informal communication between Kircher and his direct reports that might have addressed operating problems informally, before they mutated into a crisis, had become increasingly difficult. One did not simply stop in to see Mr. Kircher. One called his secretary with a request to see him. She would check his calendar and inquire about how soon he would be available and she would then call back with the day and time of the meeting. The individual would then appear at the appointed hour to make a presentation about whatever issue he was raising—it was all very formal, reflecting the increasing distance he was establishing between himself and his colleagues.

Kircher had been variously described as imperious, reserved, unruffled, forceful, strict in adhering to protocol, and never perturbed under pressure. He clearly enjoyed being the boss, and when he entered the room there was never any doubt about who was in charge. Only a few of his direct reports had the temerity to address him as "Don." For everyone else he was "Mr. Kircher." While he abhorred staff meetings and committees and considered them generally to be a waste of time, preferring to communicate directly with his direct reports, sometimes meetings could not be avoided. During the annual budget cycle, he felt that each senior vice president should have his day in court. When Kircher entered the conference room promptly at the appointed hour, all of the participants had already been present for at least ten to fifteen minutes awaiting his arrival. Those who might have already seated themselves jumped to their feet, hoping he wouldn't notice. It was rumored that late arrivals risked not being invited to the next meeting. He was polite but to the point, clearly very intelligent, and for the most part the other participants would wait for him to ask a question. He was said to have a photographic memory, probably arising from his well-known history of having completed his bar exam in roughly half the allotted time. He had one recurring habit that reinforced this mystique. When an operating manager, especially one from overseas, was making a presentation, Kircher would often stop him and ask a detailed question related to the previous year's meeting, either about something personal or an obscure point that had been raised the prior year, generally something that had not been included in the printed matter that had been distributed. Whether this was due to a photographic memory or a gimmick, it certainly had the desired effect of convincing speakers that they could never be over-prepared or hide from an embarrassing detail raised in a prior presentation.

The new Singer offices were located on the top six floors of the RCA Building at 30 Rockefeller Plaza, perfect for Kircher's vision of the Company—the most prestigious (and probably the most expensive) building in Manhattan. His offices were on the fifty-eighth floor, along with his direct staff vice presidents, the controller, treasurer, development officer, tax counsel, and personnel officer. On exiting the elevator on floor fifty-eight, one proceeded directly into a large circular rotunda highlighted by soft, indirect lighting, surrounded by part of the company's new signature art collection. Aside from the receptionist at the elevator, there was not a human in sight. There were three closed doors in the rotunda. Straight ahead was the door to the president's suite of offices that occupied roughly one-quarter of the floor. To the left was the door to his presentation room, which communicated directly with Kircher's office, and to the right was a door leading to his direct staff. Visitors sat on the curved sofas and waited to be summoned. One of Kircher's secretaries or assistants would then invite the visitor to wait in outer office beyond the rotunda until he or she was finally invited into the president's office itself. Connecting directly to the office were a dining room and a conference-presentation room for larger meetings. This was where each of the company's operating divisions rehearsed and presented their strategic plans and operating budgets for his approval.

Kircher had assembled an impressive collection of modern art to announce to both visitors and staff that Singer had arrived at the forefront of modern American businesses. Don Robbins, Kircher's early and continuing ally, had been given the responsibility for creating the collection. Robbins, an avid collector of twentieth-century art, went about it enthusiastically. On Kircher's floor, a large painting by Helen Frankenthaler hung on one side of the entry rotunda and a Paul Jenkins "ivory knife" painting hung on the other. In the center of the thirty-foot-wide domed ceiling hung a large Alexander Calder mobile. It was all very heady stuff. The art collection continued throughout the president's floor and welcomed visitors as they landed from the elevators on all of the other floors, a Robert Rauschenberg collage on one floor, a John Chamberlain crushed auto sculpture on another. Kircher was proud of the collection, which had been the subject of several magazine articles. The sixties was the era of corporate art collections as symbols of the corporate avant-garde, the most notable of which remains the public Pepsi-Cola Collection in Purchase, New York.

Kircher's private dining room, where he dined each day with the most senior officers and an occasional invited guest, was described in the *New York Times*:

Its oak-paneled dining room on the 58th floor of 30 Rockefeller Plaza has stunning views to the north (over Central Park) and east (over the East River and Long Island), but the vice presidents who lunch there take them for granted. And guests are almost never present.

> Promptly at 12:30 Donald P. Kircher, 53-year-old president of Singer's worldwide empire of products for the home, industry and business, takes his place at the head of an American walnut table and orders a very dry martini. The vice presidents are almost sure to do likewise and after the single cocktail comes a simple meal. The whole thing is over in an hour, and it is described here to keep outsiders from brooding too extensively because they can't be there. ("A Challenge for Anyone Who Feels He Must Go Everywhere," May 20, 1968)

As described by one attendee, everyone would arrive early, so as not to make Kircher wait, and each would stand behind his chair until the president arrived and sat down. The attendees, essentially the vice presidents who reported directly to him, were always juggling for seats as close as possible to Kircher's at the head of the table. (There was no chair at the foot of the table.) One recently appointed aspiring successor would usually arrive early in an effort to lock in the key position immediately to Kircher's left. He was usually successful, as most of his colleagues tired of the dance early on and the chair was eventually acknowledged as his. Kircher's old sewing colleague and fellow board member, Charles Bruder, always attuned to the relative power structure, would claim the spot to Kircher's right. The remaining participants would then join in a silent, but mutually agreed-upon dance, by which each would be seated such that the table represented the informally acknowledged power structure within the company. While the places were not assigned, they were established, and one did not take someone else's seat without causing unease or creating a potential enemy. There was always turnover in the senior ranks, particularly following a major acquisition when the newly acquired CEO, who undoubtedly thought he was probably Kircher's designated successor, engaged in a delicate dance for a priority place, much to the amusement of the others. Table conversation tended to have little business substance and consisted mostly of banter, with each VP looking for an opportunity to one-up or put down a colleague. Occasionally, Kircher himself would raise a provocative subject or ask a question, such as, "What do you guys think about so-and-so (a public figure currently in the news)?" On one occasion the subject was actually Donald Trump.

> The fifty-ninth floor was given over to the members of the controller's office: Accounting, Budgets, Internal Audit, and Manufacturing Cost. The operating divisions' headquarters staff offices were spread out between the sixtieth and sixty-third floors. Above those were the executive dining rooms, served by the

kitchen of the Rainbow Room and available to anyone in the headquarters carrying a formal title of "manager" or higher. In those days, title inflation had not yet infected corporate life, and the department managers had substantial responsibilities. The privilege of dining there was a significant perk and an indicator of one's status in the managerial hierarchy.

Now that DPK, as he was now referred to in the company, had joined the ranks of the conglomerators, it was appropriate that his activities outside of Singer, both professional and personal, reflected his success. Between 1962 and 1964, Kircher was elected to the boards of Bristol-Myers Co., General Cable Corp., Morgan Guaranty Co., Lehman Corp., and Metropolitan Life. Consistent with the Singer presidential tradition, he divided his leisure time between two residences appropriate for his status. He had initially purchased a twelve-room townhouse at 230 East Sixty-third Street that had once belonged to Huntington Hartford, heir to the A&P fortune, but he later moved to a house at 53 East Eightieth Street, closer to Fifth Avenue. On weekends, he spent time with his horses on his estate in Kingwood Township, New Jersey. The estate comprised 132 acres of secluded rolling hills and guesthouses in the horse farming and hunting country of New Jersey, the preferred weekend neighborhood of Jacqueline Kennedy.

Preparing the Stakeholders for Change

The first indication of change didn't receive much preparation. The public announcement of Donald P. Kircher's appointment as president of the Singer Manufacturing Company was made on December 5, 1957, and barely six weeks later, on January 22, 1958, Kircher announced his first acquisition, Haller, Raymond, & Brown (HRB), described in the annual report as "…a well-known research organization located in State College, Pennsylvania. It has a staff of about 350 engineers, scientists and supporting personnel and has been active in research work, largely for the military, in the field of electronic and mechanical engineering, applied physics, and weapons systems integration."

While the publicly stated primary objective of the HRB acquisition was to "…quickly to expand and strengthen our research activities in the sewing equipment field," sewing research, while strategically important, was not the driving force behind the HRB acquisition. In fact, HRB never did any subsequent research for the sewing business, which could have used some as it struggled with product development issues in the face of a declining market for sewing machines. The underlying premise was to demonstrate Singer's new commitment to technology as the force that would drive the expansion of the Company's business beyond its traditional sewing products. Kircher had undoubtedly watched with interest the feverish pace of the new conglomerates' growth through acquisition and saw how such a strategy of diversification could be viable for Singer. The company was totally dependent on a single product whose growth was limited by four important factors: (1) the declining birth rate in the United States, (2) the rise of women in the workplace, no longer interested in or able to find time for sewing, (3) the invasion of low-priced Japanese imports, and (4) the availability of ready-made, low-cost clothing.

In addition to changes in market demographics and competition, there was the very real possibility that Singer could itself become an acquisition target, and this was certainly one of the drivers for it to grow as quickly as possible, even if the Company didn't yet know exactly where it was going. Singer was still small enough with sufficient cash flow to interest the takeover artists. The Company remained the worldwide market leader in the manufacture and sale of sewing machines and was generating EBITDAs (Earnings before Interest, Taxes, Depreciation, and Amortization, a convenient proxy for cash flow from operations.) of over $50 million per year on revenues of approximately $450 million, a respectable 11 percent. Net assets of approximately $274 million were financed largely by shareholders' equity, with only $32 million of long-term debt.

Before he could implement any of his strategic growth plans, Kircher had to prepare the company for change. Any change in the corporate culture over the past 150 years had been slow and very incremental. Up until the move to Rockefeller Plaza, it was still easy to imagine Sir Douglas Alexander watching the Singer ships depart for Europe. The company had never relied on outside investors or banks, and Kircher was not yet ready to change that policy. Singer had been self-financed virtually from the very beginning, and its annual cash flow had always been sufficient for growth and generous dividends. However, if Kircher intended to embark on an aggressive acquisition program, he would soon need financing, either from a stock offering, the banks, or a high valuation of the Singer common stock if he planned to acquire companies by exchanging shares.

The company's financial reporting systems had traditionally been largely cash-based, more appropriate for a closely held private company than a large public corporation with broad ownership. If he intended to access the capital markets or exchange shares with a publicly listed company, the company would have to adopt generally accepted accounting principles that, although the gold standard, offered a substantial menu of management choices to present the company as positively as possible. In his April 1960 letter to the shareholders, Kircher announced a change to the accrual basis of accounting for installment sales, by far the largest component of the sewing machine activity. Previously, the Company had accounted for the profit on installment sales over time, as the accounts were collected. By shifting to the accrual basis, the Company could recognize virtually the total profit at the moment of sale, after creating a reserve for doubtful accounts, rather than as the customers made their payments. The result was an acceleration of reported income, which would be particularly significant in times of rapid growth. Some of Kircher's advisors worried that the conversion to accrual accounting was a critical mistake, in that it permitted management to take its eye off operations and focus on onetime accounting adjustments that either improved reported profits artificially or hid problems. Accrual accounting in conglomerates had created a panoply of tools by which management could disguise the consequences of bad decisions. Sales of fixed assets could be buried in the results as ordinary income. Changes in how inventory was recorded or when a sale was actually accounted for could create significant onetime improvements that could not be replicated in the future. Eventually, the accumulation of publicly undisclosed problems could result in an enormous onetime write-off, which itself could be used to improve future earnings by directing the reader's eye away from earnings to "results from continuing operations," which excluded the continuing cash cost of decisions management had made to discontinue certain operations, but not yet achieved. The reported bottom-line results had become increasingly inconsequential for judging management's performance. Some officers of Singer believed that the old system of counting the cash in the bank at the end of the year and comparing to the beginning of the year was not so bad after all.

At the same time as the accounting change, Kircher announced the company's intent to register its shares with the Securities and Exchange Commission, as well as to make application to list the shares on the New York Stock Exchange. Singer was viewed by both the investing community and its customers as a "faded blue-chip," the "old dowager," and Kircher felt it was important to change that image, to finally bring the Company into the twentieth century. Reporting and control systems had to be modified in order to satisfy the requirements for possible public stock offerings and bank reviews.

Kircher had not yet delineated a comprehensive strategy for growth through acquisitions, nor had he sought advice on the development of such a strategy. In considering how he might prepare an entirely new direction for the company, Kircher would have benefited from the opinions of experts outside of the implanted Singer culture that, although rich with experience and history, consisted of people who had essentially been doing things the same way for generations. His reliance on his own exceptional analytical skills as the primary contributor to Singer's strategic search, accompanied by an almost overwhelming reluctance to seek outside advice, was a significant blind spot. This tendency to reject outside objective assistance would return time and again to haunt him as the acquisition program hit rough spots. A clearer third-party assessment of the company's options would have been extremely useful. Although he had yet no clear strategy for growth, Kircher had already launched an acquisition culture, and his development officer immediately began shopping for companies, driven primarily by the conglomerate focus on improving earnings per share, rather than strategic fit.

Charles F. Bruder, the longtime head of the Consumer Products Division in the United States, had been elected to the Singer Board of Directors in 1958, the same year Kircher had been appointed president. Bruder was a stalwart ally of Kircher's and would play a considerable role in the early years of Singer's acquisition program. His experience in consumer retailing probably influenced the first two acquisitions, made in May 1960 with the announcement that the Singer Manufacturing Company had acquired the Fidelity Machine Company, Inc., of Philadelphia, a manufacturer of knitting machines for the textile, clothing, and wire and rubber industries. In June, the Company acquired the Cobble Brothers Machine Company, Inc., and Cobble Brothers Sales Company, Inc., of Chattanooga, Tennessee (collectively "Cobble"). Cobble manufactured "tufting machines and allied equipment used in the production of carpets, rugs bath mats, and bedspreads. Approximately 90 percent of Cobble's sales are to producers of soft floor covering" (Singer Mfg. Co., June 29, 1960). While both of these acquisitions were touted in the annual report as "…progress…in broadening our product line," on the surface, these products were not that different from the retail consumer sewing market. They were a baby step away from one-product dependency but they "…laid the groundwork for further advances in this direction…. Investigation of other possible acquisitions continues." In 1962, Kircher made another acquisition closely related to, but not the same as the traditional business. He acquired the Supreme Knitting Machine Company, of Ozone Park, Queens. Supreme developed, manufactured, and sold a wide variety of textile and apparel machinery. With the exception of HRB-Singer, these early acquisitions were, like the sewing business, subject to the highs and lows of discretionary consumer spending, but with some significant differences. The technology was unfamiliar to the Singer manufacturing staff, and the products were sold through entirely different channels of distribution to a different customer base. The Singer Manufacturing Company was not yet a conglomerate, and these companies didn't move it in the direction of appropriate diversification.

Two other events occurred in 1961 that allowed Kircher to begin remaking the Singer Manufacturing Company into his thus far limited vision for the future. On September 17, Stephen C. Clark died. Clark was a director of the Company and the grandson of Edward Clark, the co-founder of the Company 110 years earlier. Clark was the last direct link to the Company's origins, in that he was born before Edward Clark passed away and he had actively managed the family's affairs during the tenures of Bourne and Alexander. Then, on December 31, Milton Lightner retired as chairman of the board and Donald P. Kircher succeeded him. Lightner was the other remaining link to the past, recruited by Sir Douglas Alexander in 1927 and succeeding him as president when Alexander died in 1948. Between them, the two men had presided over the Company for over fifty-five good, but inward-looking years.

In addition to the transformation of corporate strategy, change was also apparent in Kircher's management style and his relations with his staff. Up to the point of his actual appointment as president, he had been one of them, an advisor to the president. Initially a legal advisor, he had been given a succession of special projects to complete but he remained effectively without portfolio. He was at ease in conversation with his peers, well-liked and sociable, basically a nice person but very much affected by his war experience. No sooner had he been appointed president than his relationship with those around him changed. As CEO he became increasingly remote, seemingly insecure as an appointed leader who had not grown up in the company and who lacked that "Singer culture" experience shared by those who surrounded him. Kircher had essentially moved from being an attorney to being a major company president, without any significant corporate experience in between. When combined with a strong ego, this experiential gap perhaps reinforced his unwillingness to seek advice (and potential criticism) from outside the Company. Instead, he reverted to his military experience under Patton. Here he was, now at the top, and all he had to do was issue an order and the chain of command would take action and execute it, feasible or not. Colleagues who in the past felt easy in calling him "Don" were now clearly discouraged from doing so and resented it. From then on he was "Mr. Kircher."

As there was little published financial history of the Company prior to Kircher's appointment and an even more sparse narrative history, students of the Company had to parse, infer, or guess what was going on from a close reading of the chairman's letter in the company's annual reports to the shareholders. Kircher had been appointed both president and CEO while Lightner remained chairman of the board. Prior to the acquisition of HRB-Singer, there had been no mention of diversification or acquisitions in the Kircher/Lightner joint letters to the stockholders. Lightner had made a tentative effort at diversification in 1952 when he purchased a 70 percent interest in the Thurso Pulp and Paper Company in Quebec, Canada. Rather than constituting a new strategy for the company, this purchase was little more than a continuation of the company's long-standing company strategy of maximizing vertical integration. Singer had a woodworking factory in Thurso, Canada, which processed lumber from the company-owned Thurso Woodlands into veneers and sawed logs for use in Singer's cabinet factories. Thurso Pulp and Paper was created by Singer and Perkins-Goodwin to process the waste from both the timberlands and the Thurso factory. Vertical integration to capture all of the profit had been a conscious goal of the company at the end of the nineteenth century and had linked together in an inflexible and virtually unbreakable chain that froze the way things were done and impeded efforts to modernize any single component.

Although the 1960 annual letter to the shareholders was still jointly signed by Lightner and Kircher, there appeared near the end a brief announcement of the creation of the new Special Products Division, whose mission would be "…to direct our activities in the United States outside the sewing machine field and to supervise our efforts in the direction of diversification." There it was…the first public indication that Don Kircher had other plans for the old Singer Manufacturing Company. This would have been a logical moment to go outside of the company to seek someone uncontaminated by the sewing culture who could honestly bring a new vision to the diversification program. Instead Kircher appointed H. Neal Karr, a traditionalist from the sewing business, to head the Special Products Division. Karr had also joined the Singer board of directors coincident with Kircher's appointment as president.

Nineteen sixty-one would be Milton Lightner's last year as chairman of the board of directors. He had served the company as vice president, president, and chairman for thirty-three years, from 1928 to 1961, helping Douglas Alexander steer the company through the Great Depression and World War II. Only Sir Douglas himself had served longer, guiding Singer into the twentieth century.

Kircher was taking the helm of a company that, although judged by some to be in a dying market, still had respectable results. Annual sales in 1960 of $525.9 million were up 6.0 percent. Operating income was $50.8 million, 9.7 percent of sales and 41.3 percent over the prior year. Earnings of $20.9 million were 4.0 percent of sales and flat for the year because of unusual income in both years. In 1959, the company received a partial payment of $2.9 million of claims against Russia for the appropriation of the assets of the company's Russian subsidiary during the communist revolution. In 1960, the company sold some excess land and buildings at its Elizabethport, New Jersey, factory. Without these extraordinary income items, net income would have grown by 7.8 percent.

Although the reported earnings per share, without the onetime items, was down slightly, the announcement that the company had taken the first steps to diversify its product line appears to have had an impact on how the market viewed Singer. The market price of Singer common stock in the summer of 1959 was around $49 per share, which, at a price/earnings multiple of 10.3, valued the company at $220 million. In 1960, although the reported earnings were down slightly, the improved P/E ratio of 14.0 times earnings, resulted in a market valuation of $279 million, a 26.5 percent improvement from 1959. More importantly, by the summer of 1960, Singer was well on the way to becoming a hunter rather than one of the hunted in the conglomerate battlefield. In the summer of 1959, the market capitalization of Singer had been only 60 percent of its net assets and virtually debt-free, a tempting target for an aggressive takeover artist. One year later, although the earnings had declined slightly, the market capitalization had grown by 26.5 percent, to $279 million. Although the valuation was still less than the net asset value, the market had started to take notice by valuing the company at 14.0 times earnings, an improvement in its multiple of almost 36 percent.

Notwithstanding the focus on diversification and the improved valuation of the company by the stock market, Singer's sewing machine business was still considered to be a cash cow, and the company remained a tempting target. Competition for acquisitions was fierce, and while many of the major acquisition-minded CEOs, such as Tex Thornton at Litton and James Ling at LTV, were more focused on technology companies, others, such as Charles Bluhdorn at Gulf & Western and Harold Geneen at ITT, seemed ready to shoot at anything that moved. With its healthy balance sheet and cash flow, Singer was an ideal leveraged buyout candidate, and Don Kircher had little time to lose. And if he intended to become an acquirer rather than be acquired, Kircher would need means and flexibility. He announced that the shares of the new company, The Singer Company, had been listed on the New York Stock Exchange in order to "…provide a ready and convenient market for the shares and contribute to their broad ownership." Don Kircher was going shopping.

Kircher was finally ready to implement his strategy, and lest anyone had not been paying attention, he nailed the coffin shut on the formal company of the past. The Singer Manufacturing Company, the name by which the company had identified itself since 1863, was reorganized and became simply The Singer Company. It was no longer just a manufacturer and seller of sewing machines. It had redefined itself, and over the next seven years, it would acquire forty companies, unrelated to the old core business and largely unrelated to each other. For the public, Singer was a new company, but the underlying culture remained unchanged.

Between 1961 and 1963, Kircher began formally reorganizing the company, moving away from a functional organization, with manufacturing and sales as the primary organizational units to profit centers, organized either geographically for sewing, or by product line for the new businesses. This decentralization was intended to give operating executives both control of and responsibility for their operating profit, a variation on the Geneen Model. Decisions would be pushed down as closely as possible to the customer, with the president and his staff defining overall strategy, implementation of that strategy, and setting the benchmarks that would measure progress at the level of the operating units. He had come to believe that his strategy could best be implemented by executives who, like himself, did not have a strong link to the company's past, and he went on a hiring binge at the senior staff level.

The idea of reorganizing into profit centers was a major cultural change and was, in principle, welcomed by the field organization. However, there were two critically important factors in the sewing organization that made profit centering exceedingly difficult to implement: transfer pricing and U.S. dollar reporting.

Singer sales units acquired all of their sewing machines from Singer factories, usually outside of the country where it was eventually to be sold. In order to export a sewing machine, someone had to fix a "selling price" for the factory. From the point of view of the taxing authorities in the exporting and importing countries, the price at which the machines were transferred would determine the tax eventually paid in each country. Although no real profit was made until the machine was finally sold to a customer somewhere, the authorities where the machines were made and sold were keenly interested in the transfer prices and generally required that they be the result of an "arms-length negotiation," which was patently impossible. But such a price is arbitrary and will always be considered too high by the selling organization, too low by the factories, and not credible to the respective taxing authorities.

If that wasn't confusing enough, the factory selling the machine had to price it in its local currency, say pounds sterling, while the sales organization buying the machine had to pay for it in its local currency, say the French franc (the euro didn't yet exist). As the exchange rate between France and the UK varied, the actual price that was paid or received in local currency could vary from day to day. Finally, headquarters management had little or no interest in how these "profit centers" were doing in their local currencies. It wanted to see each unit's results in U.S. dollars, since that was the result that would be reported publicly in the United States. The exchange rate between the dollar, the franc, and the sterling was also changing daily. The potential for confusion was enormous, and the result was a reporting system whose relationship to the concept of profit centering was distant at best. And with various corporate staff departments charged with minimizing the company's worldwide tax obligations, reducing its exposure to currency fluctuations, or consolidating the financial results for foreign operations to be reported in U.S. dollars to the SEC, the system resulted in an enormous communication barrier between different levels of management.

Singer was never able to develop a system that gave the sewing line managers responsibility for both manufacturing and sales or measured managers in their own local currency. It could never escape its old functional organization that kept responsibility for sewing machine manufacturing and transfer pricing at the top, almost literally the responsibility of the president. Even Kircher couldn't resist meddling in transfer pricing and was once heard to say, "If I set transfer prices in such a way as to put the profit in the factory, I can keep it. If move it to the sales organizations, they will spend it on advertising." The local controllers and treasurers spent an enormous amount of time analyzing results and explaining the local currency numbers to the executives in New York and the dollar results to their bosses in the selling country. It was an enormously complicated task to develop a profit-center reporting system in this multinational company that measured foreign managers fairly and motivated them, and Singer never succeeded at it.

Historically, the treasurer had been the Company's only financial executive. A simplified version of his primary role had been to collect and count the cash, with an accounting department to record the transactions. This was a slightly more complicated version of the system by which, according to legend, President Alexander McKenzie used before WWI. He would cross the Atlantic to the United Kingdom to visit the European offices in London and the factory at Clydebank, Scotland. He would then cross the English Channel to disembark in France and board a private railroad car for a tour of Europe to visit the Singer headquarters in the major markets. At each stop, he would stay for a few days in an apartment that had been built for him on the top floor of each company-owned headquarters building, usually at a prime city-center location, as there was always a store on the ground floor After a few days of small talk and a few fine meals, he would ask for the cash receipts for the year, by which he would judge the relative success of management and decide on any earned bonuses to be paid. He would then depart with the cash for the next country, eventually to return to New York with trunks full of cash. At the time of the Revolution in Russia, messengers were carrying out suitcases full of cash each week.

When he decided to move the corporate headquarters to Rockefeller Center, Kircher split the accounting and other financial control–related departments from the treasurer's office and placed them under Alan Drew, recently hired and promoted to the newly created position of vice president and controller. The Controller's Office was rounded out with a Budget Department, Internal Audit, Manufacturing Cost Analysis, and Data Processing. More importantly, Kircher created a new Development Office, reporting directly to him, with the theoretical responsibility of providing direction and coordination of the (strategic) planning and diversification (acquisition) programs. He proudly announced that with those organizational changes, "the average age of the Vice Presidents of the Company...is now (only) fifty-two years." Unfortunately, Kircher missed an opportunity to go outside of the company to bring in a creative new talent to head the Development Office. Instead, he turned to Charles Bruder, a senior vice president with a long history in the sewing machine business. While Kircher may have believed that he now had a coherent diversification strategy, it didn't really exist outside his own mind. Bruder had neither the inclination nor the resources to develop a set of objectives to guide the strategy, but the absence of such objectives didn't stop him. He was in charge of acquisitions, so he set out to acquire, with the only criteria being to increase the earnings per share. It was "off to the races."

- In September 1962, the Company acquired for treasury shares Panoramic Electronics, Inc., a designer and manufacturer of spectrum analyzers and microwave instrumentation equipment. This was the Company's first move into an electronics business.

- In October 1962, the Company acquired for cash Air-Marine Motors, Inc., a manufacturer of small precision motors, fans, and blowers for communications and computing equipment.

- On January 1, 1963, the Company acquired for cash Sensitive Research Equipment Corp., a designer and manufacturer of high-accuracy electrical measuring instruments.

- In September 1963, the Company acquired Empire Devices, Inc., a designer and manufacturer of electronic test and measuring equipment and microwave devices. Sensitive Research, Panoramic, and Empire Devices were transferred to the old industrial sewing machine factory in Bridgeport, Connecticut, to form the new Singer Metrics Division. One former executive characterized this move as "new wine in old wineskins."

Up to this point, Singer's acquisitions had been modest and more or less related to the company's consumer and retailing business. The apparent ease with which these companies had been acquired convinced Kircher that the company was ready for the next step. In his 1961 letter to the shareholders, his first as the sole signatory, he stated that "the success of the diversification program to date has led us to broaden our horizons and consideration is now being given to interesting fields further removed from our traditional business." Singer's forays into electronics and instrumentation were relatively modest. This was a merger of a series of small companies into a large host. However, the new Singer Company was about to make a quantum leap.

Don Kircher was not operating in a strategic vacuum. He had a vision of corporate organization and management that went beyond what he viewed as the simple risk/reward synergistic model of the conglomerates. He had hired a talented group of planners and assistants who helped him verbalize his vision for Singer at the turn of the twentieth century. At the time, Columbia University, Kircher's alma mater, was considering a series of lectures about the future of large corporations in the United States, with the expectation that they would eventually be published collectively as a book. One of Kircher's new young advisors developed for him the rationale (and the text) for an initial discourse on the evolution of the corporation in America. In 1964, that vision was the subject of a presentation at the Columbia University School of Business and a follow-up article for the *Harvard Business Review* entitled "Now the Transnational Enterprise" (Kircher, 1964). Another member of the development staff prepared the second of this intended series of articles and lectures, but Kircher lost interest after the initial public acclaim and he never followed up on it. He was possessed of a very strong intellect and he welcomed a duel of ideas, but he seemed to have little interest in the culture and environment of the enterprise and no obvious appreciation of the value of experience. The preponderance of the company's institutional experience resided in the field general managers in each country. Kircher showed no direct interest in field operations and was by choice completely isolated from them. The general managers had a vaguely good impression of Kircher, derived from the few times they might have visited New York. But their contact with him in the field was virtually nonexistent. During the eighteen years from 1964 to 1982, Kircher made but a single visit to the European organization, and that was limited to France, the largest of the sewing sales organizations outside of the United States, in celebration of the 125th anniversary of Singer's presence in that country. Even that visit was largely a social event, with a visit to the company's retail showcase, a gala banquet, and a cocktail party at the Hotel George V.

In the *Harvard Business Review* article, Kircher argued for the creation of a "Transnational Enterprise" as a natural evolution of corporate organization in response to the need for companies to diversify in order to survive. He described the drive to diversify as a result of:

- The greatly shortened life cycle of products due to accelerated technology as well as the change in their economic life.

- The increased need for companies to plan the future, leading to broader definitions of its objectives, which stimulates diversification.

- The efficient use of cash flow from stable businesses whose cash-generating ability exceeds that required to support its existing operations (i.e., Singer).

- A resurgence of entrepreneurial spirit as management is drawn to new fields and products, challenged by the opportunity for diversification.

He noted that the demand for diversification opportunities exceeded the supply and were likely to become even more restricted as such opportunities either became fewer in number or, as the result of competitive bids, were pushed beyond their economic rationale. He saw, of necessity, increased demand abroad and the consequent investment opportunities for products that had not yet reached maturity in this country. He believed that export programs were an inefficient way to satisfy such demand and the time required to expand an enterprise overseas from within was unacceptably long. Singer had taken over a century to develop its worldwide manufacturing and sales organization.

That left acquisitions and mergers as the most likely route that overseas diversification had to follow. Attempts to acquire companies abroad by outright purchase were likely to find opposition both at home and abroad. There was a strong current of economic nationalism in most foreign countries, where the notion of a "takeover" is viewed with distaste. In the United States, the continuing balance of payments deficit made it politically difficult to justify sending dollars abroad for expansion. That left mergers through exchange of shares as the most attractive solution, creating what Kircher called the Transnational Enterprise. "In idealized form these enterprises would be:

- Owned by stockholders in many countries.

- Manned and managed by persons of many nationalities.

- Operated in all of the world politically open to them.

- Run by managers trained and experienced in looking at the world as an economic unit.

- Diversified in products and fields of interest without sacrifice of those unifying principles which tie them together as unique organizations."

Aside from the questions of international ownership and diversification, Kircher was describing the Singer Sewing Machine organization. Much of what he described with respect to overseas stockholders is now routine. In 2014, non-U.S. companies raised $37 billion through the issuance of American Depositary receipts (ADRs), the most notable of which was the record-setting $25 billion raised by Alibaba. Who in 1964 would have predicted that in fifty years a Chinese company would be able to raise any equity capital in the United States, much less such a staggering amount?

Singer was for Kircher the prototype for transnational status. The company enjoyed market dominance in a mature market. It enjoyed cash flow more than sufficient to support the sewing machine business. What he believed it needed was a diversification opportunity, a business objective that was countercyclical to consumer products in an industry at the beginning of its growth cycle with a significant market position. The new business sector selected was that of office equipment, and the target company was Friden, Inc., a business equipment company with annual sales of approximately $115 million. In October 1963, shareholders of both companies approved the merger of Friden, Inc., with The Singer Company. What Kircher had failed to recognize at the time, however, was that Friden and Singer were in much the same business at approximately the same point of their product's life cycle. This was not a diversification into technology, for both Singer and Friden were manufacturers of very complicated high-cost electro-mechanical devices destined to be overtaken by competitive simplified electronic devices that would both increase their capabilities and reduce their manufacturing costs. Coincidentally, the first competitive electronic calculators were also introduced in 1963. The Singer/Friden merger would turn out to be a colossal strategic error.

The New Business Model

The search for a diversification model flowed from the following analysis of the company's primary business done by Singer's new Development Office:

- The sewing machine market was mature, and the company already had the dominant market share.

- The nature of the product required a substantial customer education effort.

- The product was no longer used as a means of fabricating functional household items, such as clothing and linens.

- The traditional method of door-to-door selling to a female customer had become increasingly inefficient, as she was entering the workforce and less and less likely to be home.

- Creative sewing as a hobby tended to appeal only to those women who did not have to generate part of the family income.

- The opportunities for technological innovation to increase market share were limited, as the new Singer electronic machines added cost and complexity, which in turn required more customer education.

- The competition from Japan was already proven at the low-tech bottom of the line, in the form of increasingly effective low-cost machines, putting pressure on the middle of the line with its higher margins.

- The prevalence of good-quality, low-cost, ready-to-wear garments relieved any pressure a woman might feel to stay home and clothe the family.

This analysis applied primarily to the U.S. market. The company enjoyed a substantial market position in many, if not most, of the countries outside of the United States, but as sure as day followed night, retailing trends in the United States found their way overseas with an increasingly shorter delay. This is not to say that the sewing machine business was dead. It still generated substantial cash flow, and cash flow that it didn't need for the sewing business but was available for diversification. The cash generated by the mature, high market share/low market growth products (sewing) should be channeled into new markets with high growth rates, especially into companies that had leading positions, preferably one of the three leaders. Ideally, these markets would be complementary to sewing and not susceptible to the same variations in the business cycle as consumer retailing.

One market that Singer overlooked, even though it had at one time enjoyed substantial market share, was that of industrial sewing. If the ready-to-wear market was suppressing demand for household sewing machines, it should have had the opposite effect on industrial machines. The demand for clothing was growing faster than the general population, and offshore manufacturing, where Singer had strong brand recognition, was booming. However, Singer was historically fixated on the household machines and very little, if any, research effort went into improving industrial machines or adapting the existing machines to a changing market. The growth in ready-to-wear production was largely off-shore, as the low labor cost countries of the Far East were virtually monopolizing clothing exports to the Western economies. It was a missed opportunity for Singer.

The Friden Merger—The First Big Step

The 1963 acquisition of Friden was Singer's first major diversification step. While the Company had made a number of small acquisitions since Kircher had begun his term as president in 1958, they did not represent significant steps toward an identified diversification objective. HRB had its own research programs, well under way prior to joining Singer, and very little of that effort was in support of Singer's existing sewing research laboratory in Denville, New Jersey. The new subsidiaries of Fidelity, Cobble, and Supreme were subjected to the same consumer retail business cycle as Singer's primary product line. Panoramic, Air-Marine, and Sensitive Research were baby steps into small technology markets.

Friden was something else altogether. With annual revenues of $115 mil-
lion, it represented 15 percent of Singer's total revenue. Friden's net income for
1963 had grown 19 percent on sales growth of 9 percent. Its foreign operations
were growing faster than its domestic and accounted for 27 percent of total sales.
More interesting was the fact that 38 percent of Friden's business was in the new
growth industry of data processing. During that year, the company had introduced the fastest small business computer on the market. For the time being,
computers were a small part of the data processing product line, which was concentrated in the manufacture and distribution of peripheral equipment used in
the preparation of data for larger computer systems. The remainder of this product line focused on small inexpensive systems for businesses that didn't require
larger and more complex units.

The bulk of Friden's sales still came from the traditional electro-mechanical
products for which it was best known, such as calculators, adding machines,
postage machines, letter openers and sealers, a check endorsing machine, postal
scales, a machine for signing, imprinting, cancelling, numbering, endorsing, and
dating checks, and other such business processing equipment. Much of Friden's
research, however, was shifting to electronic data processing equipment, particularly low-cost electronic data processing units, random access storage devices, and
advanced data and transmission systems, especially for large and widely dispersed
retail operations. At the same time, the evolution of data processing was moving
toward ever larger centralized main frames consolidating all of a company's data
at a single site, and Singer followed the trend. Although Friden was working on
the first distributive processing systems designed to move data capture, and eventual use, closer to the customer encounter, Singer as a company was moving in the
opposite direction, leasing under-sea cable capacity to transmit all of its transaction data from the western hemisphere to an immense data center in Wayne, New
Jersey.

The acquisition strategy was moving ahead full-force, and it didn't stop with
the Friden merger. Eight other technology acquisitions were either completed or
negotiated during the year. They were:

- Sensitive Research Instrument Corporation: Designed and produced
  high-accuracy electrical measuring instruments

- Empire Devices, Inc.: Designed and manufactured electrical and electronic test and measuring equipment and microwave devices

- Alemannia Maschinenfabrik GmbH: Manufactured and distributed
  flatbed knitting machines used by the textile and apparel industries

- Physical Sciences Corporation: Manufactured insulating materials for extreme environments

- Gertsch Products, Inc.: Designed and manufactured test instruments

- KLH Research and Development Corporation (KLH): Manufactured and distributed high-fidelity components, FM radios, and stereo phonographs

- Empire Electric Corp. and Wirekraft, Inc.: Manufactured and distributed electric heating devices and components

With these acquisitions, Kircher seemed to have settled on three primary target business groups:

- Data processing and business equipment

- Electronic and electric test equipment

- Products complementary to Singer's primary sewing business or products that might be distributed through Singer's worldwide retail network

In one fell swoop of twenty-four months, Singer had acquired twelve new companies. While not yet of the magnitude of Gulf and Western or ITT, Singer was now part of the conglomerate club, and Don Kircher was being noticed.

> He keeps his own horses and rides to the hounds when he has time, but Donald P. Kircher, 48, president of Singer Co., has recently been fully occupied guiding his company over the hurdles of diversification and expansion. Last week he took Singer a big jump closer to the billion-dollar club with the acquisition of Friden, Inc., a maker of office automation equipment that should fit nicely with the 112-year-old sewing- machine maker and bring annual sales to more than $750 million. Kircher has a firm rule that, within the U.S., his acquisitions must be in the high-growth area of fairly advanced technological fields. (*Time*, 1963)

The Singer Company of 1963 was dramatically different from that of 1960. With the acquisitions, sales were 50.3 percent greater, and net income had more than doubled. Based on the sales and net reported each year, the stockholders saw what appeared to be a great strategic success. Although earnings per share had dropped from $4.44 to $3.75, a decline of 15.5 percent, the market price of the company's common stock had increased by almost 26 percent, from $62 in 1960 to $78 in 1963. The early acquisitions had been paid for with cash, using the company's ample reserves and borrowing capacity.

However, the Friden acquisition had been made using the comglomerators' favorite currency, the company's own stock. Although the issuance of new stock diluted the value for the existing Singer shareholders, the reaction of the market to Singer's move into business equipment was to value the stock of this "new" company at more than twenty times earnings, giving it a market capitalization of $876 million, an increase of 214 percent. In the space of four years, The Singer Company had gone from being valued at 60 percent of its net assets to a valuation of almost 160 percent. It was no longer the tempting bargain it had been when Kircher was appointed president.

The Game Changer—General Precision

For the first time in over a century, a significant portion of Singer's revenues was coming from products other than sewing, and the non-sewing products were growing faster. Sewing machines were still the primary product line, but they were rapidly declining as a fraction of total revenues. Other consumer products were the next most important product group, and Kircher had brought in a new head of Consumer Products who was given the responsibility for all consumer products, both sewing and non- sewing. The new vice president made a concerted effort to broaden the consumer line, much as the European organization had done for years. All told, he was responsible for almost 75 percent of Singer's revenues.

Revenues from:	Percent
Sewing products	57.3 %
Other consumer products	17.3 %
Total consumer products	**74.6%**
Business machine products	13.0 %
Other industrial products	12.4 %
Total revenues	100.0 %

It was time to again redefine the major business groups in order to guide the acquisition program. The objectives seemed to be a moving target, changing after the fact with each successive acquisition. Singer had almost always been a one-product company. Less well known was the fact that it was also largely a foreign company, drawing more than half its revenues from its overseas sales organizations. In 1964, foreign sales represented 54 percent of consolidated sales and grew by 14.6 percent over 1963, compared to domestic sales growth of 12 percent. This had been diversification of a different sort, geographical rather than by product line, and historically it had worked in Singer's favor. The world was not yet flat, the economy not yet global. The Company operated, if allowed, in virtually every country in the world. Individual markets were at different stages in the development of retailing and had different rates of growth as well as risk. Countries in recession could be offset by countries that were prospering. Countries with labor strife balanced those with labor peace. The general manager of the French organization of Singer once said, albeit too simplistically, that to succeed in retailing in France, one had only to follow what was succeeding in the United States and plan for its arrival in Paris five years later. The same could perhaps have been said for the former European colonies with regard to Europe, but with a different time delay, as well as the undeveloped countries of Africa, the Middle East and the Far East. But that was no longer the case. Once women began to leave home in the Western countries to join the workforce, the market for sewing products began to slow to a growth rate that, at best, might equal that of the general population. New growth would have to be found elsewhere, and for Singer the first two markets it identified were business equipment and the non-specific "technology." Consequently, in 1964 Kircher reorganized the management structure to create three new divisions to join the traditional Consumer Products Divisions and the newly acquired Friden. They included:

1. Industrial Products Division (IPD): With worldwide responsibility for product development, manufacture, U.S. marketing, and international distribution of industrial sewing machines and related equipment

2. Technical Products Division (TPD): Responsible for the Company's activity in advanced technology and scientific fields. Presumably, this would be a basket that could catch future technology acquisitions.

3. A separate Metrics Division: Created at the Bridgeport factory to receive technology acquisitions focused on military work

4. Special Products Division (SPD): Responsible for the Company's activities in the textile machinery and certain consumer electric products fields. This appears to be an "all other" basket for acquisitions that didn't yet fit in a clearly defined business group

While these divisional definitions were sufficiently general that any newly acquired business could find a home somewhere, they at least began to focus the acquisition search effort on a somewhat smaller universe. In this context, the company made five small acquisitions during 1964. Two of the companies made products for distribution through the traditional retail store network in the United States and Europe. One manufactured test instruments with military applications and the others manufactured heating and air-conditioning devices, a new product group that was tucked into Friden for no apparent reason.

The result of the changes was a hybrid organization, some with full profit responsibility and some still functional. Sewing products continued its historical functional responsibilities, with sales organizations organized by regions geographically and worldwide manufacturing centralized in the New York headquarters. Friden and the companies acquired for the Technical and Special Products Divisions remained relatively independent profit centers, with virtually no interaction other than their respective headquarters oversight staffs. Here lay the beginnings of what would later become a significant issue for the company. The small companies that Singer was acquiring were often fiercely entrepreneurial, operated by their founders or a small number of executives functioning as an independent management team. The problem in acquiring such companies was how to retain their inherent entrepreneurial spirit and management styles while maintaining the necessary operational and fiduciary control in the parent organization. Over time, aggressive intervention by headquarters staff would become a problem.

The financial results seemed to confirm the wisdom of the Singer strategy. Sales for 1964 were up 13.4 percent, net income was up 27.2 percent (actually it was down slightly when the sale of some timberland properties in Canada and South Carolina were excluded—creative accounting). The dividend was increased from $1.70 per share to $2.00, and through the magic of an improvement in the P/E ratio, the price of the common stock had appreciated by over 16 percent.

No significant acquisitions were made for a time as the company seemed preoccupied with digesting the Friden merger. The business equipment industry was completely new to most of the Singer executives, as were virtually all of the acquisitions thus far, and the president had already identified the difficulties associated with Singer's new acquisition strategy:

> A number of factors limited the growth in earnings in 1964. The rapid expansion in sales of products other than sewing equipment through our existing distribution system and marketing outlets entailed heavy expense…. In addition, there were non-recurring expenses associated with recent acquisitions. In the case of Friden, there were large start-up costs in connection with the new and highly successful electronic calculator and other new products introduced during the year. (Singer Company, 1951–1985)

Radical change had not been a feature of the Singer sewing machine environment for over a century, and in the company's eagerness to introduce new products, particularly those with a substantially different profile than sewing machines, radical change was proving to be difficult to understand and manage. Friden alone introduced six new products in 1964. Friden sales had increased by 18 percent in that year, but without a corresponding increase in earnings.

The problems were not confined to the new acquisitions, however. The European economies were in difficulty, with a corresponding weakening of demand for sewing machines. The most serious problems, however, were at Singer's immense factory in Clydebank, Scotland, which supplied the lower end of the sewing machine line to all of the countries in Europe as well as the United States. The factory had once employed over thirty thousand employees in a fully integrated production effort from a railroad to haul raw materials to the foundry, to fabrication and assembly, to final inspection, and back to the railroad for shipping.

The city of Clydebank was historically a two-company town, with Singer and John Brown Shipping, the maker of the queens, both Mary and Elizabeth, supplying virtually all of the available jobs.

Singer factory ay Clydebank, Scotland[59]

Completely unionized and with a history of frequent, sometimes bitter, union strife, the Singer factory was in the uniquely critical position that a labor strike there would effectively shut down the production of simple low-end machines for much of the western hemisphere. And since much of the profit in the sewing machine business was captured by selling up to the more expensive machines, the quality, cost, and availability of Clydebank machines could jeopardize an already challenging sales model.

The highlight of 1966 was the fact that The Singer Company joined the "Billion-Dollar Club." Consolidated sales of $1.049 billion represented a 7.1 percent increase over the prior year. Net income increased by only 6.3 percent, apparently reflecting the continuing problems with the integration of new acquisitions and labor productivity and cost issues at the sewing machine factory in Clydebank, Scotland. While the explanation of these issues had been included in the 1965 president's letter, this year they were buried in the text for each division. It began to appear that no one had studied what would be required from Singer in order to be successful in each newly acquired business. Friden continued to expand its product line, with the addition of three new data processing products and four new adding machine and calculator products. Earnings per share increased by 10.2 percent as a result of a stock buyback program, ostensibly for use in the Company's stock option and purchase plans.

The Company returned to its acquisition program and made five acquisitions during the year, only one of which was significant, the purchase for cash of a 51 percent interest in Friedrich Schwab and Company of Hanau, Germany. The four other acquisitions continued the pattern of adding small entrepreneurial enterprises to the existing non-sewing divisions. The addition of Schwab was a curious choice. It was the second largest general merchandise catalog sales organization in Germany. Simultaneous with the acquisition, the Company announced its intent to start a similar general merchandise catalog operation in France, to be managed by the German company. The decision to acquire Schwab was a prime example of Kircher's ignorance of how a new business might fit into a completely different culture. Again and again he seemed blindsided by his insistence on the power of intellect over experience. He believed that a manager with sufficient intellect could manage anything.

The French were not very excited to discover without warning that they were to have a new French company and business reporting to another new company in Germany. Aside from the history of the two wars, the cultural and attitudinal differences between the two countries seemed to preclude identical sales, marketing, and management strategies. Beyond those differences was the question of how this new business venture would relate to the existing sewing machine organizations. One might approach the question from two points of view. First, the catalogs could represent an additional sales opportunity for sewing machines. Second, the catalogs represented an opportunity for incremental sales of other products in the sewing stores or by the sales canvassers. Both of these strategies were difficult to understand. It had been proven for over a century that the best way to sell a sewing machine, particularly a high-end sewing machine, was by demonstrating it one-on-one, followed by frequent after-sales contact with the customer to ensure that she knew how to use the machine and was actually using it. A catalog seemed to preclude such interaction. The possibility of incremental sales for the stores and canvassers was equally suspect. A large fraction of the store sales personnel's compensation was linked to sewing machines, particularly the expensive ones. In the case of the canvassers, 100 percent of their compensation was linked to sewing machines sales. Furthermore, the commission rates were set such that a salesperson had a very limited time available between the initial contact and the successful conclusion of a sale. He had to decide within a few minutes whether the probability of a sale was high enough to warrant a continuing effort or whether he would be better off moving on to the next prospect. In France, a door-to-door salesman had approximately fifteen minutes after ringing the doorbell to decide whether the probability of making a sale was high enough for him to continue pushing for a (potentially unsuccessful) demonstration or whether he would be better off moving to the next house. In primarily rural areas (i.e., most of France), travel time ate into the fifteen minutes. Furthermore, the price of a sewing machine could range from $100 to $500. It was difficult to see how a canvasser could take sufficient orders from a general merchandise catalog to equal the commission on a sewing machine. Canvassers produced the lion's share of the company's sales in France, and their productivity was highly dependent on the carefully constructed commission scale. It was a self-selecting system since the inability to make the minimum expected sales resulted in an income one could hardly live on.

Possibly the most important change made in 1966 was the creation of a group management structure. The company was moving to a profit-centered organization, which should have tended to flatten the organization chart as there would be little need for extensive staff activity between the field sales organizations and the top. Instead, Kircher announced the creation of group management for certain similar operating divisions, with a group executive and staff responsible for the various sewing machine divisions: Curiously, the European marketing organization went unmentioned in the announcement. This was the subject of much discussion and speculation among the European line managers, who concluded that this was not an oversight, but was due to the play of power politics at headquarters that had not yet anointed a winner. The following year, Europe was folded into the then renamed North Atlantic Consumer Products Group.

International Group

- Latin America Division

- Far East Division

- Africa and Near East Division

North American Consumer Products Group

- U.S. Consumer Products Division

- Canadian Division

The redefinition of product group responsibilities and diversification strategy seemed to have now become virtually an annual affair, and it was increasingly difficult to see which was leading and which was following, organization or diversification.

What was unspoken was the fact that previously these divisions had been monitored by the division staff and the corporate staff, but now they would be monitored by a new group staff, with no change in corporate-level or division-level staff units. This kind of organization seemed ripe for interference and delay in decision-making. Charles Bruder was nominally head of corporate development. In his mind, that meant acquisitions and had little to do with strategic planning. However, the staff who had been assembled around Bruder did contain some serious and talented planners, who began developing a five-year plan for the company as a first exercise. Once completed, the planning staff worked with each of the operating divisions to develop individual strategic plans. The exercise was new for the divisions, and initially process took priority over product. But eventually the divisions were judged ready to plan by business, to recognize the precise business they were in, and to plan on the basis of differential growth rates for each product business and their own position within that market. It was a time-consuming but valuable educational experience. The task was how to link the intellectual enterprise with the actual business, and that would take even more time.

The year 1967 began much as the two previous years, with continued growth in sales of 8.4 percent, net income at roughly the same level as the previous year. The company made five more acquisitions, two of which were particularly interesting. The first was Western-Stickley, Inc., a manufacturer of household furniture. Almost from its first days in the mid-nineteenth century, Singer had made its own cabinetry for sewing machines. The process had been integrated to the point that the Company had its own woodlands, harvested its own trees, transported them to its own factories on its own dedicated railroad, milled the logs, and crafted the furniture. Vertical integration was the way things had always been done, and no one gave it a second thought. The household furniture business in the United States was highly fragmented, with literally hundreds of small manufacturers spread across the country, but it was especially concentrated around the old timberlands of the Carolinas and Georgia. One day, someone on the corporate staff was considering diversifications that would fit logically with Singer's existing product lines. Curious about the furniture industry, he gathered some summary data and discovered that, lo and behold, The Singer Company was the largest furniture manufacturer in the United States. The Company had in-house all of the experience and expertise necessary to be a factor in the furniture business. Theoretically, here was a cost-free acquisition, the Wood Products Division.

The second acquisition was suggested by Joseph Smith, a semi-retired investment banker who had joined the company as the new development officer because of his previous experience in mergers and acquisitions. He succeeded Charles Bruder, who was then moved to the division of "Corporate Relations." Joe was a talented critical thinker and financial strategist. He had no portfolio, but he went wherever Kircher needed advice about some aspect of operations. Joe had completed his career on Wall Street, not in industry, and he had no personal agenda, no ax to grind. Above all he was brutally honest, so much so that in short order his encounters with other executives who might be in need of a little "deflation" became the stuff of Singer folklore. He was the only member of the president's luncheon members who dared to absent himself from Kircher's dining room to visit with the ordinary folk of the executive dining room. Once, following an unpleasant encounter with one of the other senior executives in Kircher's circle, Smith visited the executive dining room and recounted the aftermath to the table. "B. said that he wanted to meet and 'smoke the peace pipe.' I told him that I didn't smoke." He would spend thirteen valuable years with Singer until his sudden death from a heart attack in 1980.

One of the assignments Joe had worked on for his previous employer was the due diligence and proposal to acquire the General Precision Equipment Corp. for one of the bank's clients, through which Joe had developed a thorough understanding of the nature and workings of General Precision's business. The deal at the bank never went through, but the knowledge Joe brought with him when he came to work for Singer would turn out to be a considerable asset, for the acquisition of GPE by Singer would turn out to be the most significant acquisition among the company's many new ventures, the acquisition of a major player in a high-growth industry not subject to the retail business cycle. Smith began with the purchase on the open market of 14.6 percent of the common stock of General Precision Equipment Corporation (GPE), with the potential for an eventual merger. This was a major departure from the three thus-far defined business groups. Apparently GPE didn't fit neatly into the existing definition of Singer's three businesses. It designed and manufactured highly advanced systems and equipment for government military and space programs, in addition to a wide variety of control and metering devices for industrial and consumer use. On reflection, however, was GPE really outside of the defined Singer businesses? Since the first acquisition of HRB-Singer in 1957, the Company had been acquiring and warehousing technology companies in its Bridgeport, Connecticut, factory. Companies such as Panoramic Electronics (spectrum analyzers, microwave instrumentation), Sensititve Research Corp. (high-accuracy electrical measuring instruments), Empire Devices, Inc. (electrical and electronic test and measuring equipment, microwave devices), Gertsch (test instruments), and EMC Instruments, Inc. (advanced radio frequency interference test instruments) had been acquired with the intention of moving Singer into more advanced technology, hopefully with the stability that government interest in those technologies might provide. All of these minor acquisitions could now make sense by being rolled into GPE. This could be a game-changer for Singer.

In 1968 it all came together. Ever since Milton Lightner's retirement from the board in 1961 and the first tentative technology acquisitions in 1962, Don Kircher had been searching for a significant opportunity in a high-growth technology business that would complete his vision for a properly diversified Singer. GPE fit the bill. Although its margins were relatively low compared to retailing, it enjoyed a substantial and steady government contract business not subject to the cyclicality of retailing. Kircher's 1968 letter to the shareholders has a triumphant air absent from his previous letters as president:

> The year 1968 was a particularly eventful one for The Singer Company. It marked the completion of another major advance in our evolution from an enterprise engaged primarily in the production and sale of a single product to one with major operations in five broad business areas and with important commitments and capabilities in advanced technologies.... We have endeavored to discipline our diversification activities, whether by merger, acquisition or by internal development, so as to produce and maintain a well-balanced cohesive enterprise, the segments of which would be operationally related and mutually reinforcing. In setting the course of our diversification program at its inception we recognized that one of its goals should be increasing involvement in advanced technical activities. This was achieved step-by-step with the acquisition of HRB, the later acquisition of Friden and finally the GPE merger...the fifteenth largest electronic company in American industry with sales of electronic products and services

which exceed the volume of the entire company at the time the present management became responsible for the Company's direction. (Singer Company, 1951–1985)

The impact of the GPE merger on the product line and the geographical configuration of the business was dramatic. Previously, there had been three product groups:

1967	% of total
Products for the Home	64%
Products for Industry	21
Products for Business	15
TOTAL	100%
Now there were five:	1968 % OF total
Consumer Products*	44%
Industrial Products	21
Office Equipment	13
Defense and Space Systems	11
Education and Training	11
TOTAL	100%

* Of which sewing products accounted for 70%

Before the merger, Singer would have been described as a sewing machine company with a small part of its business in other lines. After GPE it had become a technology company, with significant business in sewing products. Prior to the merger, Singer's sales had been roughly half domestic and half foreign. Post-merger, Singer's sales in the United States amounted to roughly 67 percent of the total, and domestic sales were growing faster than abroad. Government sales grew from 3 percent to 17 percent of the total. In theory, if the business model was soundly conceived and correctly executed, the years following the GPE merger should have been the time to sit back, make minor adjustments, and relax while it all played out. But, as the old saying goes, "Reality is what happens while you're making plans."

Founded as General Theaters Equipment Corp. in 1936, GPE had historically focused on theater supplies and equipment and specialized lighting, later moving into visual education with the acquisition of the Society for Visual Education and the iconic Graflex, Inc. Following the end of WWII, GPE went on its own acquisition program, expanding into the rapidly growing military and aerospace testing and controls businesses. At the time of its merger with Singer, GPE was organized into nine operating subsidiaries:

General Precision, Inc., organized into three groups:

> **Aerospace Group:** Made instruments, electronic equipment, Doppler radar navigation systems, semiconductors, and communications equipment

> **Librascope Group:** Made computers information processing and control systems and optical devices

> **Link Group:** Made simulation equipment for training and industrial control systems

Tele-Signal Corp., Made data communication equipment.

Graflex, Inc., Manufactured cameras, photographic audio-visual equipment, filmstrips, and slides, and the Society for Visual Education, Inc., which made audio-visual instructional materials for educational and industrial uses. Best known historically for the famous Graflex camera, preferred by journalists

National Theater Supply Co., Dealt in theater supplies and equipment

Character Recognition Corp., Developed optical and magnetic reading devices

General Precision Systems, Ltd. (UK), Made flight trainers and simulators and air traffic control systems and equipment

General Precision Controls, Inc., Manufactured controls for home laundry equipment: valves, switches, thermostats, and other controls for home heating commercial refrigeration and automobile air-conditioning equipment and precision electric switches and fractional H.P. motors

Strong Electric Corp., Manufactured specialized lighting equipment

American Meter Co., Manufactured industrial and residential gas meters, orifice meters, liquid transfer pumps instrumentation, and pressure regulators for the gas industry

The results for GPE in the years immediately prior to the merger had been mixed. From 1960 to 1963, sales had declined by approximately 10 percent to $218 million, and net income had declined by almost 50 percent to 2.7 million. By 1965, however, sales had recovered to $241 million and net income to $5.1 million. The big improvement for GPE occurred in March 1967, when it merged with Americon Corp., which itself had just acquired American Meter Company and Vapor Corp. Thus was the frequent cascade of corporate acquisitions during the conglomerate hunting era. Everyone seemed to be either a hunter or the hunted. The combined sales of the GPE/Americon merger for 1966 were $440 million, over twice what GPE alone had achieved in 1963. Net income was $20.5 million, four times greater. The Americon merger appeared to be a home run for GPE and hopefully would pay off just sixteen months later when GPE merged with Singer.

Singer now had the final piece of its puzzle. Don Kircher had wanted to move Singer into a contra-cyclical, high-tech, non-sewing business, and he had done it in spades. On the surface, this looked like a pretty big meal to digest. Singer management had virtually no experience in any of GPE's businesses and would have to rely on the management it had acquired in addition to the "magical growth" believed to be inherent in technology. From a management structure point of view, GPE looked much like a holding company that let its individual businesses operate with a minimum of central interference. Kircher's often expressed management philosophy of decentralized profit centers appeared to be consistent with the GPE structure. The key to both was the degree of independence the operating units were to be afforded by the Singer CEO.

The GPE merger was indeed a lot to digest, and Singer, apparently suffering from indigestion, made only two small acquisitions the following year. Both fit logically into the existing primary business groups.

- Johnson Carper was a household furniture manufacturer, not unlike the previously acquired Western Stickley. Products included complete lines of living room, dining room, bedroom, and upholstered furniture, and they were distributed through a network of over fifteen thousand independent retail outlets in the United States.

- Alfred Electronics manufactured microwave instrumentation products and fit logically in with Panoramic Electronics and Sensitive Research.

With GPE, Singer now structured itself along the line of the original diversification model. The slower-growing traditional businesses of consumer and industrial products, where Singer enjoyed important or dominant market positions around the world, would be the engines to generate the cash necessary to support the new diversified businesses and future acquisitions. However, delegation of full product responsibility for the sewing business was still difficult to achieve. Since the sewing machine factories were not unique suppliers for any individual market, but rather were each supply sources for much of the world, it was virtually impossible to identify anyone responsible for the entire sewing machine business except at a level at or near the office of the president. This meant that there continued to be three levels of staff: corporate, group, and division, all monitoring, coordinating, analyzing, questioning, directing, and interfering with the actual business of making and selling sewing machines. The diversified businesses of office equipment, defense and space systems, and education and training would be the engines of growth, both in sales and earnings, hopefully without the same overlay of staff. Time would tell.

The results for 1969 were counterintuitive and did not signal a great start. Sales for the traditional businesses grew by 11 percent, while the new, diversified businesses grew by only 3.7 percent. Earnings for the traditional products grew by 15 percent, while diversified products grew by only 2.4 percent. Finally, the net profit margin in the traditional businesses was 4.8 percent of sales, while the diversified businesses returned only 2.6 percent. In his letter to the shareholders, Kircher first mentioned the two new acquisitions and then quickly switched to the sewing machine business, where, "for the first time for any company, our sales of household sewing machines in the United States exceeded one million units." The "dying market" still had a strong pulse. Office equipment results were characterized "by an accelerated rate of major new product introductions…. This reflects the increasing rate of engineering and product development expenditures…and the associated market introduction costs…(which)…will further increase in the current year." Was he already setting shareholders up for an even worse year in 1970?

Friden had indeed announced that it had introduced fifteen new products in 1969 and would continue the pace, with the introduction of at least one new product a month in 1970. The most notable new product was the Modular Data Transaction System (MDTS), a point-of-sale combination of a free-standing cash register and a computer terminal. The MDTS was revolutionary for the times and put Friden ahead of the competition in retail data processing. Until then, sales data had been gathered on paper or some other medium at the site of the sale. The data was then physically sent to a large computer facility, where the information was transcribed into a format that could be read by the computer. The MDTS was the first practical commercial application of distributed processing. While innovative, this new product effort by Friden would require substantial financial resources, and, for the time being, the traditional products had to provide those resources.

At the same time, another problem was beginning to rear its ugly head and have an effect on resource allocation. While the Company had made its largest acquisitions, Friden and GPE, through mergers, it had paid cash for the majority of the remaining companies. Since the Friden acquisition in 1963, the Singer balance sheet had begun to show the effects of cash diversification. Borrowing had increased from $149 million in 1963 to $469 million in 1969. At the same time, the average interest rate had increased from 4.5 percent to 7.7 percent, with a corresponding increase in the Company's annual borrowing costs from only $9 million in 1963 to $44 million in 1969.

The overall impact of the diversification efforts on the Company's results and the financial markets was generally positive. The earnings growth of 13 percent was rewarded by an improved price/earnings ratio, presumably confirmation of the wisdom of the GPE acquisition, resulting in a 21 percent increase in the stock price.

($ in millions)	1968	1969	Change	%
Sales	$1,755	$1,902	$ 147	+ 8%
Earnings	$ 69	$ 78	$ 9	+13%
Stock price	$ 78	$ 94	$ 16	+21%

Between 1958, when Kircher was appointed president, and 1963, the year preceding the Friden acquisition, Singer had generated a comfortable $30 to 50 million in annual cash flow. Of this amount, $10 to 15 million went to the shareholders as dividends, $10 to 15 million was used to renew fixed assets, and the balance was available to fund modest growth. Borrowings were for the most part minimal prior to 1957, and the long-term line was used primarily to fund seasonal cash needs. With only modest cash flow from traditional operations, the Company was forced to borrow not only to purchase many of the acquisitions, but to fund their growth after joining the Company. At the same time interest rates increased by 70 percent, and the combination of the two created a double-whammy, a quadrupling of borrowing costs. The time for new equity was fast approaching.

Since the beginning of the diversification program, the internally generated cash flow had been insufficient to support any ambitious growth of the newly acquired companies, much less fund any operating losses. Beginning in 1965, sales of the office equipment group, a good proxy for Friden, more than doubled. Earnings for the group were less positive, declining from $10.6 million in 1967 to $7.8 million in 1969. This was a business that would not be self-financing for a considerable time.

Total company sales for 1970 finally reached the landmark $2 billion mark, increasing by 11.7 percent in the year, but earnings declined by 3.3 percent due to losses in the Information Systems Group (Friden). Once again, Traditional Products outperformed the Diversified Products, with sales of traditional products growing by 17.6 percent and sales of Diversified Products essentially flat.

Singer made two acquisitions in 1970, both of which were a little surprising given the difficulty the company was having absorbing previous acquisitions. They were both in completely new businesses, and one, Besco, was very capital intensive.

- Layne and Bowler provided the skills and equipment necessary for finding, delivering, and metering fresh water for municipalities, water utility firms, and industry.

- Besco Group was a West Coast home builder, principally engaged in the development, construction, and sale of homes, garden apartments, and shopping centers in Northern California.

In his 1970 letter to the shareholders, Kircher justified these two acquisitions with a puzzling explanation:

These acquisitions…represent the continuing process of aligning the Company's principal field of activity and investments with current and anticipated social and economic trends. The objective is not to increase the mere mass of the enterprise…but to allocate resources selectively in those areas where increases in the application of talents and the abilities of men and the power of material investment will be of increasing importance to the societies in which we operate…. It is probable that this process will be even more important in the future as large corporations are held increasingly accountable for the qualitative as well as the quantitative effects of their operations.

The introduction for the first time of a social responsibility objective for the company was for some a publicly admirable goal and Kircher was prescient. This was seven years before Dr. Leon Sullivan had codified corporate social responsibility (the "Sullivan Principles") with regard to investments in companies doing business in apartheid South Africa. At the time, Dr. Sullivan was a member of the board of General Motors, and by 1984, his statement of principles would coalesce into a mass student movement calling for the divestment of the stocks of companies doing business in South Africa. The protests have continued through the end of the twentieth century and into the twenty-first, with similar movements addressing companies and industries deemed to be "socially irresponsible," such as tobacco, oil exploration, and fossil fuel contamination of the atmosphere. It was almost as if Don Kircher had set his company on a new socioeconomic trajectory in addition to mere earnings per share in order to associate the Singer brand with higher objectives in the public consciousness. This turn toward social responsibility seemed completely atypical of the buttoned-up, imperious, strategy-focused executive who was leading Singer through the wilderness, although in his shareholders' letter he alludes to the fact that he considers this strategy to be more of a personal philosophy than a corporate objective. While admirable, one wonders how appropriate it was at the time for a company that had yet to prove its survivability in the Wild West atmosphere of conglomerate takeovers. At least it was cost-free public relations.

Kircher further announced, "Borrowing costs were very high in 1970…(and)…we issued and sold publicly $100 million principal amount of 5½ year debentures." Did the new financial resources embolden the Company to undertake a just-announced new venture in capital-intensive housing? To coin an old phrase, was the money burning a hole in Singer's pocket?

A major feature of the 1970 report was a seven-page section devoted to "The Retailing Revolution," an explanation of the linkage that Singer was pursuing between its traditional retailing business and technology. The Consumer Products vice president had left the company the prior year. He had been hired by Kircher in the executive recruitment binge of the early sixties, when Singer was still a single-product company. He aspired to eventually succeed Kircher, but now that the strategic emphasis had turned away from sewing to technology, that possibility seemed unlikely. His future was probably doomed when articles about him started to appear in the newspapers and print journals and it turned out that he had hired his own public relations firm to tout him as a successor. His replacement as head of the North Atlantic Consumer Products Group explained that the variety of choices available to the consumer was practically infinite (this, three decades before online shopping). In Singer's case, the company was emphasizing a wide range of fabrics, notions, patterns, and sewing accessories in addition to its traditional line of sewing machines. Of the 1,400 Singer retail outlets in the United States, 350 were to be closed over the next five years because they were too small for the expanding product line. They would be replaced by newly designed stores with up to ten thousand square feet of selling space, with half devoted to new sewing-related products, principally fabrics. A similar explosion in customer choice would happen throughout the retailing environment. The task of managing this change would be daunting and would require the assistance of new technology to succeed, and Singer had developed the perfect tool for that success, the

Friden Modular Data Transaction System (MDTS). The article went on to explain how technology such as the MDTS could solve problems at both ends of retailing, by relieving the salesperson from the seemingly endless burden of transaction data recording and submission of reports, to the rapid consolidation of sales and productivity data for more rapid response. Both kinds of improvement should help create a retailing experience that would be more responsive to the customer.

In an address to the National Retail Merchants Association, Kircher said:

All of you have the same basic need, as we do, to bring the speed and power of the computer to the place where the vital action occurs—that is, where the sales person meets the customer and, hopefully, makes a sale. It is the retailing information system specialists who…must now be the interpreters between the EDP equipment suppliers on the one side, and the merchandisers and consuming public on the other. This no small task, combining as it does a thorough technical knowledge of electronic data processing with equally thorough competence in understanding the subtleties of human nature.

Here was Don Kircher's vision of the natural role of Singer's Information Systems Group for the future.

We are now entering the age during which the users of information handling equipment will assert their dominance over the technicians and it will be a period during which users' requirements will determine the direction which the electronic data processing industry will take.

And Everything Was Going So Well

The year 1971 was not a happy one for either Friden or the Company. Total sales declined by 2.1 percent, although through the magic of restating, the annual report showed an increase of 2.0 percent. Within those totals, business machines showed an increase in sales of 2 percent, but a disturbing loss of $17.0 million. While the loss was not fully explained in the president's letter, the rumor within the Company was that the costs of producing Friden's star product, the MDTS point-of-sale terminal/computer, were out of control and aggravated by insufficient volume. The retail purchase price, of around $25,000, was so high that sales were effectively limited to large network chain retailers. Friden delivered three thousand of the new MDTS systems to outside customers during the year, the largest number being a major order from Sears, Roebuck, & Co. The internal gossip was that the Company needed a major national customer to legitimize the

MDTS and had contracted to sell the machines to Sears below cost. The combined MDTS System ten point-of-sale and small computer system was the showpiece product in the annual report. However, only five thousand total machines were installed during the year, many of them in Singer stores.

In an additional effort to further increase MDTS volume, the Company took a sharp turn from outright sales to leasing the product, which could explain the decline in Information Systems revenue. Apparently the leasing volume was insufficient to warrant comment in the 1971 audit report, but it would surface in 1972. When leasing quasi-capital products, there were a number changes that occurred to both cash flow and the accounting for the transactions. First, with leasing, the company paid to build something today, shipped it tomorrow, and got paid for it later. The cash out for the product occurred before shipment, while the cash in for the sale was spread over time. In 1972, the auditors noted that the total amount of products on lease would amount to about 2 percent of sales. That may not sound like much, but for Singer, it could be an additional $44 million to somehow finance. Second, in the financial statements the Company could only record the sale as the payments were made over the life of the lease. If the lease was for five years, only one-fifth of the sale could be recognized each year. This meant that in the year when they switched from outright sales to leases, they would have a substantial drop in sales recorded for the year, even though they might have shipped the same number of units.

Fortunately, the traditional products of household and industrial sewing held their own and continued to grow, with combined sales for 1971 of $1.484 billion, including for the second time the sale of over one million sewing machines in the United States. Earnings from these products reached a record high of $74.9 million and exceeded the consolidated earnings of the entire Company. Notwithstanding the now conventional wisdom that the sewing machine market was dying in the United States, Sewing Products continued to grow, as did the other Consumer Products offered in the stores to build traffic. Between 1967 and 1971, sewing products grew from $509 million to $652 million, an increase of 28 percent. Sales of other consumer products grew from $223 million to $407 million, an increase of 83 percent. Profitability remained steady for both Sewing Products and Other Consumer Products, which appeared to be doing their job of holding up the new diversified products.

The most worrisome feature of the sewing business in the United States was that the total market for machines, while not yet declining, was not increasing, and Singer was losing market share to foreign competition, particularly at the low end of the line. While Sears Roebuck was the Company's friend with its purchase of MDTSes from Friden, it was the Company's enemy when selling inexpensive Japanese-made sewing machines from Brother Co., its Japanese supplier.

Finally, the hoped-for high growth market of the aerospace industry had yet to spread its wings for Singer. Sales of $246 million were down 2.2 percent in 1971 and were projected to remain flat for 1972. Earnings from the Defense and Space Systems Group had remained modest since the merger, ranging from 1.4 percent to 2.6 percent of sales.

On the morning of July 16, 1972, as Don Kircher was probably settling in at home to enjoy the typical New Yorker's ritual of coffee and the *Sunday Times*, he would have opened it to the following headline:

Sewing-Machine Pioneer in Trouble at Home—

Singer Unit's Sales Off 10% in 1972?

This was not the sort thing that a CEO likes to read over breakfast. The article seemed to be the product of inside information, possibly from one or more disgruntled former executives, as executive turnover was becoming disturbingly high. It dealt primarily with the U.S. Consumer Products Division (USCPD), notably with sewing machine unit sales, using data that wasn't ordinarily made public. While the author of the article provided a generally correct assessment of the U.S. sewing machine market and noted that the past problems of Friden seemed well on the way to being corrected, he referred particularly to the high executive turnover in the USCPD, which could have been gleaned from announcements of appointments and a close reading of the annual report. In any case, little of the crisis predicted in the article came to pass during the balance of the year.

A major concern was the absence of growth in the diversified products of Aerospace Systems and Education and Training Systems, which were both operating at the same level of sales as they had since 1969. Earnings for the Aerospace Group had almost doubled since 1969, but they were still quite modest in absolute terms. Earnings for the Education and Training Group had declined by 13 percent since 1969.

Finally, with exquisitely bad luck, the United States entered what was to be a significant recession, with interest rates rising to over 10 percent (1973–1975). Despite the change in the environment, Singer decided to take an even larger move into the housing market with the acquisitions by merger of:

- Mitchell Companies: A parent of twelve real estate development companies that constructed and sold single-family residential units, apartment units, and shopping centers in Alabama, Louisiana, Florida, and Georgia

- Estes Corporation: A real estate development company that constructed and sold single-family residential units, townhouses, and apartments, and the construction sale and leasing of apartment buildings in and around Tucson, Arizona

- Melody Companies: The parent of sixteen real estate development companies that constructed and sold single-family residential units, townhouses, and apartments in and around Boulder, Colorado

By the end of 1972, Singer had outstanding borrowings of approximately $448 million, with an annual interest expense of $41 million. For the long-term holder of Singer stock who bought in 1961 on the promise of a new and dynamic, young president and his plans for the future…

> The success of our diversification program to date has led us to broaden our horizons and consideration is now being given to interesting fields further removed from our traditional business.

…the results reflected in the numbers must have been a deep disappointment. While the revenues had almost tripled, as had the net income, the growth had come at the expense of the shareholders, who had seen earnings per share decline by 11 percent over the same period.

Item	1961	1972	Change
Revenues (billions)	$0.6	$2.2	+281%
Net income (millions)	$ 24	$ 88	+266%
Earnings per share	$5.33	$4.82	- 11%

In his next report to the shareholders, Kircher cautiously described the results: "The Company had a reasonably successful year in 1973. Revenue, net income and earnings per share all established new records." By the time the annual report was issued, on March 14, 1974, the country was in the middle of the major recession caused by a quadrupling of oil prices by OPEC and the high cost of the Vietnam War. The combination of factors led to stagflation, with simultaneously rising unemployment and inflation. GDP would decline by 3.2 percent, and unemployment would rise to 9.0 percent. In January 1974, well before the time Kircher had written his letter to the shareholders, the Company would already have issued an additional $100 million of 8 percent long-term debt and was undoubtedly aware that serious operational problems had once again occurred at Friden.

The irony of the 1972 *New York Times* article—"Sewing-Machine Pioneer in Trouble?"—was that it focused almost exclusively on the sewing business, an indication that the inside source(s) for the article had almost certainly been former executives in the Consumer Products Group with virtually no knowledge of what was happening in the other parts of the Company. In that article, the Friden problems were mentioned almost as an aside, along with the steps taken by management to fix the problems, all information available from easily accessed public sources. In 1973, it was the traditional businesses of Consumer and Industrial Products that were keeping the Company afloat.

Kircher described the results as "reasonably successful," moving his discussion of the Consumer and Industrial Products Groups front and center. The Friden problems were virtually dismissed, as "entry costs" of the new products. For the Aerospace Group, he addressed the lack of improved profitability, despite a significant improvement in sales, as being due to expensive prototype work in central digital computers for aircraft and space applications, which "will not be normally productive financially until unit volume production status is achieved." This was report-speak for: "Until we can make and sell large numbers at a price that exceeds their cost." There is no mention of the Education and Training Group, which apparently had been carved into pieces and moved to other business groups.

Finally, he turned to the level of debt, explaining that interest costs were consuming 84 percent of the combined profit of the Consumer and Industrial Groups. Interestingly, the audited financial statements did not consolidate the borrowings of the recently acquired Singer Housing and wholly owned finance companies. When added to the consolidated borrowings of The Singer Company, the total indebtedness was $1.03 billion, and every one-point increase in interest rates would cost the Company approximately $10 million.

By now, Joseph E. Smith, the retired banker whom Kircher had hired in the mid-sixties as a personal advisor, had risen through a series of positions as executive vice president, senior VP and CFO, and vice chairman—Policy and Programs. He was one of a small circle of officers whom Kircher would trust in speaking to the press.

On October 17, 1974, the Company announced its first deficit in more than twenty years and a net loss of $31.5 million for the third quarter. The Company disclosed the operating problems at Friden, the closure of the Netherlands factory that manufactured the electromechanical billing and accounting product line, as well as the burden that the cost of the Company's accumulated debt was imposing on operations.

A week later, a corporate profile about Singer appeared in the *New York Times* entitled "Singer's High-Key Diversification Hits a Sour Note." In this article, the author repeated the essence of the Company's third-quarter earnings announcement of the prior week and then launched into a dissection of Kircher's management style, which he had gleaned from interviews with former officers, and the operating problems, which had been explained to the reporter by Joe Smith. Kircher was not giving any interviews.

The management complaints in the article were severe:

- "Kircher…had never analyzed the acquisitions closely enough and had paid too much for them. When they failed to meet his expectations just a few months after Singer bought them, he would change the men in charge, removing the talent that had made the companies prosper originally."

- "He…bought 'fad' businesses—such as housing, defense electronics and semiconductors just at the point where those industries were poised for declines."

- "He…dismissed subsidiary managers even when top corporate management or circumstances beyond their control caused much of the difficulty."

- "Within the executive office…many subordinates feared Mr. Kircher. Others said he could be charming and courteous but also aloof and unforgiving, demanding unobtainable goals and dismissing men when they fell short."

- "…the average tenure of corporate vice presidents is less than five years."

Joe Smith's comments were directed more at what he would consider collective management decisions and operational problems and expectations.

- "For a company our size, small acquisitions are a mistake."

- "In anticipating the direction of interest rates early this year, I just under-priced like an idiot."

- "Prospects should brighten soon…(with)…no further write-offs this year."

- "Housing, normally a big contributor to earnings, should recover in the -current quarter, in contrast with many economists' views."

- "Defense products, furniture and possibly industrial sewing and knitting equipment should do better."

Significantly, the author cited one analyst's opinion that "…the board has always been impotent and in Kircher's palm, but they have got to do something to save their own neck." The article suggested that Stephen C. Clark, a great-grandson of one of the Company's founders, who possessed 200,000 shares, might push for change.

The results for 1974 were devastating. The Company was battered by both its own internal problems and the economy. At Friden, Kircher had previously announced its decision to terminate the electromechanical billing and accounting product line, a Friden mainstay that had been overtaken by electronics. The manufacturing facility in Netherlands for this product line was closed. The marketing organization was reorganized, with consolidation of branch offices and support facilities. A special provision of $30 million was made for the estimated cost of terminating this and other unidentified non-profitable operations.

Borrowing costs went through the roof. Interest expense, exclusive of non-consolidated housing and finance subsidiaries, increased from $54.8 million to $85 million. The amount of interest expense for housing and finance subs was not segregated in the announcements, but its added expense would certainly have brought the total for the year to more than $100 million. Total borrowings for the Company plus non-consolidated subsidiaries increased from $1.03 billion in 1973 to $1.12 billion in 1974.

Given the economic environment, it was not surprising that Singer Housing was suffering. Although not reflected in the consolidated sales and income of the Company, its sales were down 22 percent, and net income was down 94 percent, from $9 million to $0.5 million. Included in the drop in earnings was a $3.4 million charge related to government action concerning land development. The decline in sales was primarily environmentally driven; however, the decline in earnings also reflected inflation in labor and material costs that could not be passed along in prices, the high cost of mortgage financing, and revaluations of land parcels due to the depressed real estate market. The results for Aerospace Systems were a mixed bag, with sales up 10.1 percent and earnings down 5.1 percent, due to new product development costs.

Virtually the only bright spot in the year was in the much maligned Consumer Products Group, as sewing products grew 4.2 percent and non-sewing consumer products grew 9.2 percent. These non-sewing products now included household furniture, power tools, floor-care products, household appliances, home knitting machines, and European mail order items.

Interestingly, just as Kircher was trying to cope with the failure of his diversification strategy to offset the anticipated decline in the sewing business, an article appeared in the May 19, 1974, *New York Times* entitled "A Resurgence in Home Sewing?" Written from the point of view of suppliers of sewing merchandise such as fabrics, needles, patterns, and notions, the author made the case that the actual finished garment end of the home-sewing cycle was in resurgence. The author cited studies showing that forty-four million women enjoyed both working with their hands and the economies of sewing clothes. Almost as many sewers came from the upper income brackets as from families earning under $10,000. To satisfactorily serve the fabrics customer required a huge inventory, one that the many small retailers who entered the market could not afford. Apparently the growth of the market in the sixties and seventies attracted a large number of inexperienced retailers who saturated the market. When sales slowed in the early seventies, all retailers, large and small, took a hit due to the excess inventory. Now the major chains who specialized in fabrics, such as J.C. Penney, Woolworth, Sears, and Kresge were all showing substantial year-to-year gains. Even the traditional high-volume specialty retailers, such as Mobile Fabrics Company of Hawthorne, New Jersey, expected sales of $15 million this year, up from $13 million the previous year, and a return to its typical 4 percent net profit margin. The improvement was confirmed by fabric suppliers, such as Scovill Manufacturing Company, whose sewing notions manager reported that, "We've reached a turnaround point."

With the exception of 1974, the Singer Consumer Products Group had enjoyed net profit margins of 4.2 to 5.0 percent of sales since it began reporting separate product line numbers in 1966. Perhaps that was the norm for this market, and it was frustrating and counterproductive to make more and more complicated and expensive machines in an attempt to boost margins when there was a huge market that could be satisfied with a simple inexpensive machine. Also, given the size of the fabric inventory at the major chains, Singer had to consider whether it wished or could afford to present the massive inventory required to compete. Perhaps it would have been better off to have considered some sort of cooperative arrangement with one of the existing high-volume chains.

Meanwhile, the 1975 annual meeting of the shareholders at the Essex House in Manhattan was acrimonious. Don Kircher was at home, recovering from surgery, and the meeting was conducted by Don Robbins, his old friend and now the senior vice president and chief financial officer. Robbins had been an ally of Kircher's since the beginning of his Singer career, elected to the board in 1954 when Kircher was only a vice president, and a member of the board that chose Kircher to be president. Robbins presided over a two-and-a-half-hour session of the shareholders, whom he had hoped to reassure by stating that, "With any kind of break in the environment, we expect to do better again in 1976." The *New York Times* reported that:

> Many of the questions and comments from the approximately 800 shareholders at the meeting attacked the leadership and policies of Mr. Kircher, who has been chief executive officer since 1958. Mr. Abraham Uchitel was applauded when he said, "Mr. Kircher in the past 10 years was not the proper commander in chief of this company." Mr. John Gilbert—a stockholder who attends many annual meetings and attended this one on his 61st birthday—added: "We don't like to have the president and chairman as one person. That is one of the first things that should be done." The other major complaint raised from the floor was that of the common stock dividend, which had been reduced from 65 cents a share in the first three quarters of 1974 to 50 cents in the last quarter and 10 cents in the first quarter of 1975.

The directors' meeting followed immediately after the annual meeting, and four months later, on September 13, 1975, the Company announced that:

> Donald P. Kircher, its 60-year-old president and chairman, has taken an indefinite leave of absence from the Company because of ill health.

> Ed Graf, another old Singer hand, was appointed chief operating officer in Kircher's absence. In retrospect, it seems likely that the Singer board had presented Kircher with an offer he couldn't refuse. As described in the *New York Times* article of October 24, 1974:

> Five of the 13 board members are company employees. A sixth, Arthur H. Fredston, is a lawyer from Winthrop, Stimson, Putnam & Roberts.

Winthrop, Stimson was the firm where Kircher had worked before joining Singer and which had remained as outside counsel to Singer. The remaining members were active and retired CEOs of major companies, hand-picked for the board by Kircher, who was both chairman and president. It is possible that the outside directors, who made significant fees as directors of other large companies and who wished to continue doing so, became unwilling to risk their future employment as directors by going down with the Singer ship, and they decided to develop a fiduciary conscience. Kircher was probably made to understand that his term was about to end, and that the best way for him to accommodate that ending was to take an indefinite leave because of his health, which he did. The era of Kircher's "Transnational Corporation" was over.

What Went Wrong? Some Impressions from Within

It is always easier to challenge a strategy after the fact, to diagnose with perfect hindsight. Here, we speculate a bit on what happened during the Kircher era. What, if anything, might Kircher have done to fulfill his dream of the "Transnational Corporation"? These thoughts are observations derived from below, comments, gossip, rumors, critiques, complaints, and—hopefully—constructive observations by members of Singer management limited to sewing machine operations, those charged with the actual making and selling of the sewing machines.

Wrong diversification choices.

Friden fit the diversification model in terms of both potential for market growth and its leading product position with the Modular Data Transmission System (MDTS). The market niche, however, was a subset of the much larger market of information management, populated by technological giants such as IBM. Friden had neither the depth of technical resources nor the skill to manufacture electronic devices. A simple example of the company's inability to appreciate the importance of understanding the local culture, even in the United States, occurred when a segment of Singer's electronic equipment business was transferred to Bridgeport, Connecticut, for manufacture at the old Singer industrial sewing machine factory. A later study of the worker profile for electronics showed that the ideal employee would be female, with long, small fingers and probably of Asian origin. The primary workforce in Bridgeport at the time consisted of descendants of the Italian fishermen who had emigrated there in the nineteenth century, with relatively short, strong, and thick fingers and who could never achieve the necessary quality for sophisticated electronics manufacturing.

Inappropriate management structure.

Kircher's instinctive and often stated management philosophy was delegation, not micromanagement. His ideal organization would have been flat, with relatively few levels of management or staff supervision between him and the customer. However, it didn't work out that way. With each reorganization, another layer of management was added. In the sewing business, local sales organizations were managed in a country headquarters, which reported to a division headquarters, with a full staff of functional specialists posing questions. The division reported to the group headquarters, with its virtually identical staff posing questions of the division, and the group reported to the corporate headquarters. The result was described internally as a "matrix organization," in which executives at the lower levels in the organization had multiple reporting responsibilities, depending on their responsibilities. The controller-treasurer at a major operational sales unit might have as many as twenty or thirty direct and indirect reports, depending on who was asking the question—accounting, treasury, tax, budgets, strategic planning, data processing or general management, at any one of three organizational levels.

That management structure was particularly deadly in the case of founders of acquired companies who had joined Singer but still wished to run their companies after being acquired. The level of staff interference became a serious deterrent to the entrepreneurial spirit that had led them to success in the first place. In a few instances, these executives became sufficiently discouraged to resign, and when Singer could find no one to manage the division with the same skill and breadth of knowledge, it sold the division back to the founder at a fraction of what Singer had paid for it.

Performance disincentives.

The accounting system attempted to serve two competing objectives: measuring performance and minimizing the worldwide tax liabilities. Singer used a full (allocated) cost system, whereby the general overhead expenses of the divisional, group, and corporate staffs were charged to each field operating unit, with the result being that the local general manager had a large uncontrollable cost to overcome before he could even show a profit. Singer also used a transfer price system that, on one hand, determined the local unit's cost of sales but, on the other hand, was manipulated to minimize the Company's tax exposure by moving profit from the higher tax countries to the lower tax countries via a Swiss subsidiary taxed at less than 10 percent. Transfer prices could also provide additional currency exchange risk protection by changing payment terms for merchandise from a buying entity to a selling entity by as much as 180 days, essentially moving merchandise debt risk from one country to another.

Finally, operating units were judged on their results in U.S. dollars, while they conducted business in their local currencies, with currency valuations (exchange rates) changing daily. The results expressed in dollars could differ substantially from those in local currency, depending on the rates used for reporting various classes of assets or liabilities, with the differences virtually impossible to explain to a general manager focused on selling. The result was that the local controller ended up discussing performance with his boss as measured in local currency before administrative overhead allocations, and with his counterparts in New York in dollars after assigning headquarters' overhead costs and foreign exchange gains & losses to the local company.

Misuse of human assets.

A criticism often made of the people in the sewing machine organization was that they were inflexible and too set in their ways, that the sewing machine was such a part of their culture that they were incapable of change. In response, one might consider two factors. First, at the time of this writing there is still enormous worldwide demand for sewing machines. They just aren't sold by Singer. Second, the field general managers had enormous experience and adaptability to change. Virtually all of them had decades of Singer experience and had guided their companies through multiple recessions and wars and were capable, if asked, of helping to guide the company through the land mines it had encountered.

Imposition of arbitrary, inappropriate, and time-consuming systems.

There was a permanent conflict between senior management wanting ever more timely financial reports and the ability of the operating units to provide the data with the existing technology. The underlying assumption for requesting massive detail seemed to be that local management was either lying, stealing, or incompetent.

When corporate management decided it needed the monthly reports a week earlier, the field units, unable to generate the information with their existing systems, merely closed a week earlier. Theoretically they would then have lost a week of sales, but field units were so accustomed to such demands that they maintained a reserve for the occasion. In the fifty-two-week accounting calendar, this was termed "week zero," an extra week of sales that had been generated in some previous leap year. Gradually the unit would steal a little bit of from reported sales each week until it had reconstituted the reserve for the next cutoff change.

When the Group vice president demanded that sales for the previous week be available automatically on his desktop terminal, the field response was again typical. Each sales territory in a country would telephone the week's sales to the country headquarters at the end of each week. They would be manually added up and telephoned to the division accounting staff, who would do the same thing with the group accounting staff, who would manually enter the data on the group vice president's terminal before he got to work. He would then appear on top of everything and had the evidence that he could display, whether it be to Kircher or to a reporter, in an interview. Everyone seemed content with the system.

There were probably as many explanations for the failure of the diversification program as there were executives. Each reason was undoubtedly strongly felt and its author partially correct. There are, however, some generalizations about motivation and corporate structure that we can glean from the Singer experience. We will explore these in Chapter 14, "What We Learned."

CHAPTER NINE

Chasing the Technology Dream[60]

Joseph Flavin[61]

In September 1975, George H. Haley, president of the executive search firm Haley Associates, telephoned Joe Flavin to ask if he would be interested in the CEO's job at Singer. Flavin was a 1953 graduate of the University of Massachusetts with a Master of Science degree from the Columbia University Graduate School of Business. He had joined IBM, where he spent fourteen years, rising to the position of controller at IBM World Trade Corporation in Paris. In 1967 he joined Xerox Corporation as vice president and controller, and in 1969 he was named vice president of finance and a director. A year later he was promoted to executive vice president, and in 1972 he was named president of Xerox's international operations.

If Singer's problems were technology-based, Flavin looked to be an ideal candidate for the CEO's job. Although he had no experience in retailing, his brief time in France would have given him an understanding of how to operate in foreign cultures, where most of the sewing business took place. His management style was quite different from that of Kircher. Although Kircher could be a rough taskmaster, he was very smooth around the edges, interested in art and the cultural advantages of being a New Yorker. If a person was not in his direct line of fire, he could be invariably courteous and polite. He enjoyed socializing in refined surroundings. Joe was the cheery optimist when things were going his way, referred to by some of the executive secretaries as "Mr. Jolly-Vibes," acting as if everyone should be happy and ready to go at his bidding. When things weren't going the way he wanted, however, he could be single-minded and obstinate, with his own clear idea of what was necessary to remedy the situation…and God help you if you got in his way. In either mode, many of his colleagues had the feeling that this apparent team spirit was largely an act, convinced that he was always looking down on those who reported to him, that he always thought he knew better. This management style didn't earn him many supporters among the long-serving line managers overseas, especially since he knew nothing about the retail sewing business. He was described by George Haley as a "two-fisted operating guy and the company desperately needs leadership." In the notice of his appointment, Flavin himself said that "he expected it would take *the next few months to study all the problems* (emphasis added) and then begin to move." It had taken seventeen years to create the Singer puzzle. Time would tell whether it would be that easy to solve.

If Flavin felt at all guilty about Kircher's termination, he didn't show it publicly. He did, however, assign one of the vice presidents the task of keeping Kircher informed about the goings-on within the company. If Flavin showed little emotion about the manner in which he had succeeded Kircher, the reverse was not the case. Kircher viewed himself as a refined intellect in the tradition of the educated British or French upper classes. He was infuriated by the fact that he had been replaced by someone he referred to as a "cheap Irishman," someone not at all in his (Kircher's) league.

Transition - The Miracle-Worker

Flavin characterized 1975 as the beginning of a "transition period," and he certainly wasted no time getting started. His appointment became official on December 1, and on December 11 he informed the board that he planned to "get rid of the business machines division." He was moving faster than his colleagues could keep up with, as at the same time a company spokesman had responded to a press query by saying that "I can assure you that nothing of any consequence will happen to the business machines division. We are not negotiating its sale to anyone." When asked, an outside director of Singer said, "I don't know what Mr. Flavin has cooked up. I figure he's been deciding just what business Singer is in. He wasn't hired to do nothing." This director also said that he would be "surprised" if there was any proposal to drop the business machines operation soon.

Meanwhile, Flavin had decided to close the San Leandro, California, headquarters of Friden and move it to a new location in New Jersey. The engineering staff was cut in half, and the accounting staff had been given until the end of January to decide whether they wanted to move to New Jersey. A former Singer executive in the business machines division said that "three-quarters of the business machines people I knew are no longer with the company." Along with the fourth-quarter results, Ed Graf, the acting COO, announced that Singer would discontinue the Graphic Systems Division and had signed contracts for the sale of Schwab A.G., the German mail order company, and the Water Resources Division. Later he also announced that the Company would probably close the household appliance factory in Leini, Italy, eliminating about two thousand jobs. It was breathtaking.

On January 31, 1976, just eight weeks after his appointment as CEO, Flavin announced that Singer had lost $414.6 million in the fourth quarter and $452 million in all of the previous year under Donald Kircher. Flavin was invoking one of the now-habitual tools of any new CEO hired to deal with major problems—to make all of the major unpleasant organizational changes on day one and provide a huge reserve to cover the cost of those changes. This accomplished a number of goals:

1. It placed the blame for the results squarely on the predecessor.

2. If estimated generously, it created a reserve much larger than realistically necessary, which became a cushion of discretionary profit that management could tap from time to time to conceal future problems.

3. It classified any future costs of the closed operations as "discontinued operations," leaving earnings from continuing operations as the number to highlight to the public, even if the actual reported earnings per share were much lower when all of the costs were accounted for.

4. It changed the format for presenting financial information, making it difficult to construct any meaningful time series of results to determine what was actually going on.

The audited financial statements contained more and more footnotes. They would typically indicate unusual events and changes in accounting that were not discussed elsewhere. They were a good place to hide bad news, as they were typically read only by securities analysts, if at all. For the previous fifteen years, Singer's audited statements and footnotes never exceeded eight to nine pages in the annual report. The 1975 annual report devoted twelve pages to the audited statements and footnotes alone. In addition, there was for the first time a "Management's Discussion and Analysis of the Summary of Operating Results," presented by the auditors. This discussion appeared in the last pages of the annual report and was, if anything, more obscure than the footnotes. Such an in-depth analysis would be of primary interest to the shareholders and should have probably been part of the chairman's letter or at least appeared at the beginning of the annual report. Flavin was displaying the skills he had learned as controller at IBM and Xerox.

Nevertheless, Flavin had to write an annual report letter for 1975. He began by announcing that the Company was struggling under a heavy debt burden

(Kircher's fault). He then announced the cessation or sale of business in Tele-Signal, Water Resources, European Mail Order, and the Business Machines Division (Kircher's strategy). These actions had caused the Company to record a provision of approximately $400 million (Flavin's cushion). In addition, he had sold all of the existing and future consumer accounts receivable to the General Electric Credit Corporation. The result of these efforts had solved, on paper, the Company's most pressing problems, with the result that the fourth-quarter loss of The Singer Company was $414.6 million (the largest single quarter loss in U.S. corporate history).

Organizationally, Flavin consolidated all worldwide sewing products operations into a single Sewing Products Group and redefined the reporting business groups, making it extremely difficult for analysts both inside and outside of the company to understand its history. He further stated that:

> …you will see that Singer has a strong position in many fine areas of business with extremely good prospects for growth and profit (sewing products?). Having addressed our major operating problems, we can now concentrate on our fundamentally good businesses.

It was as if the mere act of reporting the problems had solved them. The notes to the financial statements consisted of long and largely undecipherable details of the accounting impact of the above decisions, which permitted the Company to split its results between "Continuing Operations," for which operating statements were provided in detail, and "Discontinued Operations," which would appear on future income statements as one- or two-line items deducted after determining "Income from Continuing Operations," the measure by which Flavin expected to be judged.

Operating units were redefined with a shuffling of certain units from one group to another, making any sales or income comparisons with the results of the Kircher years impossible. Income in the operating reports was also redefined, with the same result. "Continuing Operations" were what Flavin argued should be the basis for judging his performance. Things looked a lot better this way, since the measure he proposed excluded all of the losses from discontinued operations necessary to arrive at the publicly reported loss of $451.9 million. Meanwhile, during all of this disclosure and rhetoric about the company's problems, the sewing machine business still seemed to be holding up the fort.

At the 1976 shareholders meeting, Flavin was all optimism. He announced that Singer had signed agreements with TRW and International Computers to take over the worldwide marketing and servicing operations of the business machines division, and said, "We have had good indications up to this point that the worst is over. We have our major problems behind us"…and…"I feel that our reserves established last December are clearly adequate." Finally, he noted proudly that in the past four and a half months, he had closed, consolidated, or made plans to consolidate thirteen facilities, resulting in the termination of seventeen thousand employees, and that the TRW/International Computer agreement would result in an additional five thousand employees being transferred to those companies, bringing total employment at Singer down approximately 20 percent.

Joe Flavin's letter to the shareholders and the accompanying financial statements for 1976 were very difficult for the lay reader to translate, filled as they were with business-speak and conglomerate accounting. By focusing only on continuing operations, he avoided any additional unpleasant news arising from the businesses he had decided to discontinue. He could put them aside, implying that whatever happened had been Kircher's fault and he was just cleaning up the mess. He then suggested the possibility of restructuring the sewing business, seeming to warn of major cost-cutting in the core business. Finally, he noted that the various provisions and agreements made in 1976 had made the financial statements difficult, if not impossible, to understand but rather than try explaining them, he merely referred the reader to the lengthy footnotes at the end of the report where all of the relevant facts were buried in accounting text.

On the positive side, the company now had only three primary business activities, and sewing was still number one, described by the chairman as "an excellent business with good potential."

Primary Business Groups:

1.   Sewing Products

2.   Products Manufactured for the Consumer

3.   Products and Services for the Government

The strategy for the sewing business was focused on advanced electronic systems that could theoretically simplify sewing and add to profit margins. That was it— no mention of the undeveloped world or emerging nations, the largest and fastest-growing segment of the world population, for whom the sewing machine was not a luxury but a necessity. To use electronics, one must have electricity.

The non-sewing consumer products received a lot of strategic attention and led the reader to believe that Singer was still essentially a manufacturer and retailer of consumer appliances and a supplier of controls and measurement devices in support of other manufacturers of large consumer items such as home appliances, automobiles, and heating and air-conditioning. Finally, technology products and services received a mention, primarily because of the contra-cyclicality of those businesses relative to retailing.

Recovery—Still a Retail Sewing Business

The first year of Joe Flavin's "Recovery Period" seemed to be a return to the original concept surrounding Don Kircher's diversification strategy of the late 1960s, before he got ambushed by the Friden business. The success for the year was pretty much guaranteed, starting as he did with over $400 million of potential losses already behind him. Of note, however, is the fact that although revenues and income from continuing operations were 18-19 percent higher than they had been in 1973, every other performance measure was down:

1976	1973	Change
Sales	$2,284.8M	$1,936.0M	+18.0%
Income—Continuing Operations	$ 74.5M	$ 92.3M	-19.3%
Income—Reported	$ 94.2M	$ 94.5M	- 0.4%
Earnings per share	$ 5.11	$ 5.32	- 3.9%
Common stock price	$ 22.00	$ 47.00	-53.2%
Dividends	$ 0.25	$ 2.45	-89.8%

It was Flavin's strategic narrative that recalled Kircher's original purpose, to find diversification opportunities that released the primary sewing retail business from its cyclical uncertainties. The first text that leaps out from the discussion of products in the annual report is:

WITHOUT A DOUBT ELECTRONICS IS

THE KEY TO THE FUTURE OF SEWING

This might have been reassuring to sewing products managers who had their doubts. While a tad overstated, as electronics was only relevant to the developed markets of the United States and Western Europe, this statement nonetheless seemed to identify the direction Flavin wished to take the Company. Home appliances would take an important role, particularly in the developing countries where the Singer store had traditionally presented a much broader product line than just sewing.

Beyond sewing products, the so-called Products Manufactured for the Consumer presented significant growth opportunities, particularly where Singer enjoyed a significant market position, such as the manufacture of the Craftsman line of power tools for Sears, the manufacture of electro-mechanical controls for a large portion of the automobile industry, and furniture combined with Singer's near monopoly of the sewing machine cabinet business. However, these products were still closely linked to the vicissitudes of the retail environments in individual countries. Those environments, now quite different from one country to the next, would inevitably become more interdependent as trade linked those countries.

The New York Times, Wednesday, June 14, 1978—

"Singer Co. Is Moving to Stamford to Surprise of New York Officials"

Not only was this a surprise to NY officials, but it was a surprise to many of the Company's employees. Singer's headquarters had been in New York since its founding in 1852, and it was considered the quintessential New York Company. After all, Edward Clark himself had started, and his successor Frederick Bourne had completed, the building of the Dakota and had given each of his grandsons an entire adjacent city block of New York City with which to amuse themselves. Avid and competitive art collectors, the two would go on to help found both the Metropolitan Museum of New York and the Museum of Modern Art. Isaac Singer was a notorious man-about-town, leaving numerous scandals in his wake. The Singer Manufacturing Company had a rich history in New York, and the Singer Building had been one of New York's iconic skyscrapers.

Flavin, a resident of New Canaan, Connecticut, explained that the operating costs would be lower in Stanford, that the work environment would be pleasant, and that the living and working environment for employees would be favorable. The gossip within the Company was that Flavin had paid $250 thousand for a consultant's study that had reviewed Atlanta, Dallas, and the New Jersey and New York suburbs. Atlanta and Dallas were for show, as the Company had its largest U.S. factory, its R&D lab, and its data center in the metropolitan New York area. The real choice was between Connecticut and New Jersey. Flavin lived in New Canaan, so it was no surprise when Stamford, Connecticut, emerged as the victor. Employees suspected an even more Machiavellian reason, that the move accomplished two important objectives: It reduced Flavin's commute time, and it resulted in a substantial voluntary reduction in expensive headquarters staff. Historically, the Company had strong links to New Jersey, and for decades, when the Company was called the Singer Manufacturing Company, the executive ranks had been heavily populated by manufacturing managers. In the

United States, they came from the Elizabethport factory, and outside of the States they came through Clydebank, Scotland. The many vice presidents and senior staff of the New York office were more or less evenly divided between New York and New Jersey residents. Many were nearing retirement and were little inclined to undertake a major household move. No matter which choice was made, Flavin could lose up to half the headquarters population, if not immediately certainly within a year or two, so why not stay close to home? The New York City officials were annoyed by the absence of communication about either the "study" or the announcement, but there was little they could do about it.

> The close of 1978 marked the completion of the Company's recovery period. Over the last two years, the primary emphasis has been the improvement of our balance sheet. The year 1979 brings the beginning of a period when that emphasis will change and focus on long-term opportunities for selectively developing Singer businesses.

In his annual letter, Flavin described the results as "mixed," with sales growing to $2.5 billion and operating income from continuing operations (there was that distinction again) declining by 19 percent. Since there wasn't much else to talk about, he described the primary success of the year to be a substantial reduction in the Company's consolidated debt. Product success, in what has historically been a consumer retail company, was largely unmentioned. Before beginning an interesting analysis of the state of the worldwide market for sewing machines, Flavin launched into a detailed description of the problems he had encountered at Singer's largest sewing machine factory in Clydebank, Scotland, a principal source of both household and industrial machines. What was described as "manufacturing problems," primarily at Clydebank, had created an absolute loss of $9 million on a 10 percent sales increase. Flavin was not the first CEO to be frustrated by Clydebank, as it had been a historic source of concern. A virtual city, it once had over thirty thousand employees working in Singer's total integration style, from railroad to foundry to final assembly. Historically, there had been only two employers in Clydebank, Singer and John Brown Shipping, builder of the "queens," the pride of British luxury liners. By 1978, John Brown had closed and Clydebank had become a single-company town. Strongly unionized, the workforce had been resistant to change and quick to take labor action.

Flavin described the market for sewing machines as being essentially two distinct markets. The first, and the primary challenge from his point of view, was that of the developed countries. He called this the "Mature Markets," as if they were approaching their end of life, a market in which the woman was more likely to be in the workplace than at home and for whom the sewing machine was a high-cost discretionary purchase. While he paid lip service to the need for sewing education, his focus was clearly one of cost reduction in both manufacturing and distribution. The declining demand in the United States would be dealt with through marketing and technology. The second market was that of the developing countries, where the sewing machine was still more of a household necessity than a discretionary purchase and in some countries an important, if not the primary source of income. Demand in these countries continued to grow with the population. The underlying text was that manufacturing cost reduction was highly dependent on unit volume, and it was the declining volume in the United States and Western Europe that was threatening the Company's ability to compete on the basis of price.

At this point it is useful to return to one of the basics of the Core Model developed by Edward Clark in the nineteenth century. The sewing machine was still probably the most complicated electro-mechanical home appliance ever invented, and it did not sell itself. Sales required intimate face-to-face contact with the customer, a high level of initial and continuing customer education, if the customer was to extract maximum value and satisfaction from the machine. Technology alone would not sell the product. It might have permitted the company to sell at higher margins, but until it cut the fabric, threaded itself, and traced the desired pattern without human intervention, it would require continuing demonstration and support. It was the critical encounter of the salesperson and customer that determined the success of the sales effort. The nature of direct versus indirect selling was critical to that encounter. For indirect selling to succeed, independent agents must have a strong reason to support the critical encounter. The ability to find an appropriate balance between independence and a shared motivation to manage the encounter would determine indirect distribution success.

Flavin's apparent feeling of discontent with sewing was obvious when he enumerated the actions already taken, or to be taken:

- Restructure sewing operations in Japan, Portugal, and Iran

- Reorganize and consolidate controls

- Restructure manufacturing operations at Clydebank, Scotland

- Phase out production of some industrial machines at Clydebank

- Modernize the remaining portions of Clydebank

- Reduce the labor force at Clydebank by almost half

- Review the remaining manufacturing operations

- Reduce the number of sewing machine models offered

- Restructure or close a number of retail outlets

- Increase indirect selling channels

- Introduce new sewing classes

- Introduce a new advertising program

- Introduce a new marketing program

- Introduce the TOUCH-TRONIC 2001 machine in the United States

The year 1978 marked the return of the multi-layered financial statements, with significant reserves for new closings and restructurings, changes in prior reserves for closings and restructurings, changes in tax benefits, etc., etc. The net income reported for 1978 was down by 33 percent, with the reasons all buried in the audited statements and footnotes. It was more interesting to look at the operating income, more accurately the direct contribution, for each product group. The contribution didn't reflect any allocation of general corporate expenses nor the cost of any "discontinued operations." Flavin's concern with sewing products was understandable. While every product group had a sales increase over prior year, only the group, Products Manufactured for the Consumer (excluding sewing) had a contribution growing faster than sales, a "scale advantage." Sewing Products had a 24 percent decline in its direct contribution on a 4 percent sales increase.

For the coming "Development Period," from 1979 to 1982, Flavin's explicitly stated goals for the company were:

1. Revenue growth of 10 percent or more per year.

2. Operating income of at least 10 percent of sales.

3. Debt/equity ratio of no more than 0.6 to 1.

4. An "A" credit rating for the Company's funded debt.

Development – Sewing or Technology, a False Choice?

The first year of Flavin's "Development Period" was the beginning of the end of Singer as a sewing machine company. The Company reported a sales increase of 5 percent, but a decline in reported net income of $155 million, from a $58 million profit in 1978 to a $98 million loss in 1979. In his letter, Flavin attributed the loss to the creation of yet another reserve of $130 million, established to cover the costs of restructuring the sewing machine factories in the United States and Europe, as well as changes in the distribution system for sewing machines. Sales of the other products had fair to modest increases, but 11 to 14 percent declines in contributions to profit. Once again, the only major achievement for the year seemed to be the further reduction of the Company's debt. Notably, the Government Group now appeared at the top of the product group listing, ahead of both Products for the Consumer and Sewing Products.

More importantly, Flavin had apparently run out of patience trying to correct the ills of the sewing business in the developed world, and now he was proposing steps that would have a dramatic impact on the future of the Company's sewing machine business. Specifically, he planned to:

- Phase out all operations of the Clydebank, Scotland, factory and attempt to sell the facility

- Restructure operations at the Karlsruhe, Germany, factory to move from the integrated manufacture of electronic and top-of-the line sewing machines for Europe (historically the most profitable machines sold by the European countries) to the assembly of certain machines and the production of precision parts requiring highly skilled labor for top-of-the-line machines (presumably made and/or assembled elsewhere) and third parties

- Restructure operations at the Monza, Italy, factory for the same kind of specialization of parts manufacturing and assembly of a limited number of machines as at Karlsruhe

- Expand production of the Anderson, South Carolina, factory to manufacture the arms, beds, and electronic components for top-of-the-line machines for both the United States and Europe

- Restructure operations at the Elizabeth, New Jersey, factory for a reduced level of integrated manufacturing and the transfer of certain operations to other locations

These programs implied massive changes to the way Singer had manufactured sewing machines for the past century. Traditionally, each factory manufactured a machine or series of machines completely, from component manufacture to final assembly, the fully integrated process developed to produce machines of the highest quality while taking advantage of the economies of mass production. This reorganization implied that factories would basically become parts manufacturers for machines to be assembled elsewhere, and machine assemblers would receive parts manufactured elsewhere. It implied a degree of coordination between assembly and the sources of parts supply not seen in the past. It also assumed that no factory would be completely responsible for the production of a high-quality working sewing machine. The proprietary interest and pride that each factory might have had in its products was no longer. Also, if the primary problem of manufacturing was cost, none of the affected factories was in a low-cost labor market, yet Singer had many factories that were in such markets.

On the distribution side, the actions proposed were to:

- Accelerate the program begun in the United States to change the configuration of, convert to dealerships, or close marginally profitable or unprofitable stores. Extend the same program to Europe. Reduce the number of Company-owned stores by converting them to dealerships and other indirect channels of distribution.

- Further reduce distribution expenses for industrial sewing machines, primarily through marketing changes.

The move from direct to indirect distribution was precisely the reverse of the strategy inherent in the Core Model developed a century earlier. Lack of control could evolve into competition with oneself, as non-exclusive dealers sought the broadest array of sewing machine brands to offer. Adequate demonstration, essential for closing sales, especially for top-of-the-line machines, could become problematic, resulting in declining margins as the product mix shifted downward. It would seem that careful exploration of some novel combination of direct/indirect sales might have been wise before plunging in on such wholesale change.

Because the sewing machine business seemed to be the primary concern, it is useful to examine its history since Flavin's appointment as CEO. Since 1975, the last full year under Don Kircher, worldwide sales of Consumer Sewing Products had grown on average by about 3 percent per year. This was not far from the growth anticipated in the original strategic planning model, which relied on slow regular growth and cash flow from the sewing business to fund the acquisitions and growth of non-traditional products. The data for Consumer Sewing Products were not separated between North America and Europe. However, based on the explanations in the Annual Report, the decline in Consumer Sewing profitability was largely due to a sales decline in the United States and manufacturing cost problems in Europe, principally at the Clydebank factory. This suggested that demand in Europe was still at acceptable levels, but that the cost of a wholly controlled distribution network was becoming unacceptable. Flavin concluded his letter with a rather ominous prediction for sewing:

The expenses associated with the changes in the Company's North American and European sewing marketing organizations and the inefficiencies associated with the restructuring of our factories will have an adverse impact on the operating performance of those operations in 1980 and 1981.

He remained buoyant about Products for the Consumer, "which continues to show good potential," but somewhat circumspect about Products for Government, "which shows prospects for growth and stability."

The New York Times, May 9, 1980—

"Vacancy Filled as Singer Elects a New President"

William Schmied, 51 years old, has been elected president and chief operating officer of The Singer Company, a position that had previously been vacant. Joseph B. Flavin, also 51, continues as chairman and chief executive officer of the Stamford, Conn., corporation. He has held those titles since 1975.... Mr. Schmied is stepping up at a troubled company.... Once a Wall Street favorite, Singer has seen its stock decline from a high of 93¼ in 1972 to yesterday's close of 8½ in trading on the New York Stock Exchange.

When interviewed, Schmied, previously executive vice president in charge of Products and Services for Government, more or less let the cat out of the bag as to where the Company was going:

My greatest attention will be given to sewing because that's what's given us the most difficulty.... What I need to do is get the same detailed knowledge that I have of our government products area and give it some guidance.

By essentially ignoring the existing wealth of talent and knowledge about the sewing machine business, was Flavin trying to inject a breath of fresh air into the traditional business, or had he decided that the technology products for government would be where the Company was headed? The latter would be instinctual for someone who had spent his entire professional life at IBM and Xerox.

If there was any remaining doubt about where Joe Flavin intended to take the Company, it was easy to see by comparing the list of primary product groups for 1980 and 1979:

1980	1979
1. Products and Services for Gov't	Sewing Products:
2. Products Mfg for the Consumer	1. **North America & Europe**
Sewing Products;	2. Africa, Latin America, Far East
3. Africa, Latin America, Far East	3. Industrial Sewing Products
4. **North America & Europe**	4. Product Mfg for the Consumer
5. Industrial Sewing Products	5. Products & Services for the Gov't

The sewing machine business had been replaced by Products and Services for the Government and Products Manufactured for the Consumer. Within Sewing Products, North America and Europe were now just barely above Industrial Sewing, the least important product. Notwithstanding the change in product emphasis, the worldwide sewing business still generated 49 percent of the Company's total sales and 33 percent of its direct contribution to profit. North America and Europe had a combined loss at the direct contribution level of $46 million, without which the rest of the sewing business would have contributed 53 percent of the direct contribution to profit.

Products and Services for the Government had a strong increase in sales of 26 percent, with an improvement in contribution of 31 percent. Products Manufactured for the Consumer had only a 2 percent increase in sales and an 11 percent decline in contribution. Singer was described in the joint Flavin/Schmied letter as:

> ...a better balanced company. It is the Company's balance of expertise in aerospace and marine systems, an important group of U.S.-based consumer businesses, and an outstanding consumer marketing organization in the developing world that provide the diversity and strength for Singer to become a more profitable and effective competitor.

It was as if the North Atlantic sewing business had been wiped from the face of the earth.

In January 1980, the country entered a brief recession of six months' duration. The GDP declined 2.2 percent (peak to trough), and unemployment peaked at 7.8 percent in July. More importantly, the Federal Reserve under Paul Volcker raised the prime interest rate dramatically to fight inflation, reaching 17.25 percent in March. Singer's consolidated debt increased slightly in 1979 and

1980, but the effect of the increase in interest rates increased the burden on the Company from $59 million of interest expense in 1978 to $78 million in 1980.

The sewing business in the United States and Europe continued to take most of the hits in the marketplace and was subjected to the most draconian actions. Manpower had been reduced in the United States by 30 percent in 1980 alone. In October, Singer announced that it would end the production of household sewing machines at its Elizabeth, New Jersey, plant, resulting in the layoff of 850 employees. Constructed in 1873, little more than twenty years after the Company was founded, the plant was then Singer's largest and the world's largest single product manufacturing facility. A Company spokesperson said that Singer estimated that since 1972, the demand for sewing machines in the United States had dropped as much as 50 percent. Others, however, disputed this and contended that demand remained high, but that the Singer product had not been able to meet the market need. At Sears, a saleswoman with twenty-three years' experience said that "people are sewing more than ever, largely because the cost of clothing is skyrocketing." This contradiction between the internal management belief and the evidence outside of the company was never objectively tested. Kircher's reluctance to seek outside expert advice had apparently permeated the Singer culture, and Flavin never engaged an outside market research expert to test the underlying assumptions.

Meanwhile in the United States, approximately 175 independent dealers had been added to the distribution system to counterbalance the phasing out of 150 Company-operated stores. In Europe, selling and administrative expenses were reduced by an amount roughly equal to the decline in sales. However, the loss of $46 million included approximately $19 million of onetime costs associated with the manufacturing and distribution restructurings. Without these costs, the loss of contribution for 1980 would have been $27 million, a slight improvement over the 1979 loss of $31 million. However, lest anyone in the organization think that the worst was over, James J. Johnson, the new executive vice president, Sewing Products and Consumer Durables, said in the annual report:

> Our objective for this part of our business is to attain profitability as quickly as possible. Perceptions concerning the past size of the business or concern about the future market share will not be allowed to reduce the speed of achieving this most important objective.

In other words, don't get in the way!

Page one of the 1981 Annual Report said it all:

> The Singer Company develops and produces aerospace and other high-technology systems for government and industry, and manufactures or markets

sewing and consumer durable products in the United States and approximately 100 other nations. It has an especially extensive distribution network in the developing world. Singer was founded in 1851 and now maintains headquarters in Stamford, Connecticut.

That year was another difficult one for Singer. The recession, with persistent inflation, high interest rates, and unfavorable exchange rate fluctuations, created a difficult business environment. Worldwide sales of sewing products declined by 6 percent, with a 22 percent decline in the United States and Europe partially offset by an 11 percent increase in Africa, Latin America, and the Far East. Contributions to profit for sewing declined by 40 percent, with the greatest decline occurring in Africa, Latin America, and the Far East for a change. A slight worsening of the losses in Europe was attributed to currency losses, as the full effect of the cost-reduction steps taken over the past two years more than offset the fall in demand.

The list of accomplishments in Flavin's letter to the shareholders seemed to suggest another change in strategy:

1. "Aerospace/high technology operations grew strongly and accounted for a greater share of total corporate sales and earnings." The expectation was that this group would represent more than half the Company's revenues in 1982.

2. "Substantial cost reductions were made in North American and European sewing under the continued restructuring of this business." Everything seemed still focused on cost reduction, with no mention of a change in sales or marketing strategies.

3. "Additional production efficiencies and improved use of assets were achieved in domestic consumer product activities…. We continue to consolidate and trim operations." Boilerplate. The future did not look good for Products Manufactured for the Consumer.

4. "Sales of sewing products and consumer durables increased in the Africa, Latin America and Far East markets." Although this group represented only 23 percent of total Company revenues, it generated 65 percent of the total contribution to operating income.

5. "Aggressive balance sheet management held debt below planned levels."

Aside from Aerospace, this description of progress was pretty hard to decipher. The Company apparently had a successful strategy for the sale of sewing products in the developing world, where it manufactured its own product line and distributed it through the same variety of distribution networks that had been used, even perfected, in those countries for years. Yet there was no discussion of whether or not those solutions could be replicated in North America and Europe. Were there product line issues? Product pricing issues? Manufacturing cost issues? What was it about the nature of the distribution system(s) in the developing markets that made them unsuitable for the developed markets? The absence of an explicit analysis of the differences between the developed and developing markets appears to have generated a self-fulfilling prophecy, where the apparent failure of a sales and marketing strategy in the developed countries drove continued cost-reduction programs, which in turn imperiled sales volume as retail outlets were sacrificed. Was this a strategic withdrawal of Singer from the sewing machine business in favor of technology as the driving, or even the only, mission of the Company? The uncertainty of direction that had been a defining characteristic of the Kircher presidency seemed to have been institutionalized and raised questions about the company's survival.

The 1980–1982 recession was particularly damaging to the business environment. What began as a relatively mild recession, from January to July 1980, turned into a double-dip recession just as it looked as if the economy was about to improve. Paul Volker's use of the prime rate to fight inflation continued as the prospect of inflation appeared to be aggravated by Iran's Revolution and the subsequent uncertainty in production that forced oil prices up. In 1980 alone, there were forty separate increases in the prime rate, peaking at 21.5 percent on December 19, 1980. The following year was not much better, with the prime rate hovering around 18 to 19 percent for most of the year and dropping only to 15.75 percent by year's end. At the end of 1981, Singer had total borrowings of almost $600 million, including nonconsolidated subsidiaries. Each percentage point increase in the average borrowing rate could cost the company as much as $6 million a year, on pre-tax net income of approximately $60 million.

This year marked the end of Joe Flavin's "Development Period." The letter to the shareholders sounded like the beginning of the end of Singer as a sewing machine company:

> Record sales and earnings of the Products and Services for Government Group once again demonstrated the strength of its technological base and leadership in key market areas.

> While the North American and Europe sewing operation experienced lower overall results due to the recession, the major development in this area was the essential completion of programs to restructure manufacturing facilities and modify the distribution network.

In the United States, we have converted…(all of)…our Singer-operated retail stores…into dealerships.

We have reduced the Singer operated stores in Europe to approximately 700, compared with 1,350 in 1979.

…We closed the Karlsruhe, West Germany, and Elizabeth, New Jersey, plants…. We also continue to restructure facilities in France and Italy.

In total, since 1979 we have closed or converted to dealerships approximately 1,375 retail stores, eliminated approximately 4 million square feet of manufacturing space, and reduced the work force by about two-thirds.

Products Manufactured for the Consumer continues to be on cost control and asset management.

The Africa, Latin America and Far East Group was affected by the pervasive economic downturn and currency devaluations…. We have instituted cost reductions in the areas affected by the recession, and…are continuing to shift from retail to wholesale distribution.

To put it succinctly:

- Technology is where we're going.

- North Atlantic sewing is out.

- Products for Consumers are on hold.

- Sewing for the rest of the world is uncertain.

The euphemism, "…modify the distribution network," to which Flavin alluded in his list of accomplishments for 1982, was, in fact, the brutal termination of the cadre of long-serving managers of the large European sales organizations.

The Sewing Business Is Dull and Difficult

In 1980, the door-to-door sales organization in France followed a cadence of sales relationships that hadn't changed substantially in almost a century. In order to sell a sewing machine, a canvasser had to make five demonstrations. In order to make five demonstrations, he had to knock on seventy-five doors. The compensation system was a combination of a fixed portion plus a commission, with the commission rate such that in order to make a threshold livable income, the canvasser had to sell approximately fifteen machines per month. In terms of work pace, this meant that he had approximately fifteen minutes from the time he knocked on a door to determine the probability of a demonstration or move on to the next house. The best salesmen sold twenty or thirty, even forty machines a month. Those who couldn't maintain the pace left.

The French company was managed by Jacques Ehrsam, the latest patriarch of a family that had led Singer for almost a century. Jacques's grandfather, Adolphe Ehrsam, had been the first general manager of La Compagnie Singer, appointed on November 1, 1888. Under his tenure, France had been the first non-English-speaking sales subsidiary to successfully introduce the Singer business model developed in Great Britain and the United States. Adolphe died in 1924 and was succeeded by his sons, Maurice and Henri, as co–general managers. Henri died in 1937, and Maurice continued as general manager until 1947, when he was succeeded by his son, Jacques, then only thirty years old. Although very young, Jacques benefited from his father's counsel, for Maurice lived another twenty years. But the junior Ehrsam was determined to make his own mark. He had begun as a technician and had received front-line sales and marketing training in the United States, Italy, and France. His direct knowledge of life at the level of customer contact soon made him a hero to the store managers and door-to-door salesmen, a reputation he would carry with him throughout his Singer career. For Jacques, the salesperson encountering a customer was always right until proven otherwise. Under Ehrsam, La Compagnie Singer became the largest sales and marketing organization in the Singer world outside of the United States, with annual sales of over 275,000 sewing machines in the 1970s. The three generations of Ehrsams had shepherded the company through World War I, the Communist Revolution, the Great Depression, and World War II, protecting the company's assets and reconstituting the organization after each trauma. They, along with the other senior European managers, could have taught Joe Flavin something about managing change, but he never asked. He summarily fired Ehrsam and the other country managers without so much as a face-to-face conversation. Jacques had been expecting the end to come and had used his extensive network of Paris connections to gather sufficient financial commitments to acquire La Compagnie Singer. Flavin refused. Ehrsam then upped the ante to include all of Europe. Flavin again refused. While he wanted to be done with the sewing business, Flavin seemed to believe that the entire worldwide business was worth more than its parts, or that the worldwide business would be difficult to sell without its second-largest sales organization.

The year 1983 was the first with generally good news all around. For a while, it looked as if Singer might reestablish itself as a sewing machine company. Although total company sales were essentially flat, operating income improved by 65 percent to $106 million. The reported net income improved from a loss of $3 million in 1982 to a profit of $32 million. The key achievements were:

- Aerospace Electronics continued strong growth.

- North American and European Sewing significantly improved performance as a result of restructuring.

- The North American Consumer Products Group now included the North American sewing business, which was folded into this renamed group, and there was no longer a separately reported world-wide sewing business.

- The International Group now included European sewing machines and had made "excellent progress in realigning its worldwide operations to reduce costs...."

With the reshuffling of North American and European sewing operations, Flavin would no longer have to deal with any executive responsible for any part of the sewing machine business. North American Sewing was now part of Products for the Consumer, and European Sewing was now part of a new International Group, more focused on consumer durables than sewing for its growth.

The New York Times, July 12, 1984—

SINGER'S SHIFT INTO HIGH TECH

After nearly a decade of selling off unprofitable business lines, closing plants and investing heavily in new lines of aerospace and military products, The Singer Company appeared to have completed what a journalist described as one of the most thorough corporate restructurings in recent memory.... "This is a company whose whole culture was built around the sewing machine," Joseph B. Flavin, the company's chairman and chief executive, said.... "As hard as we tried, that couldn't be changed overnight."

"Singer has been in a turnaround mode for years," said Morton Langer, an analyst for Bear Stearns & Company, "and they've finally made it."

Joe Flavin was riding high. His strategy of moving the Company out of the sewing machine business and into technology was finally paying off. The highlights in his annual letter to the shareholders were bullish:

The Government Products Group, our principal business, again posted record sales and income and, as expected was accounting for approximately one-half of total revenues at year-end.

The North American Consumer Products Group (which now included sewing) asserted its strengths in favorable markets to register higher sales and an even sharper gain in earnings.

The International Group (no mention of European sewing) improved its performance substantially, despite the persistence of adverse conditions in many of the major economies in which it functions.

We continued to reduce debt in 1984. Consequently, our financial condition is now stronger than at any other time in the past decade.

From the very beginning of his tenure, Joe Flavin had seemed to view the sewing business as a liability. He was a technology executive who had little interest in learning the nuances of selling sewing machines nor their unique place for the past 125 years in the eyes of women the world over. He never engaged the operating managers in a discussion of the changes in either products and/or distribution that the company was considering. The field managers were as aware of the problems as Flavin and his staff, and experience had taught them that one size did not fit all in the Singer universe. There was a wealth of untapped sales management experience in the field among those who knew how to survive in a rapidly changing environment. Arrogance by Flavin and his newly hired staff permeated the headquarters organization, with often seriously negative consequences.

It was true that the culture had been built around the sewing machine. More precisely, it had been built around the sewing machine culture country by country, creating the belief that Singer was, in fact, a local company. Flavin had spent considerable time as the controller of IBM World Trade in Paris, and his experience there should have given him a sense of the tolerance and humility that the successful management of such an organization required. If he understood the implications that certain behavior by his staff were having on local operations, he didn't share it with them. One example in particular stood out. Flavin had just hired a new vice president who decided to make a first tour of the principal Singer offices in Europe…by private company jet, of course. Paris was to be his first stop, as it always seemed to find its way onto the itineraries of visiting New York executives, even if the primary destination was elsewhere in Europe. At the same time, a Singer factory near the expected landing site of the Singer airplane was experiencing a labor action, with the usual back-and-forth of the company pleading penury and the employees pleading poverty. The union leading the action was affiliated with the French communist party and was led by a young, good-looking, and charismatic representative who fit perfectly the profile for an interesting interview on the evening TV news. Remember that one of the century-long strategies of the Singer business model had been to create the belief in France that

Singer was a French company. The fact that it was American was not a secret, but neither was it ever mentioned in the press. In the midst of all this, a jet landed near the factory with the big red Singer *S* on its tail, and emblazoned on its side, in English, of course, was:

WHAT'S NEW FOR TOMOROW IS AT SINGER TODAY

Both the young labor leader and the airplane appeared in the local papers and in the evening television news.

The Singer Company Annual Report 1985:

"Aerospace Electronics: A Decade of Growth"

The results for the year substantially confirmed that the turnaround was complete and the Company was firmly on the electronics growth curve, now including new acquisitions:

- Net income increased for the third consecutive year.

- The aerospace electronics operations recorded their tenth straight year of higher revenues and again increased their share of corporate sales.

- Singer accelerated its expansion in aerospace electronics by entering into a definitive agreement to acquire Textron's Dalmo Victor Division, which develops and produces electronic warfare systems.

- Most of the direct sewing marketing operations in Europe, Africa, and the Middle East were sold to independent distributors.

- The balance sheet was further strengthened.

Finally, in case anyone might have thought that the Company still had any desire to remain in the sewing machine business, Flavin announced, "…the Board of Directors authorized management to investigate the possibility of combining our sewing and furniture operations into a separate company with the intention of distributing the new company to Singer shareholders as a special dividend."

Q.E.D.

In February 1986, Singer announced publicly its intent to spin off its sewing machine operations into a new company, which would be a manufacturer of sewing machines and furniture and would be allowed to use the Singer brand under a licensing agreement. Only the old company would use the Singer corporate name. In the second quarter of 1986, Singer Company formed the new company, called SSMC, Inc., and in July 1986, it completed the spinoff as a special dividend to the holders of the Company's common stock, while retaining 15 percent of SSMC's common stock together with a class of SSMC preferred stock. Singer reported its own results for 1986 without SSMC, but it did not issue an annual report, for reasons which will become clear.

And that was it.

This 135-year-old company, America's first multinational corporation, was no more. While Flavin retained the name of The Singer Company, it was no longer a sewing machine company. It might even have been a mistake to retain the corporate name for his new aerospace company. No one living would ever think of Singer as anything other than a sewing machine company, as the brand was so well-embedded in the culture of over 180 countries. Aerospace and high technology had no general meaning in the Singer name, and by retaining that name, Flavin had done great harm to both his technology company as well as whoever would continue to sell sewing machines under the Singer brand in the future. Having transformed a company that had once employed nearly one hundred thousand people around the world into one that employed only twenty thousand, principally in the United States, the Company had almost certainly left a bad taste in the mouths of those ex-employees, their families, and their friends around the world. The legacy of factory closings devastated many communities, and the absence of prior notice left many embittered governments, particularly in Western Europe, where the culture and in many cases the law, required companies to work with government officials in such cases. The trademark, while still valuable, undoubtedly suffered. The sullied brand had probably been the Company's greatest asset.

It is interesting to compare the results for 1986, the first year without sewing, with those of 1985, the last year that included sewing as well as those of 1974, the last full year under president Donald P. Kircher, as a way of better understanding the changes that Joe Flavin brought to the Company during his twelve years as CEO of Singer.

SALES: ($ Millions)	1986	1985	1974
Sewing Products	$ 0	$ 568	$1,541
Information Systems	$ 0	$ 0	$ 277
Aerospace	$1,431	$1,279	$ 376
Products Manufactured for Consumers	$ 295	$ 569	$ 393
TOTAL COMPANY	$1,725	$2,416	$2,587

Kircher's acquisitions of Friden and General Precision gave him footholds in two new industries: information systems and aerospace. Despite having introduced the first distributed processing component in the form of the terminal/cash register called the MDTS, the Company had been ill-equipped to compete with the IBMs and Hewlett-Packards of the information systems world. Friden was Kircher's nemesis, and it brought him down. Flavin immediately eliminated it to avoid the same result. Aerospace, on the other hand, turned out to be a technology winner, right up Flavin's alley, and he devoted the time, energy, and resources necessary to develop it. Also, Singer's existing base in the manufacture of consumer products, such as power tools for Sears and household furniture from the Company's experience in making sewing machine cabinetry, was a modest growth opportunity. The sewing machine business was clearly not Joe Flavin's cup of tea. It was a non-starter from the day he arrived. It wasn't a business he understood, and he had little desire to learn. The only question had been how and when it would disappear. Looking at the resultant 1986 sales mix, one might wonder if by undoing Kircher's diversification effort to free the company from the dependence and risk of being a one-product company, Flavin hadn't gone full circle and remade Singer into another one-product company.

When viewed through the eyes of a shareholder who might have owned stock for the long-term, the results were improved, but still not stellar. The goal of a 10 percent operating return was as far from reality as it had been in 1974. Net income was positive, yet static. The outstanding debt had been reduced by more than half, with a corresponding improvement in the debt/equity ratio. Earnings per share were down, probably as a result of executive stock option awards for the turnaround. The stock price was up, but the P/E ratio was not what one might expect for a successful technology company. The market didn't appear to be valuing the new Singer as a technology company. Perhaps it was too soon to judge the longer-term results of the transformation. It could also have been that the securities analysts were having a difficult time relating the Singer name to anything other than sewing machines. The result, nevertheless, was a market capitalization of just under one billion dollars, less than the value in 1964, when the Company acquired Friden, and in 1968, when it acquired General Precision. The fact that Singer was now a much smaller company, with space-age technology and no retail businesses, had not gone unnoticed. Could the Company have become undervalued?

The Final Challenge

Singer's Offices Move to New Jersey

Montvale, N.J.—The Singer Company said it had moved its executive offices here from Stamford, Conn., possibly for protection from a hostile takeover bid…. ("Singer's Offices Move to Jersey," August 21, 1987)

Singer would not comment on the move, but in New Jersey, Singer would be protected by one of the nation's toughest anti-takeover laws, which stipulated that any investor buying at least 10 percent of a New Jersey company's stock in a hostile takeover attempt had to wait five years before completing the merger. The noise on Wall Street was unsettling, and Flavin was gearing up for a battle.

Business and the Law; States Protect Merger Targets

> FACING an unfriendly takeover attempt from T. Boone Pickens, the Texas oilman, and his Mesa Limited Partnership, executives of the Singer Company decided last week to do what any other besieged warrior might do: seek a safe harbor....

> Singer's move was perhaps the most graphic example of a trend by companies on the defensive in takeover battles to rely on favorable state laws. (Stephan Labaton, August 24, 1987)

Pickens Is Considering a Big Stake in Singer

(Thomas C. Hayes, August 8, 1987)

T. Boone Pickens was a notorious corporate raider and greenmailer who was most active during the 1980s. Using his company, Mesa Petroleum, as a base, Pickens would make solicited and unsolicited buyout bids, along with other more traditional merger and acquisition activities. Although many of his bids were not consummated, the publicity surrounding his offers frequently created interest in the target company's stock. By taking a significant ownership position in the target company, Pickens and his shareholders often reaped substantial gains, even if the deals were not concluded. His interest in a company was taken by the market to mean that he had found the target company to be undervalued. Among his better-known takeover targets of the era were Newmont Mining, Diamond Shamrock, and Koito Manufacturing, Ltd.

> Pickens announced today that his Mesa Limited Partnership owns the equivalent of 4.4 percent of The Singer Company and may buy up to 15 percent of the aerospace and electronics manufacturer.... Mr. Pickens could easily finance the purchase of all of Singer's 21 million shares.... A takeover could cost as much as $1.3 billion.... Singer's common stock jumped $.625 today, to $51.50, with more than a million shares traded....

> Joseph B. Flavin, Singer's chairman and chief executive, declined to comment on the Mesa announcement.... In jettisoning the sewing-machine business, Singer's revenues and profits both fell last year (1986).... In the second quarter, ended June 30 (1987) Singer took a charge of $45 million

to cover cost increases on several military contracts…. It lost $20.2 million in the quarter… (Thomas C. Hayes, August 8, 1987)

Then, Out of the Blue—

Joseph B. Flavin Is Dead at 58;

Led Overhaul as Singer Chairman

> Joseph B. Flavin, chairman and chief executive officer of the Singer Company, died yesterday at Norwalk hospital. He was 58 years old and lived in New Canaan, Conn.

> Mr. Flavin joined Singer in 1975 and oversaw its evolution from the world's best-known manufacturer of sewing machines to a military contractor…that draws 80 percent of its revenues from aerospace electronics. (James Barron, October 8, 1987)

Stocks End Mixed in Wild Day

> Singer, which has been the subject of takeover rumors, rose 1 7/8 to 55. The company's chairman and chief executive, Joseph B. Flavin, died unexpectedly yesterday morning. This heightened speculation on Wall Street about the company's vulnerability to a takeover. (Phillip H. Wiggins, October 8, 1987)

What would take place over the next six months was a drama worthy of a prime-time soap opera. It is perhaps best told through the *New York Times*' headlines.

CHAPTER TEN

Life Without Joe

William Schmied[62]

The unexpected death of Joe Flavin thrust Bill Schmied into the limelight with the combined responsibility of running the Company and fending off one or more anticipated takeover attempts. Schmied had joined Singer in 1969 to run its Kearfott division, a developer of inertial guidance systems acquired in the General Precision acquisition of 1968, and he had been appointed president and chief operating officer of the Company in 1980. When Schmied had joined the Company, aerospace operations represented only 12 percent of the business. By 1987, that business sector produced 80 percent of Singer's revenues. When asked about the possibility of a takeover attempt, Mr. Schmied said Singer had a "strong defense," including a greenmail provision. Before his death, Flavin had moved the corporate headquarters from Stamford, Connecticut, to a statutory presence in Montvale, New Jersey, in response to T. Boone Pickens's announced interest in Singer. Schmied pointed out that "New Jersey has a pretty stiff anti-raider law that makes it pretty tough for a raider to come in and strip the company of assets in order to pay for buying the company."

Less than two weeks later, on Monday, October 19, 1987, stock markets around the world crashed, in what became known as "Black Monday," losing huge corporate value in a short time. The New York Stock Exchange experienced a 23 percent decline, dropping 508 points to 1739. A degree of mystery is still associated with the 1987 crash. Potential causes cited for the decline included program trading, overvaluation, illiquidity, and market psychology. Whatever the cause, the crash provided some interesting opportunities for takeover specialists.

MARKET TURMOIL; Pickens Sees Plunge Spurring Takeovers

("Market Turmoil," October 28, 1987)

> ATLANTA—Depressed stock prices could lead to new corporate takeovers "within a week or so," T. Boone Pickens, the Texas oilman, said here today.
>
> "If companies were attractive targets when the Dow was at 2,500, they will be even more attractive with the Dow at 1,800."

Apparently waiting in the wings was a little-known but aggressively ambitious aspiring takeover artist named Paul Bilzerian. Whether he had been following the price of Singer shares or had taken a clue from Pickens's publicly announced interest in the company, he began to purchase Singer stock.

Bilzerian Holds 9.9% of Singer

> Paul A. Bilzerian, who has made repeated takeover attempts but never ended up owning his targets, disclosed yesterday that he owned 2.1 million shares, or 9.99 percent, of the outstanding common stock of The Singer Company.
>
> Mr. Bilzerian, who could not be reached for comment, told Reuters that he had paid an average of $43 for each of his Singer shares.
>
> The stock dropped $10, to $34.625, in the market plunge Oct. 19, and continued to fall in later days…. After his announcement yesterday, the stock closed at $42, up $9.75.a rise that presumably wiped out most of Mr. Bilzerian's losses.
>
> Mr. Bilzerian said that he would soon decide whether to go ahead with an offer for Singer but that he did not as yet have a financial advisor. He said that he had not yet talked with Singer management. ("Bilzerian Holds 9.9% of Singer," October 30, 1987)

WHO THE HELL IS Paul Bilzerian?

CORPORATE RAIDER: PAUL BILZERIAN;

A SCRAPPY TAKEOVER ARTIST RISES TO THE TOP

> CLASSMATES vividly remember their first glimpse of Paul A. Bilzerian at Harvard Business School's opening session in 1975.
>
> "Everyone was wearing jackets and ties…and this guy sticks his head in five minutes late. He's wearing blue jeans that look like he's been mining coal and a Stanford sweatshirt with holes in the elbow…"

Mr. Bilzerian, a takeover artist, can laugh about all that now. Today he has made at least $45 million…

Mr. Bilzerian's burst into the nosiness elite has not been without risk. Takeovers are nothing if not a game of bluff, and takeover artists have provoked wrath for treating companies as so many chess pieces…(his)…skill in accumulating huge blocks of stock in takeover candidates have thrust him under the scrutiny of the (SEC)…he received an SEC subpoena in March regarding four of his public deals…

Documents provided by Mr. Bilzerian suggest that…he might have been acting…in a way that was not adequately disclosed. The SEC is also studying the $125,000 paid by Mr. Bilzerian—purportedly for investment banking services—to Jefferies & Company, the West Coast stock broker that settled charges relating to the Wall Street scandal earlier this year. Boyd Jefferies, the firm's former chairman, has pleaded guilty to two felonies that involved the use of phony invoices…

Already people who once spoke freely about their liaisons with Mr. Bilzerian have grown cautious about linking themselves to him…he has remained somewhat of a mystery…until recently, his Florida base of operations consisted of a rented phone in the rear of a hardware store in one of his shopping centers…to…(his critics)…Paul Bilzerian's desire to own a company is an act…He has always been tight-lipped about his backers and his net worth…

One fact about his past is clear: Mr. Bilzerian was practically born to be a corporate raider. (Alison Leigh Cowan, May 24, 1987)

Although Bilzerian was not in the same league as Pickens, he was brash and very ambitious. Never having succeeded in completing a major deal, he was perhaps emboldened by Pickens's attraction to Singer into making an offer, even though he lacked the ability to finance such a transaction. His confidence was such that he would figure it all out when the time came.

Takeover Activity Resuming;

SINGER GETS HOSTILE OFFER

Paul L. Bilzerian, a Florida takeover investor with a history of unsuccessful takeover bids, offered $50 a share yesterday for The Singer Company. Singer…advised its shareholders to hold off action until it completes its review of the proposal by November 16…

Analysts noted that the (Singer) stock had dropped almost to $28 in the recent market collapse. But yesterday Singer rose $3.125 a share, to $47.25...Mr. Bilzerian said that his investor group would consider selling Singer's defense and electronics businesses...He added that the deadline for tendering the shares is Dec. 1...He (Bilzerian) said that most of the financing for the offer was in place..." (Alison Leigh Cowan, May 24, 1987)

Not to be outdone by an amateur, Pickens decided to climb on board to see what might happen. Even if Bilzerian failed, his takeover attempt would drive market interest and almost certainly an increase in the price of Singer common stock. For the time being, Pickens was content to let Bilzerian take all of the risk while he (Pickens) had very limited downside exposure.

Mesa Gets 9.9% Stake in Singer

T. Boone Pickens...announced today that he had increased his stake in the Singer Company to 2.1 million shares, giving him a 9.9 percent interest.... "We bought the stock based on its potential for appreciation of value... Mesa may buy more stock, sell its stock, make a tender offer for the company or seek board representation or control of the company through the board...for the time being, Mesa does not plan to seek to acquire or to obtain control of the company." (Peter H. Frank, November 10, 1987)

Singer management, nervous about the unwelcome interest in a merger, started going through the motions of inciting a bidding war. If it was going to be acquired, it would be by mutual consent, and then by anyone other than Bilzerian, who had made it clear that he wasn't interested in the survival of Singer as such. He had made the calculation that if he could find sufficient short-term financing to close a transaction, he could quickly sell off enough components of the company to both repay the lenders while leaving a substantial gain for himself.

Singer Acts to Bar a Bid by Bilzerian

...The Singer Company said yesterday that the directors had instructed senior executives to open discussions with potential buyers—including those who have indicated an interest in the company...It said that the alternatives included the sale of one or more operations, liquidation of the company, a joint venture, the placement of a block of securities with a friendly suitor or some other form of restructuring.

It said that it had also reached new agreements with officers to give two years' severance pay to five top executives and one years' pay to eight others if they were dismissed or lost status after a change in control...

Singer contended that the offer contained "many uncertainties," including terms that Shearson Lehman Brothers would not provide financing for the offer if the New Jersey Shareholder's Protection Act was deemed applicable to the offer...Mr. Bilzerian did not respond yesterday to a request for a status report on his financing arrangements. (Robert J. Cole, November 14, 1987)

Singer's attempts to find someone, anyone, to acquire it and avoid a Bilzerian breakup were falling on deaf ears. Flavin had made much of Singer's problems with the sewing business, and few were eager to take on those problems in return for the one or two technology units that were most appealing to them.

No Singer Bid from Allied Signal

Allied Signal said that it would not expand its military-contracting businesses, an announcement that analysts interpreted to mean that the company was no longer a potential suitor for the Singer Company.... Singer (shares) slipped 37.5 cents to $49.25. ("No Singer Bid from Allied Signal," November 18, 1987)

Singer in Talks

Pressing its defense against a $1.1 billion takeover bid from Paul A. Bilzerian, The Singer Company said it had begun preliminary discussions with a number of domestic and foreign companies...and had been furnishing these suitors with confidential data on Singer. ("Singer in Talks," November 20, 1987)

Seeing the difficulty Singer was having trying to find an interested substitute for himself, Bilzerian believed that his takeover attempt had a good possibility of succeeding. There remained a critical problem, however. He did not have sufficient funds or investor commitments to close a transaction, so Bilzerian began to try selling parts of Singer before he actually owned them.

Bilzerian Talks on Singer Bid

Paul A. Bilzerian, the Florida investor, disclosed that his financial advisors had contacted unidentified third parties about purchasing all or part of the military electronics and training systems divisions of the Singer Company.... Mr. Bilzerian also said that Singer officials were prepared to meet with him to discuss his $50-a-share tender offer.... Singer has previously rejected Mr. Bilzerian's offer. ("Bilzerian Talks on Singer Bid," November 21, 1987)

Although Singer had no desire to be acquired by Bilzerian, it agreed to provide him with certain financial information so long as he agreed to not increase his ownership position, allowing the company to stall while it continued what was becoming a frantic search for an alternative suitor.

Offer from Singer

> Paul L. Bilzerian, the Florida investor, said today that The Singer Company…had offered him access to certain nonpublic information if he agreed to purchase no more of the company's shares for 18 months. ("Offer from Singer," November 25, 1987)

Convinced that the company was worth more than Bilzerian's offer, Singer continued to resist in an effort to buy time in order to find another partner whose goal was to invest, rather than carve up the company and sell the pieces.

Singer Seeks a New Buyer

> The Singer Company said today that it was talking with potential buyers about being acquired…. They do not include Florida financier Paul Bilzerian…. Some analysts have said that Singer may be worth as much as $60 a share. Its stock closed Wednesday at $53, up 25 cents. The company's search for a new suitor suggests it is determined to steer clear of Mr. Bilzerian, who failed last summer in an effort to acquire Pay N Pak stores. ("Singer Seeks a New Buyer," November 27, 1987)

By now, Bilzerian seemed convinced that Singer would be unable to find an alternative to his bid and that management's concern had shifted from outright resistance to maximizing the economic value of whatever transaction ensued in order to avoid any risk of litigation from its shareholders. He offered a choice that he thought would respond to that concern.

Bilzerian Seeks Auction for Singer

> An investment group led by Paul A. Bilzerian, a Tampa, Fla., financier, has…proposed that The Singer Company be auctioned to the highest bidder by Dec. 15…. Singer…said on Wednesday that it was not ready to respond… Under the proposal, the Bilzerian group would be allowed to participate in the auction and, in return, it would extend its offer of $50 a share until Dec. 15. ("Bilzerian Seeks Auction for Singer," November 28, 1987)

Singer management seemed to confirm that its primary objective was litigation risk avoidance, saying it would only agree to a transaction at a price greater than the current market price per share.

Singer Committed to Sale or Merger

> The Singer Company said it wants to be bought or merged with another company by the end of the year…

> "We want the best price for the company," a company spokesman…said, noting that today's closing price of Singer shares, at $51.50, down $1.50, was still above Mr. Bilzerian's $50-a-share offer. ("Singer Committed to Sale or Merger," December 1, 1987)

Singer continued to resist the offer, while Bilzerian challenged the validity of the company's takeover protection under New Jersey law. Singer's options were narrowing.

Singer to Decide on New Partner

> The Singer Company…said that it planned to decide on a new partner by Dec.21…. (Singer) also said that it and Paul Bilzerian…had agreed to suspend their Federal court battle over Mr. Bilzerian's $1.05 billion offer until then…. A company spokesman said that the agreement did not mean that Singer had begun negotiating with Mr. Bilzerian, who has filed suit challenging a New Jersey law preventing a new owner from selling major portions of a company for five years after gaining control. ("Singer to Decide on New Partner," December 2, 1987)

Singer finally accepted the probability that it was going to have to deal with Bilzerian and announced that it would consider his offer, subject to his ability to demonstrate that he had the financial resources to close. Singer shares dropped and were finally below Bilzerian's offering price.

Singer Invites Bilzerian Bid

The Singer Company said late last night that it had notified Paul A. Bilzerian, the Florida investor, that he could complete his pending tender offer for the company if he could arrange the necessary financing and promptly complete the deal….

> In a statement issued last night, Singer said that its board did not have a sufficient level of confidence in the availability of Mr. Bilzerian's financing to recommend a tender offer….

> Singer's shares closed at $49…down 50 cents. ("Singer Invites Bilzerian Bid," December 21, 1987)

Now Bilzerian had a major problem. He did not have sufficient commitments to complete the deal. The banks showed little interest in financing a brash newcomer with insufficient equity and serious uncertainty that he could complete the expected selloff of Singer's businesses at prices that would permit them to be repaid. Now it was Bilzerian's turn to stall, as Singer shifted the pressure to him.

Amid Doubt, Bilzerian Extends Bid for Singer

> Amid growing uncertainty that he can raise the money, Paul A. Bilzerian, the Florida investor, extended his offer yesterday to buy The Singer Company for $50 a share, or $1 billion in cash, until 5 P.M. tomorrow….

> "Discussions with Bilzerian," said Singer in a statement, "have not given the company a sufficient level of confidence in the availability of Bilzerian's financing to cause the board to recommend the tender offer…," telling shareholders to "make their own determinations." (Robert J. Cole, December 22, 1987)

Bilzerian Remains Silent on Financing

> The Florida investor Paul A. Bilzerian gave no word about whether his partnership had obtained the financing it needed for his extended $1.06 billion bid to take over the Singer Company. ("Bilzerian Remains Silent on Financing," December 23, 1987)

Pickens to the rescue! T. Boone Pickens had been content to sit on the sidelines as Bilzerian did all the work for him. If Bilzerian failed to find financing, Pickens could step in and acquire Singer at the price of Bilzerian's offer. But Pickens had an even better idea. He could provide Bilzerian with the interim financing he needed to close, in return for which he could extract conditions from Bilzerian that would assure Pickens of a virtually risk-free high return.

Bilzerian Obtains Financing for Bid to Acquire Singer

> Paul A. Bilzerian, the Florida investor, announced yesterday that he had raised most of the money for his cash offer to buy the Singer Company….

> And in a surprise development, Mr. Bilzerian disclosed that he was negotiating with T. Boone Pickens, the Texas oilman, to invest $150 million in the venture…. The emergence of Mr. Pickens seemed to almost assure that Mr. Bilzerian will be successful…even though Singer was not yet ready to concede anything.

Moreover, a successful takeover is expected to touch off a dash among other major military suppliers for a piece of Singer, with Ford, General Motors, Chrysler, Boeing, Rockwell, General Electric and Litton Industries all expected to show interest…. A consultant to Mr. Pickens declined further comment…(but)…insiders said that deals of this kind typically provide that in exchange for their help, investors get a return on their money plus a share in the profits when various parts of the company are sold. (Robert J. Cole, December 24, 1987)

Bilzerian could now taste success—but not so fast. By now it was apparent that Pickens's financing offer was the only game in town, and Pickens was tightening his terms. Bilzerian continued to look for alternatives while he stalled Singer, who by now was demanding a response.

Bilzerian Extends Offer for Singer

The Singer Acquisition Company, the concern formed (created)…to take over (Singer)…extended its $50-a-share tender offer…until Monday….

Mr. Bilzerian said he was still discussing the sale of $150 million in junior subordinated notes with various parties, including Mesa Limited Partnership, a concern headed by T. Boone Pickens. ("Bilzerian Extends Offer for Singer," December 31, 1987)

Bilzerian stalled again, going so far as to claim he was in talks with another investor who (presumably) was willing to provide the necessary investment on terms more favorable than Pickens.

Bilzerian, Investor End Their Talks

The Florida investor, Paul A. Bilzerian said he had ended negotiations with an unidentified investor who he said had previously given an oral commitment to purchase $150 million in stock to help Mr. Bilzerian complete his $1 billion bid for The Singer Company….

An individual close to Mr. Bilzerian said he was still negotiating with various parties, including Mesa Limited Partnership…concerning the same $150 million…. ("Bilzerian, Investor End Their Talks," January 6, 1988)

If Bilzerian hoped to complete his first major deal, it was finally time to bite the bullet—which he did. The disclosure of Pickens's terms would await the final closing and would show that at the end of the day he could actually make more than $50 million on the transaction than Bilzerian, with little or no risk.

Bilzerian's Singer Bid Aided by Pickens Loan

> A $1 billion hostile takeover of the Singer Company seemed assured yesterday as Paul A. Bilzerian…announced that T. Boone Pickens…had agreed to provide the last $150 million needed to finance the deal.
>
> The Pickens group owns 2.1 million shares of Singer…so…its profit on just the stock should exceed $6 million. Its overall profit, however, is expected to approach $50 million because of the hard bargain that it drove with Mr. Bilzerian.
>
> Mr. Bilzerian said in a telephone interview that he planned some sales of Singer assets but hoped to meet with William F. Schmied, Singer's chairman, "in the next day or two" to discuss details.
>
> As for Mr. Schmied, who is 59 years old, Mr. Bilzerian said, "If he's willing to stay, we'd like to keep him." Acknowledging that he himself had never taken the helm at a major company, Mr. Bilzerian remarked: "I don't expect to run the company. I don't really want to." (Robert J. Cole, January 7, 1988)

From this point, the rest of the takeover consisted of formal acceptances and votes to approve the merger agreement. Schmied would stay for the transition and asset sales, for which he would presumably be well compensated.

Singer Board to Meet on Bid

> The Singer Company said yesterday that its directors had called a special meeting to consider a $1 billion takeover bid from Paul A. Bilzerian, the Florida investor.
>
> Mr. Bilzerian said yesterday that his group had approved the merger agreement and that he expected Singer to approve it, too.
>
> Asked about the future status of Singer's chairman, William F. Schmied, the company declined comment. Others close to the negotiations said that Mr. Schmied had agreed to stay while the assets were being sold….
>
> Mr. Bilzerian…had said that…he planned to dispose of the company's military business. Analysts said that, in addition to his basic $1 billion cost, he would assume Singer's $500 million debt, but could possibly recover everything by selling just the plants that do military work.
>
> On this basis, Mr. Bilzerian could keep Singer's remaining operations at no cost. Among those are tools made largely for Sears, Roebuck

& Company and gas meters sold to utility companies. ("Singer Board to Meet on Bid," January 13, 1988)

Singer Backs Bid

The Singer Company's board of directors approved a once-hostile $1.06 billion takeover bid by a group led by Florida investor Paul A. Bilzerian, and it recommended shareholders tender their stock. The Montvale, N.J., military electronics company said in a statement that its board considered the $50-a-share offer "fair and in the best interests of the company." In November, the board had rejected the offer and challenged it in court. Later, Singer put its challenge on hold and said it would acquiesce if Mr. Bilzerian could come up with the financing. The Tampa, Fla., financier has said he has the commitments. ("Singer Backs Bid," January 14, 1988)

Bid for Singer Extended

The investor Paul A. Bilzerian has extended his $50-a-share offer for The Singer Company until next Monday amid talks with Singer's banks about the company's credit status after the $1.06 billion proposed takeover. He also said Tuesday that almost 15.7 million of the 21.1 million shares had been tendered. ("Bid for Singer Extended," January 28, 1988)

Once Pickens had provided Bilzerian with the additional equity for the purchase, other investors and the bankers looked more favorably on the transaction and their exposure as Bilzerian began to dissect the company.

Singer Funds for Bilzerian

Paul A. Bilzerian…said today that he had obtained about $505 million in financing for his offer.

Mr. Bilzerian raised $355 million of senior subordinated debt and another $150 million from the Mesa Holdings Limited Partnership, a group headed by T. Boone Pickens, the Texas oilman.

In addition, Mr. Bilzerian expects to sign an agreement today with a bank syndicate led by NatWest USA for $540 million of debt. The execution of that agreement will complete the arrangements for the financing of the tender offer, which is valued at more than $1 billion. ("Singer Funds for Bilzerian," February 1, 1988)

The ordeal was finally over. The necessary shares were tendered by the stockholders. The financing agreements were signed. And the acquisition of The Singer Company by Paul Bilzerian was complete.

Singer Offer Ends

> The company established by Paul A. Bilzerian to acquire The Singer Company said that it had accepted more than 17 million shares in response to its tender offer of $50 a share, which expired Wednesday. The Singer Acquisition Company said it now owned about 90 percent of the aerospace and military electronics company. ("Singer Offer Ends," February 5, 1988)

And so it goes (with apologies to Kurt Vonnegut). The prospect for the survival of The Singer Company was over. The future of the sewing machine business under the Singer name was uncertain. The sewing business was still alive, but on life support.

CHAPTER ELEVEN

The Deconstruction of Singer

Paul Bilzerian[63]

Paul Bilzerian was running hard. He had a two-item agenda that he had to complete quickly. First, he needed to complete his plans to cash out on the Singer transaction in order to relieve pressure from the banks that had helped finance the takeover. Second, he wanted to make sure that his profits from the Singer takeover were not at risk of forfeiture in the investigations and litigation being conducted by the federal prosecutor and the SEC into some of his business transactions prior to the Singer takeover attempt. He would be preoccupied with these two concerns simultaneously for the next two years, and they are commingled in many ways. They are easier to understand separately.

Picking over the Bones

By March 30, 1988, the Singer/Bilzerian transaction had closed, Bilzerian had moved into the CEO's office at the Company's headquarters in Stamford, Connecticut, and he had replaced Bill Schmied as president and chief operating officer with Joseph J. Campanella, a former president of Sperry Aerospace. Schmied, who had helped build the aerospace and electronics businesses for Singer, had little interest in remaining. Bilzerian said that, "Now with Singer approaching the divestiture of those operations, it is understandable that Bill should wish to relinquish his responsibilities." Bilzerian indicated his desire to sell all of the company's military as well as the common and preferred shares of SSMC, Inc., which it still owned following the distribution of 70 percent of the shares of SSMC to the Singer shareholders as a special dividend. He also indicated that, for the time being, he intended to retain the power tool business that supplied Sears, Roebuck & Company and the gas meter division. William F. Andrews, the chairman of SSMC, indicated that he had already begun negotiating a purchase.

Bilzerian lost no time with the non-sewing components of his $1.06 billion acquisition:

- **July 5, 1988**: Singer announced an agreement to sell its Motor Products Division, the manufacturer of Sears' power tools, to Ryobi Ltd., of Japan, for approximately **$325 million**. A Singer spokesman said that, "Everything is up for sale, and potential buyers are examining the assets." The sale, if fully used to pay down the company's debt associated with the takeover, would reduce that debt by over 60 percent. ("Singer Agrees to Sell Motor Products Unit," July 6, 1988)

- **July 8, 1988**: Singer announced an agreement to sell its Link flight simulation and training systems division to CAE Industries of Canada for **$550 million.** ("Singer Agrees to Sell Flight Simulation Unit," July 9, 1988)

- **July 8, 1988:** Singer agreed to sell its education division for **$20 million.** ("Singer Agrees to Sell Education Unit," July 9, 1988)

- **July 15, 1988**: Singer announced the sale of its electronic systems division to the Plessey Company PLC of Britain for **$310 million**. ("Singer in Agreements to Sell 2 More Units," July 15, 1988)

- **July 15, 1988**: Singer announced the sale of its HRB-Singer division to the Hadson Corporation of Oklahoma City for about **$145 million**. ("Singer in Agreements to Sell 2 More Units," July 15, 1988)

- **July 29, 1988**: Singer announced an agreement to sell its American Meter division to Ruhrgas A.G. of West Germany for **$132 million**. ("Singer Divestment," July 29, 1988)

In less than four weeks, Bilzerian had concluded agreements to sell six units of the company for a total of approximately $1.5 billion (remember that the purchase price was $1.06 billion).

How He Did It

By the end of August 1988, Bilzerian had either closed or signed deals to sell seven of Singer's twelve businesses for a total of $1.7 billion. The five remaining businesses, along with some other non-operating assets, such as the stock of SSMC, Inc., were estimated to be worth at least another $632 million. Thus, after paying taxes, acquisition costs, and interest, Bilzerian's partnership would end up with at least $90 million, of which half would go to Bilzerian.

In a lengthy feature article in the *New York Times* entitled "How Bilzerian Scored at Singer," the author listed the following series of events that combined to create a "perfect storm" and allowed Bilzerian to succeed (Cowan, August 24, 1988):

1. The death of Joe Flavin, who would have fought the takeover with his considerable determination and skill. The successor management had little stomach for a protracted battle.

2. The October 1988 stock market crash, which frightened away potential rival bidders.

3. The insistence by Singer, or its investment banker, Goldman, Sachs & Company, that the company be sold as one piece. Potential friendly buyers did not relish having to break up the company to have the one piece they really wanted.

4. The change in the tax laws. On December 16, the very day when bids were due, Congress eliminated the provision in the tax code that permitted corporate liquidations to be tax-free, rather than taxable as either ordinary income or capital gains. Congress exempted any outstanding tender offers, such as Bilzerian's. The tax difference for Singer would have been an additional $175 million.

Bilzerian's sales pitch was intense. "…Mr. Bilzerian and senior management distributed more than 300 brochures in five countries, conducted slide-show briefings for some 70-odd finalists and opened a 'data room' with important documents available to buyers when the talks turned serious" (Cowan, August 24, 1988). During the process, Bilzerian changed his mind with regard to the Power Tool and Meter Divisions, which he had originally intended to keep as a base for further acquisitions. Instead, he preferred to cash out while he could.

Whenever a transaction as complicated as this winds down, it is always interesting to see just how each of the participants made out. The following table provides a good idea of how it went:

Results of the Singer-Bilzerian Transactions

Acquisition cost:	millions
Purchase of stock and options	$1,060
Repayment of existing Singer debt	650
Financing and other fees	103
Interest expense ($800,000 a day)	100
Severance payments	20
Total acquisition costs	**$1,933**
Divestitures:	
Motor Products	$ 325
Career Systems Development	20
Link Flight Simulation	550
HRB Singer	145
Electronic systems division	310
Dalmo Victor	175
American Meter	132
Kearfott	175
Remaining assets:	
Librascope	(These 4
Link Industrial	(Est 375
Link Miles	(in
Simuflite	(total
Mitsubishi Precision (40% stake)	Est. 40
SSMC	Est. 42
Total divestitures	**$2,289**
Estimated gain before taxes	**$ 356**
Taxes	Est. 100
Profit after taxes	**$ 256**
For Shearson Lehman	$ 26
For T. Boone Pickens	$ 52
For Bilzerian partners	(1/2 to Paul Bilzerian) $ 178

Staying Ahead of the Law

Paul Bilzerian had only a few months to enjoy his newfound wealth, for on December 22, 1988, the world would read:

Bilzerian Is Indicted over Deals

> Paul A. Bilzerian, the Florida investor who captured the Singer Company earlier this year, was indicted yesterday on 12 counts of violating securities and tax laws, conspiracy and making false statements to the Government. None of the charges relate to the acquisition of Singer.

The government contended that Bilzerian hid illegally hid his accumulation of stock in takeover targets by using secret accounts at the Jeffries & Company stock brokerage and then selling his holdings after the price of the stocks had risen. This investigation was publicly known and had been kicking around since the spring of 1987 and referred to Bilzerian's accumulations of stock in Cluett, Peabody, & Company, H.H. Robertson, & Company, Hammerhill Paper Company, and Armco, Inc. Bilzerian had made a $7 million profit for a group of investors on the sale of his Cluett, Peabody stock. He was said to have purchased 20 percent of Hammerhill through a secret account, made a tender offer for the remaining shares, and then sold his shares to the International Paper Company for a profit of $58 million. A week later, Bilzerian entered a plea of not guilty. He was released on a $500,000 bond and was ordered to surrender his passport. In April 1989, one of the twelve counts in the indictment was dropped.

In May 1989, jury selection began for a trial on the remaining eleven counts. Bilzerian's lawyer was expected to argue that no one had ever been tried criminally for these activities, which had always been dealt with as civil cases. Interestingly, the federal prosecutor in this case was one Rudolph W. Giuliani. The SEC indicated that it was conducting an investigation with the possibility of also bringing civil charges. As the case opened, Bilzerian contended that he had believed that he was in compliance with the law. If convicted, Bilzerian would be the first takeover artist tried for securities fraud since Ivan Boesky in 1986. Boyd L. Jefferies, implicated in the Boesky trial, was to be a primary witness in that of Bilzerian. In his trial, Bilzerian's primary defense was his own testimony. The judge prevented him from saying he believed that the documents he had sent to the SEC were true, ruling that he could not offer such a defense unless the Government was permitted to ask him about the advice he received from his lawyers, which is usually covered by attorney-client privilege.

On June 8, 1989, the Bilzerian trial went to the jury, and on June 9, 1989, he was convicted of nine counts of securities fraud, conspiracy, and making false statements to the Government. In response to a question following the trial, the jury foreman said of Mr. Bilzerian's testimony, "It wasn't that hot. There was not too much credibility."

On June 29, 1989, coincident with a lawsuit against Bilzerian by the SEC, he resigned as chairman and chief executive of the Singer Company, and on August 26, Walter A. Drexel was named chairman and chief executive of the Singer Company. Drexel had been a former chairman and CEO, vice chairman, and president and chief operating officer of Burlington Northern, Inc., and had come out of retirement for the appointment ("New Singer Chairman Is a Railroad Retiree").

On June 30, 1989, the Government filed a civil suit against Paul Bilzerian, seeking the disgorgement of $3.1 million in what it said were the illegal profits Bilzerian made in an attempted takeover of Pay N Pak Stores, Inc.

On September 27, 1989, Paul A. Bilzerian was sentenced to four years in prison and fined $1.5 million for the convicted nine counts of securities fraud, conspiracy, and other crimes. The judge said that his conviction was stiff in part because he believed that Bilzerian had perjured himself when testifying, saying that, "I do believe that if Mr. Bilzerian had not testified at all at the trial, his sentence would not be what it was." On January 3, 1991, a Federal appeals court upheld Bilzerian's conviction, and on April 10, 1991, the Securities and Exchange Commission won a court order barring Paul Bilzerian from future securities law violations and indicated it would now seek over $30 million in illicit profits from him (Kurt Eichenwald, September 28, 1989).

In October 1989, while free on appeal, Bilzerian changed the name of the Singer Company to Bicoastal Corporation and moved it to Tampa, Florida. The essential transactions necessary to ensure profitability for all concerned in the takeover had been completed. Since Joe Flavin had apparently vested all of the trademark rights to SSMC in the spinoff of the sewing business, the Singer name no longer had any substantial value to Bilzerian. Relocating to Florida, on the other hand, did have substantial value. Now Bilzerian's primary concerns were staying out of jail and preserving as much of his net worth as possible. Florida is one of several states with advantageous "homesteading" laws, designed to protect one's principal residence from seizure in bankruptcy. In Florida's case, the law provides for an unlimited homestead exemption, which doesn't cap the value of a home subject to the exemption. In citing that law, Bilzerian joined the ranks of other known people with financial difficulties who have availed themselves of the law, such as Kenneth L. Lay and Jeffrey K. Skilling, of Enron; O.J. Simpson; and Burt Reynolds.

Paul Bilzerian's house in Florida[64]

Finally, on October 16, 1992, Federal District Judge Robert Ward reduced the prison sentence of Paul Bilzerian to twenty months from four years. Bilzerian had been denied parole and because of the denial said that he had sentenced Mr. Bilzerian with the expectation that he would be paroled after serving one-third of his sentence and that he was shortening the term to meet his "original sentencing purpose" ("Judge Reduces Bilzerian Term," October 17, 1992).

And Now, Back to the Singer Sewing Business

During all of Bilzerian's travails, he still held the largest block of shares in SSMC, effectively controlling the company. Apparently there were businessmen in the world who didn't think that the sewing machine business was dying. The possibility that he might yet have valuable additional assets to sell piqued Bilzerian's interest, and to protect his control of the business, on February 6, 1989, he filed for permission from the antitrust regulators to raise Singer's stake in SSMC to more than 50 percent. In a separate filing, Vincent Tan, a Malaysian businessman, disclosed that companies that he controlled had acquired a 9.2 percent stake and might seek control. A week later, a company called Semi-Tech Microelectronics Far East Ltd. of Hong Kong made a $30-a-share cash offer for SSMC. So, within the space of a week, there were three bidders vying for control of this "dying business." And one of these bidders was an electronics company who would like to enter the sewing machine business. Irony abounded ("SSMC Attracts New Suitors," February 7, 1989).

The Singer board accepted the $30-a-share offer of Semi-Tech, only to have Vincent Tan come back, saying that he was prepared to offer more, and requested the same material that had been provided to Semi-Tech. Meanwhile, on February 27, Bilzerian, assuming that the sale to Semi-Tech was going forward, proposed transferring Singer's trademark and cash to Semi-Tech for SSMC's furniture business, an offer that Semi-Tech refused a week later. Bilzerian continued to talk with Tran about an alternative bid ("Malaysian Invesor May Bid for SSMC," February 9, 1989).

Then Bilzerian joined Tran to begin a joint tender offer at $33-a-share, causing the Singer board to reconsider the Semi-Tech offer, advising in a statement that a special committee of the board would consider the offer and advise its shareholders by March 10. On March 1, Semi-Tech raised its offer to $34-a-share. In response, Mr. Tran raised his offer to $37-a-share ("Semi-Tech Bids More for SSMC").

Finally, Semi-Tech raised its offer once more, to $38-a-share, for a total value of $206 million, as part of an agreement between Singer, Bilzerian, Tran, and Semi-Tech. Under the terms of the agreement:

1. Semi-Tech would acquire control of the company for $38-a-share.

2. Mr. Tran would have the right to purchase SSMC's Malaysian operations for $30 million cash and certain royalty payments.

3. Bilzerian would assist Semi-Tech in the transaction with $15 million in subordinated financing.

4. Bilzerian would acquire SSMC's furniture division for $40 million and sell all of the rights to the Singer trademark to Semi-Tech ("Semi-Tech Is Winner: $38 a Share for SSMC").

The Singer Company (now Bi-Coastal) was finally out of the sewing business, Semi-Tech (now Singer) was in the sewing business, Bilzerian (Bi-Coastal) was now in the furniture business, and Vincent Tran was SSMC's (Singer's) dealer in Malaysia. It was all very confusing, but everyone seemed happy with the way it turned out.

CHAPTER TWELVE

Confusion

Semi-Tech Microelectronics Although even less well known than Paul Bilzerian in the U.S. takeover world, James Henry Ting was very well known in the Hong Kong business community. The owner of Semi-Tech, Ting began his career as a small electronics manufacturer in Canada. Semi-Tech had developed a reputation for buying and successfully rebuilding companies in difficulty. Born Ting Wei in Shanghai in 1951, he moved with his family to Hong Kong in 1958. There, his father started a small garment business, but he died when James was thirteen. After high school, Ting moved to Australia, married an Australian woman, and immigrated to Canada, where he studied engineering at the University of Toronto. In 1981, he started a computer assembly company, Toronto-based Semi-Tech Microelectronics. Semi-Tech went public on the Toronto exchange in 1986. The company grew through acquisitions as Ting traveled between Toronto, Hong Kong, and the United States. In 1987, he negotiated a deal with a Chinese state-owned electronics group to sell them a 10 percent stake in Semi-Tech for $5 million. At virtually the same time, Ting negotiated a $270 million contract with the Chinese Ministry of Electronics Industry to manufacture computers in China and Canada. In the process of organizing his business interests, Ting had become highly adept at constructing a network of interlocking offshore companies. They would eventually become useful as a means of concealing the actual ownership of these companies and, more importantly, the movement of funds among them.

Yet Another Miracle Worker

Ting's ambition was to assemble a group of well-known retail distribution companies into a global manufacturing and sales network along the lines of a Japanese *keiretsu*, with consolidation of all of their manufacturing in China. As the essence of Ting's plan depended on the draw of world-class brands, he was naturally drawn to the Singer name. The actual manufacture and sale of sewing machines probably meant less to him than the power of the brand and the legitimacy the Singer name could bring to his enterprise, and the acquisition of Singer in 1989 became the linchpin of Ting's strategy. It was not an entirely crazy idea as far as the sewing machine business was concerned, and by the early 1990s it looked to the public as if Ting had turned the sewing business around. In June 1991, he announced that Singer (SSMC) was going public, with the sale of 15.6

million shares to be sold at a price between $16 and $19 a share. If successful, the offering would raise between $250 million and $300 million, which would be used to retire the debt he had raised for the Singer buyout. In the press release, Ting noted that SSMC had approximately 35 percent of the global market for sewing machines, in addition to which it marketed major household appliances through its nearly one thousand retail stores.

At the same time he decided to relocate and rename the company. Since its acquisition, the Singer Company had been located in Hong Kong, having been actually purchased by Semi-Tech Global, a subsidiary of International Semi-Tech Microelectronics, Inc. Ting announced that Singer's headquarters would be moved to the Netherlands Antilles, and its name would be changed to the Singer Co. N.V. and listed on the New York Stock Exchange. By August 1991, Ting was feeling less bullish about the offering and announced that the expected selling price of the shares would now be between $14 and $16 a share and the amount raised would be between $218 million and $250 million. No further mention was made of the New York Stock Exchange.

In 1992, Singer N.V. reported a sales increase of 29 percent to $818 million and a net income increase of 43 percent, to $62 million, with a net operating margin of 7.6 percent. In 1985, Flavin's best year, Singer had reported total sales of $2.4 million and net income of $83 million, with net operating margin of only 3.4 percent. Furthermore, Singer's total sales for that year included all of the product groups, of which sewing products accounted for only $568 million. It certainly looked like Ting had discovered something that had eluded Flavin. In March 1992, an article appeared in the *New York Times* that was very bullish about the future of sewing in the United States. In it, the author cited the Simplicity Pattern Company, which had a sales increase of 15 percent in 1991:

All About/Sewing in the Gray 90s, Women Are Headed Back to the Bobbin

> Most people in the industry credit the recession with the resurgence in home sewing. But many are hopeful that a more fundamental change in the American psyche will keep the industry buoyant long after the economy recovers…. This is part of the more global reaction to the self-indulgent 80s…. People aren't throwing money around like they did five or six years ago. (Stephanie Strom, March 29, 1992)

> While even the most talented are reluctant to wear a garment they had made for themselves, there is no such reluctance when it comes to baby clothes and home decorating. The new technology has rendered automatic the most arduous tasks, such as threading the needle and cutting the fabric. The creative home-sewer can even scan in a picture from almost any source,

such as a magazine, newspaper or photo, commit it to memory, accept the sewer's orders on color changes within the design image and produce a garment. "Singer reports that five years ago, 30 percent of its North American customers were first-time users, compared with 50 percent now." Because of their high pre-tax profit margins, all three of the major pattern companies had been acquired in leveraged buyouts, with some changing hands several times. (Stephanie Strom, March 29, 1992)

Singer N.V. seemed to confirm the turnaround. Results for the sewing business in the four years since Ting had acquired it from Bilzerian showed a marked improvement. Sales had grown by 78 percent, net income by 130 percent, and the net operating return on sales had improved from 6.8 percent to 8.7 percent.

Year	(Millions) Sales	Percent change	Net income	Percent change	Oper return
1994	$1,132	+ 8.8%	$99	+9.7%	8.7%
1993	$ 1,045	+10.0%	$90	0.0%	8.6%
1992	$ 951	+16.2%	$90	+44.6%	9.4%
1991	$ 818	+28.8%	$62	+43.4%	7.6%
1990	$ 635	n/a	$43	n/a	6.8%
1990–1994	**+78%**	**+130%**	**+28%**		

In July 1992, Singer N.V. announced that it would enter a joint venture with the Butterfly Company, run by the provincial government of Shanghai, to build a sewing machine factory in China. The venture, to be called Singer (Shanghai) Sewing Machine Co., would also set up retail stores in China to sell Singer products. Singer would finance the construction of the four-hundred-thousand-square-foot facility at an estimated cost of $20 million and own 70 percent of the enterprise, the largest domestic concession yet granted by China to a foreign joint venture. All machines would bear the Singer name, and production would ramp up in three phases. The first year would have twenty thousand kits supplied by Singer and assembled there. The changeover to full manufacture would occur in the second year, with a target of two hundred thousand units, and in the third year the factory would operate at its full capacity of four hundred thousand machines a year. Financing would come from the Singer Credit Company, a finance company formed by Singer and Semi-Tech ("Sewing Machine Venture Is Planned by Singer for China," July 30, 1989).

In August 1993, once again needing funds to continue his ambitious plans, Ting met in Canada with a group of investors in an effort to raise $850 million using a mix of common stock and zero-coupon bonds. The source of the funds would turn out to be the Bank of Canada's Dominion Securities and Kidder, Peabody. The use of the funds was less clear. The securities would be issued by Semi-Tech, his Canadian holding company. Semi-Tech (Canada) would send the funds to Semi-Tech Global (Hong Kong), which would invest them in Singer's developing marketing and manufacturing network. With the proceeds, Ting acquired, through Semi-Tech Global, 72 percent of the shares of G.M. Pfaff A.G., a German manufacturer of sewing machines with a long history of fierce competition with Singer at the high end of the household sewing machine line in Europe. A restructuring program was put in place to improve productivity, including outsourcing, relocating certain manufacturing facilities, focusing on developing countries for growth, and workforce reduction for efficiency. Pfaff's sewing machine operations had collapsed in the late 1980s, and it had begun to lose money. Its historic focus on industrial and high-end household machines had ill-equipped it to compete in the growth opportunities of the emerging markets. Singer would manage Pfaff for Semi-Tech Global for a fee. Singer and Pfaff would cross-source each other's products and cooperate on new product designs.

Ting was hardly devoting all of his time to Singer, as he was still focused on his goal of using Singer's brand name and global distribution network to build Semi-Tech into his own "*keiretsu*." Between 1986 and 1995 he had acquired, in addition to Singer, Sansui Electric Company, Kong Wah Holdings in China, and Akai Holdings Ltd., which itself had 160 subsidiaries. Ting's empire grew too quickly, however, and he had become more and more overextended. His ability to fund any losses by one of his companies in the event of a disaster was becoming seriously compromised. As he dug himself deeper into a potential hole, he kept changing the legal structures of his companies, moving their headquarters from one tax haven to another, and then moving large amounts of money between them. He had also learned the tricks of conglomerate accounting, which he used to hide suspect transactions and render the financial statements more and more difficult to understand.

Warning Signs

Times columnist Reed Abelson analyzed the Singer financial results for the past few years and came to several worrisome conclusions:

INVESTING IT;

Singer's Success Requires Reading Between the Bottom Lines

Analysts rave about the company's consistent earnings, which have risen for 23 consecutive quarters. And…Ting…wants people to consider the stock…as much a blue chip as DuPont or Coca-Cola. Only Singer isn't the real thing. Without doing anything illegal, and with the blessing of its independent auditors at Ernst & Young, the company employs a myriad of tactics to raise its profits. Nearly a fifth of the $98.5 million that the company earned last year came from sources other than basic operations. (Reed Abelson, May 14, 1995)

It sounded like the good old days in New York and Stamford. Abelson listed several of the signals that should have reminded investors to look deeper into the results:

- Netherlands Antilles: Financials needed only to be filed annually instead of quarterly—and even then with as much as six months' delay.

- Profits were too predictable: Virtually impossible with a company that does business in as many foreign currencies as Singer. Management would forecast earnings, but not sales???

- Incestuous relationships: Ting controlled both Singer and the holding company, Semi-Tech, and he was chairman and CEO of both companies. Only two of the eight directors were independent of Semi-Tech. One-eighth of Singer's net income was the result of dealings with affiliated companies, including $12.2 million in management fees, royalties, and $5.3 million of "interest income" from Semi-Tech Global.

- Included in the reported 1994 profits of $98.5 million were an unusual amount of one-time-only gains. These included a $4.7 million investment gain, foreign exchange gains of $600,000, asset sales of $4.8 million, the $5.3 million of interest income, and $2 million of consulting fees.

- Cash flow was questionable: The Company reported $46 million more of cash flowing in than had flowed out the previous year. However, $132.2 million came from increased borrowings, not operations. The operating cash flow was negative $29 million.

- Installment credit sales were threatening liquidity: Credit was extremely liberal in countries that represented half of the company's sales. In Turkey, for example, 100 percent of the sales were on credit, and in Thailand 85 percent were on credit. Overall, accounts receivable grew from 33 percent of total sales to 40 percent, and the length of time it took to collect those receivables increased from 105 days in 1993 to 146 in 1994.

In November 1995, The Singer Company N.V. announced that it would buy back the Singer Furniture Company, which it had spun off in the 1980s, as well as the Italian operation that made sewing machines. This might have been an indication of strong earnings and cash flow on the part of Singer N.V., except that the entity selling these units was Semi-Tech Global, a subsidiary of Semi-Tech Microelectronics. Apparently, Ting was going to buy from himself something he had sold to himself in the 1980s. The final price was to be determined by an appraisal under a 1991 agreement between Singer and Semi-Tech (Global or Electronics?). All of this was reported with a straight face as arm's-length transactions ("Singer to Buy Back Furniture Operation," November 14, 1995).

In 1997, the countries where Singer had its primary business activity entered a collective financial crisis, and sales of consumer appliances in Asia plunged. At the same time, Moody's downgraded the debt securities of Singer N.V. and Semi-Tech Corporation from senior to Ba1, noting that:

> ...expectations for the company's profitability and debt protection measures will remain under pressure...(and)...reflects concern about the predictability of Singer's overall business model as it expands further into emerging markets while attempting to shore up profitability in more established markets such as the US and Europe. (*Moody's*, February 19, 1997).

It went on to express concern, not only about Singer and Semi-Tech, but about Semi-Tech's other holdings, Akai, Kong Wah, and Sansui ("Moody's Downgrades Ratings of the Singer Company N.V. (Senior to Ba1) and Semi-Tech Corporation (Senior Secured to B1)," February 19, 1997).

Meanwhile, back in the United States, journalists optimistically covered the apparent resurgence in the sewing products markets:

Sewing: 30 Million Women Can't Be Wrong

> Today, nearly one-third of the country's adult female population—more than 30 million women, mostly college educated, between ages 24 and 54—are revving up their sewing machines....

> In 1992, $5.1 billion was spent on sewing and related supplies, up 21.4 percent from $4.2 billion in 1987.

> Faith Popcorn, the consumer-trends oracle who ennobled yuppie couch potatoes in the late 1980s by coining the word "cocooning" for their stay-at-home ways, sees sewing as an example of the thoroughly 90s do-it-yourself creativity she calls "ego-nomics." (*New York Times*, March 1997)

The article went on to attribute the change to an increased interest in sewing one's own clothes, driven by the Fashion Institute of Technology, the virtually instantaneous production of patterns for designer clothes, the increased cost of fashionable clothes, and do-it-yourself champions such as Martha Stewart.

In November 1997, Singer announced its acquisition of G.M. Pfaff A.G., the German sewing machine manufacturer from Semi-Tech Global. The public rationale was that the obvious synergy would significantly lower costs. This appeared to be another transaction between Ting and Ting as, once again, the participants were all owned or controlled by him. Approximately two-thirds of Pfaff's 1996 sales of $448 million were industrial sewing machines. Singer would purchase an 80.5 percent interest in Pfaff for $157.5 million, $82.5 million in cash and $75 million in Singer preferred stock. It was not clear where the cash would come from at Singer—more borrowing? This appeared to be a move to accumulate cash in Semi-Tech Global, which would then presumably be remitted to the parent holding company ("Singer to Acquire 80% Stake in German Manufacturer").

By this time the auditors for both Semi-Tech and Singer had become increasingly nervous. Ernst and Young, the auditors for Semi-Tech when it had raised the $850 million in 1993, resigned, and in September 1998, the Singer auditors Deloitte and Touche suspended their audit. In December 1997, Singer had appointed Stephen H. Goodman as chief executive and president of Singer N.V. and announced that it would close some plants and dismiss 5,968 workers, or 28 percent of its labor force. Singer would take a charge in the fourth quarter of $186 million. This appeared to have closed the accounting door on Singer's operations, but the horse (the cash) was already out of the barn. That same month, another article appeared in *The Motley Fool*, a publication of an investment advisory service, titled "Singer N.V.: How Did It Find Trouble?" In it, the author noted the confusion arising from the Semi-Tech/Singer corporate structure, the Pfaff transaction, the apparent closing of the sewing machine factory in Brazil, and the moving of production out of Germany to the nations of Eastern Europe for lower cost but higher risk—recalling the risk of expropriation that Singer had experienced in Russia during the revolution. Finally, the writer said, "Investing was supposed to be easier than this. With Singer, picking a good brand name with a battered stock price is not enough. Now one has to balance the fiscal solvency and political climate of where the next shop will open" ("The Singer Company N.V.: How Did It Find Trouble?" December 12, 1997).

The year 1998 was a continuation of the wreckage that had begun in 1994. Although sales had been relatively constant throughout the five years, the company was now losing over $200,000 a year. It looked like the grand plans for the sewing business were beginning to come apart.

Year	Sales	Net income	Operating return
1998	$1,260	$(207)	-16.4%
1997	$ 1,100	$(238)	-23.8%
1996	$ 1,308	$ 29	2.2%
1995	$1,223	$ 84	6.9%
1994	$1,132	$ 99	7.5%

Reliving a Bad Dream

While observers were speculating about the state of affairs at both Semi-Tech and Singer's sewing machine business, the corporate reality became clear. Akai Holdings Ltd., Semi-Tech's main Hong Kong subsidiary, had posted a $1.75 billion loss. In Germany, Pfaff filed for bankruptcy, and on September 14, Singer announced that it would seek bankruptcy protection under Chapter 11 while it devised a reorganization plan. The retail and manufacturing businesses would continue to operate ("Singer Files for Chapter 11," September 14, 1999).

Chapter 11 of the U.S. bankruptcy law was the most desirable jurisdiction for the Singer N.V., as the company was concerned about whether the courts of other nations would recognize the U.S. proceeding and enforce the plan against creditors who might assert that they were not subject to U.S. jurisdiction. Unfortunately, Ting had created such organizational complexities in an effort to minimize taxes that filing in the United States was not a simple matter. Singer N.V., which had begun as SSMC, Inc., the U.S. manufacturer of sewing machines, had changed its name initially to the Singer Company, then to Singer N.V., as well as changing its place of incorporation to the Netherlands Antilles. Simultaneously, it moved its headquarters to Hong Kong while retaining its administrative office, the functional headquarters, in the United States. By the time Singer filed for bankruptcy, it had changed, reorganized, or sold various units of its operations such that three-quarters of its employees were in Asia, Europe, Africa, or the Middle East. By virtually any standard, Singer was no longer an American company, and its parent, Singer N.V., was a Netherlands Antilles company. The next succession of steps were as confusing as Semi-Tech's accounting.

To solve the problem, Singer filed a motion seeking authority to create a new wholly owned U.S. subsidiary of Singer N.V. called Singer USA LLC (Singer USA). After Singer USA was formed, the proposal was to transfer all of Singer NV's assets (Singer NV's equity interests in its subsidiaries) to Singer USA and to cause Singer USA to guarantee all of Singer NV's liabilities. Thereafter, Singer NV's sole asset would consist of its equity interest in Singer USA.

The next step would be for Singer USA to file its own chapter 11 petition, thus bringing Singer USA within the protection of the U.S. bankruptcy court. The final step was to propose a chapter 11 reorganization for Singer USA that eliminated Singer NV's equity interest and issued 100 percent of the new equity in Singer USA to Singer USA's creditors, i.e., the holders of the obligations of Singer NV that Singer USA had guaranteed.

Stripped of its legalisms, Singer's strategy was to replace the Netherlands Antilles corporation with a newly minted U.S. one and bankrupt the new corporation immediately. The New York bankruptcy court confirmed Singer's plan, and it appears that no one challenged it elsewhere, either by ignorance or oversight (Lynn M. LoPucki, 2005).

During the bankruptcy proceedings, the court uncovered a curious set of transactions between Singer and its related companies, some of which have already been discussed. "In one, Singer paid $157.5 million to Akai, Ting's Hong Kong flagship, for shares in G.M. Pfaff—twice the value of Pfaff's publicly-traded shares. Pfaff then became a chronic money-loser, dragging down Singer. Singer also put down a $50 million deposit to buy an antiquated Russian sewing machine factory. The deal never closed, but Akai, according to court documents, kept $44 million of the money. These transactions came after Akai had already taken $1.1 billion out of Singer through stock and bond issues. The bankruptcy court found that the deals fatally weakened Singer" (*Bloomberg Business Week*, August 5, 2002).

At the start of 1999, audited statements showed Akai with $2.3 billion of assets and $262 million of cash. By year's end, the company had taken a write-off of $1.75 billion. When the court-appointed liquidators arrived on the scene a few months later, they found that Ting's "…companies had no businesses, staff or premises; the directors' records had huge gaps in them; and most of the directors and officers of Akai had left Hong Kong."(*Bloomberg Business Week*, August 5, 2002).

In December 1999, the Ontario Securities Commission issued a cease-trading order against James H. Ting and the other officers of Semi-Tech Corp. The OSC said that Semi-Tech was in arrears in its annual and interim filing obligations and had also failed to disclose any material information in respect of the affairs of Semi-Tech, Singer, and Pfaff ("Dishonored Dealmaker," August 5, 2002).

The failure of Akai was the largest corporate collapse in Hong Kong history. In June 2000, Ting sold his $5 million Hong Kong compound there and hadn't been seen in the city since meeting with creditors in 1999. Sources said that he was probably in mainland China, the place of his birth. Repeated efforts to reach him through his representatives were unsuccessful ("Dishonored Dealmaker," August 5, 2002).

CHAPTER THIRTEEN

A Savior?

SINGER N.V. [65]

Steve Goodman had been hired by Ting at the end of 1997 to be the president and chief executive of Singer N.V., although, through his control of Singer, Ting effectively remained Goodman's superior. Prior to joining Singer, Goodman had been a managing director of Banker's Trust Company. Now with the bankruptcy and reemergence of Singer N.V. (and the disappearance of Ting), Goodman became in reality the senior officer of Singer N.V. ("Singer Reorganizes and Emerges from Bankruptcy," September 16, 2000).

Cleaning It Up

Goodman shepherded the company through the trials of Chapter 11 and the reemergence of Singer as a functioning company. Under the Reorganization Plan, the outstanding shares of the Old Singer were cancelled and substantially all of the shares of Singer ("new Singer") were issued and distributed to all of the holders of unsecured claims approved by the court. Except for Goodman, none of the directors of Old Singer were appointed to the new board, all of whom were approved by the Creditors' Committee of Old Singer. Under the protection offered by the court, Singer had been allowed to continue as a stand-alone going concern throughout the bankruptcy proceedings. In the first Disclosure Statement issued by Singer N.V. in September 2001, the company reported its results for the first two quarters of operation since its reemergence ("Singer N.V.," September 2001):

Six months ended

(Millions)	June 30, 2001
Revenues	$217.6
EBITDA	$ 27.7
Interest expense	$(14.3)
Net income	$ 4.1
Total assets	$482.0
Debt	$226.2
Sh. Equity	$103.4

The company was profitable, with an operating return on $217.6 million of sales for the six months of 12.7 percent. More than half of the operating income was going to cover the cost of the borrowings, but all in all, it was not too bad considering what the company had just gone through.

It appeared that Goodman had saved Singer. But what exactly had he saved? When Don Kircher became president of the Singer Manufacturing Company (SMCo) in 1958, he inherited a company that had remained essentially unchanged for over a century. Singer manufactured and sold sewing machines and that was it. The Company might have added some factories and expanded into markets as they became more open, but Singer had pretty much covered the world during that period. Based on the financials, the surviving Singer was a pale shadow of its former self.

Ironically, the 2002 financial results of the new company for its first full year of operations were very similar to the financial results of the Singer Manufacturing Company for 1958—if one ignored the impact of forty-four years of inflation. The notable difference was the shift of a substantial portion of the shareholders' equity into borrowings.

Operating entities	Old Singer	New Singer
	1958	2002
$ Millions:		
Sales	$362	$ 338
Net income	$ 15	$ 19
Total assets	$445	$ 469
Borrowings	$ 48	$ 192
Shareholders' equity	$310	$ 122
Percent:		
Net return on sales	4.3%	5.7%
Return on year-end equity	6.4%	15.6%
Per share:		
Net income	$ 2.41	$ 2.35
Dividends	$ 2.20	$ 0.00

When the results in absolute terms for 2002 are compared with those of 1958, the sales, net income, and total assets are not substantially different and the net return on sales had actually improved, from 4.3 percent to 5.7 percent. If the results for 2002 were adjusted to reflect forty-four years of inflation since 1972, the result would be a Singer Company that was but a shadow of its former self. The sales of the company would have declined by 85 percent, and earnings would have declined by 80 percent. Curiously, the return on shareholders' equity would have substantially improved, but that would only be because the shareholders' equity had declined so much from the cumulative losses. Finally, dividends would have disappeared and the earnings per share would have declined by 96 percent because of the combination of the losses and the dilution of the shareholders' equity as a result of using the Company's stock as the vehicle for acquisitions. The common shares were not to be listed on any exchange, but were to be traded on the so-called Pink Sheets. Not surprisingly, the largest single asset of the new shareholder's equity of Singer N.V. was the Singer trademark, which was valued by an appraiser at $85 million. After having been battered about by the machinations of five CEOs over the course of fifty-odd years, the Singer brand remained the core of the Company's value.

The evolution of the organization was even more dramatic. The following chart demonstrates both the ambitions of Don Kircher as he pursued the conglomerate version of Singer, and the destruction of the basic sewing business as the direct manufacturing and distribution organization was reduced from 169 operating entities to twenty-two.

OPERATING UNITS*	Singer Mfg Co	Singer Co.	Singer N.V.
YEARS	1958	1972	2001
Sewing & Consumer Products:			
Production & Research	35	37	4
Sales Offices:			
United States	43	43	1
Europe	45	45	5
Far East	26	26	9
Latin America	18	18	3
Total sales offices -	32	32	18
Sewing Products	**167**	**169**	**22**
Consumer Products		9	
Total Sewing and Consumer Products	167	178	22
Industrial Products	25		
Office Equipment	2		
Defense & Space Systems	4		
Education & Training		4	
TOTAL OPERATING UNITS	**167**	**213**	**22**
NUMBER OF EMPLOYEES	**90,000**	**100,000**	**17,483**

Wrapping It Up

In April 2004, Singer N.V. announced its results for the year ending on December 31, 2003. Stephen Goodman appeared to be making some progress. Although the company was in breach of several covenants of the loan agreement with the Bank of Nova Scotia, enough progress had been made for the bank to waive them for the time being (Singer N.V., April 2004).

	2002	2003	% change
Millions			
Annual sales	$ 337.7	$ 382.8	+13%
Annual net income	$ 19.1	$ 20.3	+ 7%
Total assets	$ 469.0	$ 511.5	+ 9%
Borrowings	$ 192.3	$ 193.1	0%
Shareholders' equity	$ 122.4	$ 122.4	0%
Percent			
Net return on sales	5.7%	5.3%	
Return on yr-end equity	15.6%	16.6%	
Per share			
Net income per share	$ 2.35	$ 2.56	+9%
Shareholders' equity	$15.16	$15.41	+2%

Ready to Go Again

On October 1, 2004, Goodman announced that as of September 30, 2004, Singer N.V. had sold its worldwide sewing machine business and the ownership of the Singer trademark to KSIN Holdings, Ltd., an affiliate of funds managed by Kohlberg & Company, a U.S. private equity firm. KSIN would still have the right to use the Singer trademark as the exclusive distributer of Singer-branded sewing machines in its retail business, consisting of select emerging markets in Asia and Jamaica. Under the agreement, Singer N.V. would cease to use Singer in its name, which would be changed to Retail Holdings N.V. (RHNV). Its shares would continue to be traded on only the "Pink Sheets" under the symbol

RHDGF (Singer N.V., 2004; "Kohlberg Unit Buys Singer Brand and Business," October 2, 2004).

The total consideration that Singer N.V. received in the transaction consisted of approximately $134.6 million, of which approximately $65.1 million was cash, $22.5 million of unsecured subordinated notes, and payoff or assumption by KSIN of approximately $47.0 million of sewing-related debt. Of the $65.1 million of cash that Singer N.V. received, $26.3 million was used to repay in full the Bank of Nova Scotia debt. A balance of approximately $36.9 million in cash was uncommitted, but possible uses included investing additionally in the retail sewing business in its exclusive territories, a partial buy-back of the company's common stock, cash dividends, or investing in new businesses.

Goodman had pulled it off. He came out of it debt-free after selling a business that was in default on many of the bank covenants with the Bank of Nova Scotia, was extremely tight on working capital, had severe restrictions on the compensation for himself and the other executives running the company, and had no uncommitted assets. In addition, he retained exclusive rights to the fastest-growing sales region in the Singer world.

What Did KSIN Buy?

Frederick Bourne said it best:

> Our machines are of no value to the public until we make them so, our reputation as producers being of the most value…. The fact that it is made by this company is what gives it a reputation and nothing else.

The business that Kohlberg & Company bought consisted of the Company-owned marketing operations in the United States, Brazil, Canada, the Czech Republic, Hungary, Denmark, Sweden, Italy, Mexico, the Middle East, and Africa, South America, the Caribbean, and Turkey, as well as the manufacturing facilities in Brazil and China. In addition, they acquired a network of independent distributors and dealers in over one hundred additional markets. Singer N.V. booked an accounting loss on the sale of approximately $34.5 million, reflecting the difference between the consideration of $134.6 million received and the book value of the assets sold and liabilities assumed. That difference was primarily the goodwill associated with the Singer trademark (Singer N.V., 2004).

In the final analysis, it was the Singer brand that turned out to be indestructible, the brand that had taken 150 years to develop, reinforce, disperse, and repeat. It was the brand that had convinced Donald Kircher that the Company was well enough known and respected that he could play in the big leagues of the conglomerates, even though the expansion was dependent on the continuing success of the sewing machine business. It was the brand that had convinced Joseph Flavin he could venture outside of the sewing business while ignoring the Company's cultural connections with Singer's past and its worldwide audience. It was the brand that convinced Paul Bilzerian that he could easily sell the undervalued non-sewing assets that remained after the Kircher and Flavin debacles. And it was the brand that convinced Joseph Ting he could convince the public and investors that he was really a legitimate businessman. And finally, Kohlberg & Company were convinced that the brand was worth saving.

CHAPTER FOURTEEN

Re-Birth?

Who Is Kohlberg & Company?

 [66]

Jerome Kohlberg Jr. co-founded Kohlberg & Company in 1987, retired in 1994, and passed away in 2015. He is best known as the senior founding partner of the firm that continues to bear his name, Kohlberg Kravis Roberts & Co. ("KKR"), one of the preeminent leveraged buyout firms in the country. Born in New York City in 1925, Kohlberg attended high school in New Rochelle, New York, and went on to receive a BA from Swarthmore College in 1946, an MBA from the Harvard Business School, and an LLM from the Columbia Law School.

In 1955, Kohlberg joined Bear Stearns, rising to the level of senior partner. He was in charge of the investment banking and corporate finance activities. In 1969, he was joined by two recent college graduates, Henry Kravis and Kravis's cousin, George R. Roberts. At the time, Kohlberg practiced an investment banking technique that he called "bootstrap acquisitions," seeking undervalued companies and helping the companies' management borrow sufficient capital to buy out the business for themselves. Seeing this as an opportunity that didn't interest Bear Stearns and was largely overlooked by the investment banking community, Kohlberg and his two young colleagues left Bear Stearns in 1976 to form KKR. For the next six years, KKR created a series of limited partnerships for the purpose of acquiring companies that were underperforming or undervalued. They would reorganize them, sell their underperforming assets, and then sell them. Typically, they would put up 10 percent of the buyout price from their own funds and borrow the rest from investors by issuing "junk bonds," frequently through Drexel Burnham Lambert.

Over time, Kohlberg became unhappy with Kravis's focus on ever larger leveraged buyouts, his willingness to attempt hostile takeovers, and the KKR practice of helping management buy up the stock of a publicly traded company and take it private. Management would then attempt to improve the profitability of the company through layoffs and the sale of unused assets or underperforming subsidiaries. They would then take the company public in a new IPO that would yield substantially more than they had originally paid for the stock (Jerome Kohlberg Jr., 2014).

Unwilling to participate in the evolution of the KKR strategy, Kohlberg left the firm in 1987 to form Kohlberg & Company with his son James A. Kohlberg, the firm's current chairman. Since that time, the company "… has organized seven private equity funds, through which it has raised $5.3 billion of committed capital." Kohlberg has completed transactions with an aggregate value of approximately $9 billion. Its focus continues to be on middle-market companies "…where it can work in partnership with senior management to identify growth opportunities and implement fundamental operating and strategic changes, resulting in substantial increases in revenue and cash flow."

Holdings of Kohlberg & Company at May 1, 2015, were:

- AGY Holding Corporation: A manufacturer of high-performance materials

- AM Conservation Group: An integrated provider of energy-efficient services and products

- Aurora Products Group, LLC: A manufacturer of burial, cremation, and technology products for the funeral industry

- BioScrip, Inc.: A provider of home infusion therapy

- Chronos Life Group: A life settlement products and services company

- Concrete Technologies Worldwide, Inc.: A manufacturer of capital equipment for the production of concrete pipes and manholes

- E+ Cancer Care: A leading operator of outpatient cancer care centers

- Katy Industries, Inc.: A manufacturer of janitor and sanitary products

- NBG Home: A global designer, manufacturer, and marketer of home décor products

- Nellson Nutraceutical, LLC: A contract formulator of branded and private-label nutraceutical products in the United States

- Performance Sports Group, Ltd.: A leading designer, marketer, and manufacturer of hockey, lacrosse, baseball, and softball equipment

- Pittsburgh Glass Works, LLC: A leading manufacturer and supplier of windshields and sunroofs

- PPC Industries, Inc.: A manufacturer of specialty plastic solutions for medical/pharmaceutical, food processing, and niche industrial applications

- Risk Strategies Company: A commercial property and casualty and employee benefits insurance brokerage firm

- Sabre Industries, Inc.: A leading provider of engineered structures for the electric transmission and distribution ("T&D") and wireless communications end markets

- SP Plus (f/k/a Standard Parking Corporation)

- Stanadyne Corporation: A manufacturer of fuel pumps and fuel injection equipment

- Troon Golf, LLC: A third-party management company centered around golf and golf-related hospitality

- SVP Worldwide, LLC: The largest consumer sewing machine company (Kohlberg & Co., 2015).

The sewing machine business had been rejected by a series of presumably intelligent and capable executives, either because they didn't believe in the future of sewing machines or they didn't know how to make money in the business. Don Kircher had a pessimistic view of the future of sewing. The changing role of women after the war, the aggressive competition from Japan, and the emergence of attractive and inexpensive ready-to-wear garments convinced him that the opportunity for growth in the market was limited. Joe Flavin found the sewing machine business dull and difficult. A product of IBM and Xerox, he was naturally drawn to the technology field, where he saw unlimited growth potential. The sewing business was a grind for him under the best of circumstances. Paul Bilzerian had no interest in any of the Singer businesses. For Bilzerian, they were merely chips in a poker game that he had won. All that remained was to cash them in with the highest bidder. James Ting was an empire builder, trading on the renown of the Singer brand to assemble a patchwork of companies with no unifying theme. Ting lacked the ability to manage the empire, and when it began to collapse, he ran with whatever he could grab on the way out. Stephen Goodman was a caretaker of the brand. Financially trained, he apparently had no desire to operate the company, but he was smart enough to allow those with the necessary operational experience to bring the much-reduced company back to modest profitability. As soon as he found a buyer interested in Singer, he was content to withdraw into his own business model, built around a subset of the sewing business, the emerging markets of Asia. He created a loyal and ambitious base of entrepreneurs in each of the countries that he retained by selling them a significant equity interest in the local company, while he retreated to manage a lean financial holding company.

Why Would Anyone Buy Singer?

First, the market for sewing appeared to be emerging from the doldrums, with significant growth opportunity ("Sewing Machine Markets in the World—Market Size, Development, and Forecasts," April 2015; Laura M. Holson, July 2012).

In 1997, James Ting was being chauffeured around Hong Kong in his Rolls-Royce while simultaneously trying to prop up his empire with the purchase of Pfaff for twice the price Pfaff's stock commanded on the Frankfurt Stock Exchange. At the same time, there was the first indication of optimism for the sewing machine market. In a *New York Times* article entitled "Sewing: 30 Million Women Can't Be Wrong," it was reported that "...nearly one-third of the country's adult female population...more than 30 million women, mostly college-educated, between the ages of 24 and 54...are revving up their sewing machines" (March 2, 1997). The reasons cited for the renewed interest in sewing were: (1) relaxation, citing a study that concluded that sewing reduced heart rates, blood pressure, and perspiration rates; (2) styles and sizes in colors not available in stores; and, finally (3) to save money. Here was the "creative sewing" motivation that in the 1970s Singer had counted on to revive its sales of high-end machines in the United States and the developed countries of Western Europe. The motivation took longer to develop than expected, but the trade organizations seemed to feel that it had finally arrived. The shift was helped by the new emphasis on do-it-yourself projects championed by the likes of Martha Stewart and promoted seemingly everywhere by a whole new coterie of project-oriented magazines and TV shows.

Second, all of the problem businesses had either been closed and written off or sold. The bloodbath had taken the better part of thirty years to recede, but it appeared to be finally over. Singer was back to its original core business with significant modifications along the way. It had closed all of its major factories, moved most of its production to China and Brazil, and transformed most of its direct, company-owned, and operated distribution network into a network largely made up of free agents and exclusive dealers.

Third, the price was ridiculously low. In the reorganization plan for Singer's emergence from bankruptcy, the court valued the Singer trademark at $85 million, based on independent appraisal. At $65.1 million, Kohlberg was effectively paying for less than the value of the brand. Everything else was either paid for by the debt holders or was free. Or, conversely, Kohlberg had purchased all of the tangible assets for $65 million and had acquired the brand for nothing.

Fourth, both seller and third-party financing were available. The stated purchase price of $134.6 million of purchase price consisted of $65.1 million of cash, $22.5 million of subordinated promissory notes, and the assumption by KSIN (Kohlberg's holding company) of $47.0 million of sewing-related debt. Since the debt could be repaid from operations, Kohlberg had put up only about 48 percent of the stated purchase price.

Fifth and most importantly was the Singer name. The brand was the critical asset that Kohlberg must have really been seeking. Singer was still one of the most recognized brands around the world, with an image of quality and dependability that remained largely undisturbed despite thirty years of tumult. The brand was so strong that it had tempted CEOs to use it to sell products far removed from the basic sewing machine business. Kohlberg seems to have decided that the sewing business had an attractive future and that the best way to enter that market was with the Singer brand.

What Did Kohlberg Actually Buy?

The entity that Kohlberg purchased was the worldwide Singer sewing machine business, less its 56.8 percent equity investment in the Singer retail distribution business in Singer Asia Ltd. (Bangladesh, India, Indonesia, Pakistan, the Philippines, Sri Lanka, Thailand, and Vietnam), and its 100 percent equity investment in Singer Jamaica Ltd. Those investments remained with Singer N.V., which was renamed Retail Holdings N.V. In the year prior to the sale, Singer N.V. had revenue of $383 million and an operating income of $34 million. A breakdown of the revenue and operating income split between Singer and Retail Holdings N.V. for the year before the acquisition was not available. However, since the Retail Holdings' relationship with its Asian holdings were as equity investors, the results were probably reported as income from affiliates, below the operating income from Singer operations, which would show the following results for the year ending on December 31, 2003:

	Twelve months Consolidated	Less equity In affiliates	Singer as acquired
Revenues	$382,793	0	$382,793
Operating income	$ 33,397	0	$ 33,397
Income—affiliates	$ 5,800	$(5,800)	$ 0
Operating income	$ 27,597	$(5,800)	$ 21,797
Percent of revenue	5.7%		

While an operating return of 5.7 percent is nothing to brag about, it is an order of magnitude better than anything the Singer Company had seen in quite some time. Kohlberg's cash purchase price was about five times the EBITDA, a bargain if you believed in the future.

How Did Kohlberg Manage the Company?

Singer N.V. was acquired by a Kohlberg entity called SVP Worldwide—and the meaning of the name will become clear. The Kohlberg representative on the SVP board of directors is Samuel P. Frieder, the managing partner of Kohlberg & Company. Given his extensive background in corporate finance, his membership on ten of the nineteen boards currently in the portfolio, and his responsibilities for originating and executing new investments, it is unlikely that Mr. Frieder would have much time to devote to the minutiae of the sewing machine business. He would properly rely on the senior management of SVP and other colleagues at Kohlberg who had some relevant experience.

In 1993, Joseph Ting, the then owner of Singer, had acquired control of the household sewing machine business of G.M. Pfaff A.G. Subsequently, he had been obliged to relinquish control as part of his 1999 bankruptcy, and Pfaff had been sold to the Swedish VSM Group, which owned the Husqvarna Viking brand of sewing machines. Following its acquisition of Singer in 2006, Kohlberg acquired the Swedish VSM Group and it now manages the three brands jointly under a holding company created for the purpose, called SVP Worldwide (Singer–Viking–Pfaff). As result of these transactions, Kohlberg united all but one of the old competitors of the European high-end sewing machine market, along with Singer's worldwide distribution network, to sell the full line of sewing machines. Only Elna, the Swiss manufacturer of high-end industrial machines, escaped, as it had been sold in 2006 to the Janone Sewing Machine Company of Tokyo. The headquarters of SVP Worldwide is now located in La Verne, Tennessee.

Now that Kohlberg had assembled a powerhouse product line and an international distribution system, what were Kohlberg's plans for the company? The combination of brands allowed the company to provide products across all price points. While historically Singer has produced a full line of machines, it is best known for sturdy and simple sewing machines for beginners, simple enough to be used in third-world countries lacking electricity. Pfaff and Husqvarna are aimed at experienced seamstresses and industrial users. Some of these high-end machines can cost several thousand dollars, can sew detailed embroidery or quilting work, and can be computerized. As for manufacturing, plants have historically been spread across the globe. In January 2010, SVP announced a shift in manufacturing from its Swedish plant to a Chinese facility the company had owned for some time.

Kohlberg & Company is a private equity firm, with the emphasis on "private." It does not comment on the business strategy for any of its holdings, and it is not required to announce any financial results. The public must glean what it can from the generic statements issued by the company. Here is the complete statement concerning the company's existence, mission, and ownership:

About SVP Worldwide

SVP Worldwide is the world's largest consumer sewing machine company and source of the SINGER, HUSQVARNA and PFAFF sewing machine brands.

As a global leader doing its business through affiliated companies in over 180 countries, SVP Worldwide specializes in the design, manufacture and distribution of innovative consumer and artisan sewing, quilting and embroidery machines, accessories, embroidery designs and software.

Ownership

SVP Worldwide is owned by Kohlberg & Company. The global enterprise is headquartered in Hamilton, Bermuda with regional administrative offices in the U.S. and Sweden. (Kohlberg & Co., 2015)

The only information of potential use in guessing about the company's plans is the number of countries in which the company operates. The 2010 version of this statement indicated operations in 190 countries. By 2014 this had been revised downward to 180. Beyond this brief statement, all of the other SVP press releases have been promotions for new machine models, software, and marketing events.

That is, until…March 12, 2014.

Ready to Go Yet Again—Any Takers?

Exclusive—Kohlberg Looking to Sell Singer Sewing Machine Company: Sources

The Singer sewing machine company, largely credited with helping develop the U.S. fashion industry by allowing clothes to be made more cheaply and efficiently, is exploring a sale that could fetch more than $500 million, three people familiar with the matter said today....

The company has roughly $65 million in annual earnings before interest, taxes, depreciation and amortization (EBITDA), the sources said. It sells its products in more than 170 countries and has a greater than 30 percent global market share, according to the Kohlberg website. ("Exclusive—Kohlberg Looking to Sell Singer Sewing Machine Company: Sources," March 12, 2014)

Curiously, no mention is made of the Husqvarna or Pfaff brands being up for sale. It is Singer and only Singer, not SVP, which Kohlberg is trying to sell. A suggested price of $500 million with an EBITDA of $65 million suggests that Kohlberg has made impressive strides in improving the profitability of the sewing business. However, without an analysis of the complete financial statements, it is impossible to tell.

In April 2015, a research firm by the name of Market Research Store issued a report entitled "Sewing Machine Markets in the World to 2019—Market Size, Development, and Forecasts." At a cost to single users of $13,634, the report was beyond the resources of this author. Nevertheless, some of the statistics included in the summary designed to sell the report should certainly been of interest to Kohlberg:

- The expansion of the global sewing machine industry is forecasted to reach 3.7 percent p.a.

- Between 2008 and 2014, the market increased with an average annual growth of 7.5 percent.

- Currently, automatic sewing machines account for 36.4 percent of global demand.

- Bangladesh, China, India, the United States, and Vietnam represent the largest sewing machine markets.

- The strongest annual growth is forecasted to occur in the United States (12.4 percent), Bolivia (8.3 percent), the Philippines (7.6 percent), Vietnam (7.4 percent), and Kyrgyzstan (5.4 percent).

If these forecasts turn out to be remotely true, the sewing machine industry will soon enter a period of growth that it hasn't seen in over fifty years, and Kohlberg may have been a perceptive buyer of a world-class brand.

One can find an indication of how the global sewing machine market has evolved during the Kohlberg ownership by examining the results of Retail Holdings N.V., the part of the old Singer N.V. that Kohlberg did not buy. Since Retail Holdings has significant publicly traded minority interests in each the countries where it does business and it is obliged to publish an annual report that identifies its results by country, a comparison of the evolution of revenues over the past nine years provides an interesting picture.

	2005 Revenues	2013 Revenues	Percent change
Thailand	$122.5m	$ 110.0m	- 10%
Sri Lanka	$108.2m	$ 196.6m	+ 82%
Bangladesh	$ 26.8m	$ 83.9m	+313%
Pakistan	$ 19.2m	$ 23.7m	+123%
India	$ 7.2m	$ 36.4m	+505%
Philippines	$ 7.6m	—	—
Indonesia	$ 1.0m	—	—
Vietnam	$ 0.8m	—	—
Other	—	$ 1.6m	—
Total	$293.3m	$452.1m	+ 54%

Overall growth has been stronger than predicted for the global market for sewing machines. This should be viewed with caution, since in 2013 sewing machines represented only 14 percent of the total revenues of these countries. The balance consisted of home appliances (49 percent), consumer electronics (17 percent), IT products (6 percent), and furniture (3 percent). These are much more general household appliance stores than sewing centers. Nonetheless, Retail Holdings N.V. generated pre-tax income of $27 million in 2013, 6 percent of revenues, following the same product strategy that Singer was using in these countries fifty years ago. With the right mix of products, distribution networks, and entrepreneurial motivation, it seems to have worked.

CHAPTER FIFTEEN

Conglomeration Today

Who Succeeded in the Conglomerate Wars?

Don Kircher was a casualty of the conglomerate movement, whether due to a faulty strategy, poor implementation, or just plain bad luck. But he was not alone. None of the pioneers of the movement came out unscathed. Some have disappeared completely, along with their companies. Others have presided over a long, slow retreat until they are today a shadow of their former selves. And a few have adapted, turning their backs on the conglomerate model in an effort to make their way forward with that which they knew best—their original core businesses ("Multiple—Textron, Litton, LTV, Gulf & Western & ITT Histories," 2014).

Royal Little (Textron)

Little's tenure at Textron began in 1928, with the founding of Special Yarns Corporation, and it ended with his retirement in 1962. However, the company was founded as, and remained, an acquisitive textile company for the first twenty-four years of its existence. It wasn't until 1952 that Little and his company had the means to launch what was arguably the world's first conglomerate by making acquisitions outside of Textron's core business (Funding Universe). He was a compulsive acquirer who preferred to look for targets of opportunity rather than follow a defined diversification plan. His stated policy was to "be sure to pick a company whose board of directors isn't smart enough" to fight back (Funding Universe). Little was insightful enough to recognize his weaknesses, and in 1956 he hired a banker, Rupert Thompson, to calm his impulses to shoot at any moving target. With Thompson's help, he built what would eventually become a well-diversified manufacturer of tools, industrial machines, consumer goods, plastics, appliances, and helicopters (Bell Aircraft).

Little retired at the top of his game in 1962. Thompson succeeded him and continued to build the company through acquisitions until 1968, when he was diagnosed with cancer and retired. Thompson was then succeeded by G. William Miller, who attempted to follow the company's diversification strategy but failed in attempts at major takeovers of United Fruit, the Kendall Company, and Lockheed. By 1978 he had apparently become more interested in politics than acquisitions and Textron when he was appointed the chairman of the Federal Reserve

Bank. His tenure at the Fed was cut short when barely a year later President Carter appointed him to be secretary of the treasury.

Miller was replaced by Joseph Collinson, who was soon replaced by the team of Bob Straetz as chairman and Beverly Dolan as president. These men were more inclined to divest problem companies rather than attempt to turn them around, and they began to sell anything not related to aerospace or technology (a strategy remarkably similar to Joe Flavin's philosophy at Singer). They would dump, without notice, any division that didn't perform, and they ended up consolidating the business around Bell Aerospace, where they tried to develop a commercial market for helicopters. Textron itself was the target of an unsuccessful takeover by Chicago Pacific Corporation in 1984, and in 1985, from a desperate need to reduce its debt, Textron announced its intent to sell Bell Aerospace and transform itself from a conglomerate to an operating company.

Royal Little's most lasting legacy to the conglomerate universe was his belief that the management he acquired was at least as important as the businesses their companies were in. Once acquired, he would manage those businesses as a portfolio, with a small staff to oversee their financial results, and he would delegate almost all of the operating decisions to the managers he had acquired. With the Bell Aerospace announcement, Textron was abandoning Little's philosophy.

Fortunately, the company's financial position improved and the sale was postponed. Textron reorganized into two operating units: Bell Aerospace and Textron Marine Systems. The company went on to renew its conglomerate strategy and by the late 1980s had evolved into a company with thirty-two operating companies in three groups: aerospace, commercial products, and financial services. By 1992, revenues reached $8.3 billion, with aerospace contributing over thirty-seven of the company's profits, financial services contributing 43 percent, and commercial products contributing 20 percent. It remains one of the most successful conglomerates today.

Tex Thornton (Litton)

The rapid expansion of Litton required more attention to the management of the enterprise than Thornton was able or willing to give. He often acquired talented management with the new companies, but many chose not to remain. Some became discouraged by Thornton's failure to deliver on his pre-acquisition promises of resources for development. Others were content to cash out and pursue other interests. Whether by a carefully considered management philosophy or the fact that he had little or no interest in day-to-day operations, Thornton professed belief in a decentralized and largely autonomous management structure, rather than an extensive headquarters where the significant operational decisions would be made by functional staff at the top.

Thornton's strategy of growth through acquisition by finding "bargains" inevitably caused earnings to suffer. If companies were "bargains," there was often a good reason for it. Some were run by families who wanted to cash out, and Litton lost their management skills. Some had innovation problems and were being outperformed by their competition. Some were in dying markets. By 1967 profits flattened and the stock price peaked. It became more and more apparent that the growth in earnings had been the result of some very creative accounting and not the value added of the company. By 1967, Litton was a giant in the military electronics business, as it had been in 1954, but not much more. Never discouraged, Thornton continued to promote the bold ideas that had characterized Thornton's Litton, and investors continued to support the company.

Then, in 1968, the company reported a decline in its quarterly earnings and the illusion ended. Within three months, the company's common stock lost half its value (Sobel, p. 74). Late the same year, Litton announced a further earnings disappointment for the first quarter of the following year. Thornton blamed the decline on "deficiencies of management personnel." Not surprisingly, senior managers began to look elsewhere for opportunities. The fantasy that Litton was and would continue to be a growth company had been exposed. Finally, in 1972, after three years of declining profits and a forecast that the company's sales would revive, the Company recorded a loss of $2.3 million. Thornton replaced his president with an engineer whom he hired to reduce the number of subsidiaries and improve its technological competence. In 1981, Thornton died of cancer at the age of sixty-eight. By 1986, Orion Hoch, who succeeded Thornton as chief executive officer, had overseen the divestment of fourteen major unprofitable and unrelated businesses representing over $1 billion in sales. Litton exited the industries of business machines, publishing, medical products, office furniture, and microwaves. As the company unloaded its losing businesses, it coalesced around the successful ones, and by end of the 1980s it finally became the sophisticated technology company Thornton had imagined it to be, heavily concentrated in the defense industry. This single industry focus has left Litton open to the constraints of the national defense budget, as well as a contentious relationship with Washington, D.C.

James Ling (LTV)

Over time it became apparent that Ling's total company wasn't growing any faster than the individual acquisitions. In 1969 Ling–Temco–Vought was caught up in an anti-trust suit and was required to sell Braniff Airways and Okonite. When the economy began to decline in 1969, LTV's growth halted, and it was obliged to sell several businesses to service its growing debt. In 1970, Ling was temporarily replaced by Robert Stewart, another Ling–Temco–Vought executive, until a replacement for Ling could be found. Ling was demoted to president and he resigned six weeks later. His ultimate replacement was W. Paul Thayer, of the company's aerospace division, who immediately began to dispose of the unprofitable divisions and remove all the others from public trading. Ling–Temco–Vought had until then been essentially an investment portfolio, with substantial private investors in each division. As such, it was not an operating company in the sense that the parent (a holding company) could shift resources from the successful to the less successful divisions. The company restructured its debt and began to acquire as much as possible of the minority shareholdings in each division, and on May 5, 1971, the company's name was changed to LTV.

By 1977, Thayer had reduced the company to three core businesses: steel (Jones & Laughlin), meat packing (Wilson), and aerospace (Vought). All three businesses were cyclical, and all three cycles went south in 1977, resulting in a loss of $39 million on sales of $4.7 billion. Ling was subsequently sued over the sale of unregistered securities. From then on, the company went through a series of spinoffs, divestitures, and, surprisingly, acquisitions, until, with the acquisition of Republic Steel, it ended up primarily in the steel business. In 1986, unable to compete with massive imports from Japan, LTV finally filed for Chapter 11 bankruptcy, where it remained for over seven years, one of the longest and most complicated cases in U.S. business history. In 1993, it emerged as predominantly a steel producer, with thirty thousand fewer employees and a $3 billion pension shortfall. It had settled its debt with stock and began once again to acquire companies, this time in steel.

Charles Bluhdorn

Over time, Bluhdorn became known more as a manipulator of companies and their results to produce apparent growth, rather than someone who was creating new value from G&W's growth (Sobel, p. 101). Additionally, as the accounting profession required a more accurate distinction between earnings derived from the normal operations of a company and onetime items or accounting changes that were not part of operations, it became clear that there was no small amount of indirection in the G&W results.

By 1969, the luster was gone. As the poor quality of the earnings became apparent, G&W's stock price, which had peaked above 64 in 1969, at around twenty times earnings, dropped to 171/2, notwithstanding the fiction of reported "stable" earnings. The manipulation of earnings attracted the attention of both the anti-trust department and the accounting profession, which asserted more and more discipline concerning how financial results were portrayed honestly to the public. G&W's stock dropped thirty points, reducing its market capitalization by $500 million and its P/E ratio to a dismal eight times earnings. The one bright spot was Paramount, near bankruptcy when G&W had acquired it, which had its highest box-office revenues in history. In 1977, it bought Madison Square Garden, apparently paying double the market price primarily to acquire the Garden's underlying real estate portfolio. G&W went through a series of SEC investigations, which also contributed to a continuing credibility gap that depressed its P/E ratio. In 1983, Bluhdorn died of a heart attack while returning from a business trip. He was succeeded by Marvin S. Davis, who streamlined the company, focusing on three business groups: entertainment, financial services, and consumer products. He restructured management, sold the businesses not in the three primary groups, and liquidated the company's large stock portfolio. Davis continued to sell segments of the business, culminating with the sale of its entire consumer and industrial products business for $1 billion cash. The sale left G&W with an entertainment and financial services company with over $10 billion of assets, producing $3 billion in sales and $400 million in profits.

Harold Geneen

Frustrated by the anti-trust regulators in his attempt to purchase the ABC television network, Geneen sought to grow by acquiring companies outside of the telecommunications industry. During the 1960s, he acquired over three hundred companies in such diverse businesses as the Sheraton hotels, Wonder Bread, Avis, and the Hartford Insurance Company. Over the decade of the 1960s, sales grew from $700 million to $8 billion and profit from $29 million to $550 million.

Geneen's belief in his mastery of his own environment also led him to meddle in politics, both domestic and foreign. He was involved, along with his friend and CIA director John McCone, in the 1964 coup in Brazil. (McCone later was hired by ITT.) He used what today would be considered a PAC to buy the 1972 Republican National Convention's location in San Diego. And in 1973, ITT in Chile apparently helped the military coup against Salvador Allende. High interest rates had begun slowing ITT's growth, and by the late 1970s Geneen was removed. Rand Araskog, the new CEO, began to dismantle the ITT holdings. Faced with over $4 billion in debt that had accumulated under Geneen, Araskog embarked on what *Financial World* would later call "a gigantic corporate garage sale the likes of which the world will probably never see again." From 1979 to 1983, he sold businesses worth $200 million each year, and by the end of 1984 he had divested sixty-nine subsidiaries for nearly $2 billion, which was used to pay down the Geneen debt. In so doing, Araskog created an attractive takeover target and had to fend the corporate raiders off while he continued his sales festival, reaching a total of one hundred subsidiaries sold by 1986. He split the remaining subsidiaries into three profitable core business groups in which ITT was a market leader: insurance, finance, and industrial engineering. By 1990, ITT's debt-to-equity ratio was down to 0.3. The business was profitable but undervalued by Wall Street, which has always had a difficult time trying to figure out what business or businesses Geneen was actually in. Finally, in 1995, Araskog split the company into three separate public companies: ITT Corporation, ITT Hartford, and ITT Industries.

- ITT Corporation would merge with Starwood Hotels and Resorts Worldwide in 1997, and, in 1999, it would drop the ITT name in favor of Starwood.

- ITT Hartford would continue as a major insurance company and would eventually drop ITT from its name altogether.

- ITT Industries would operate under this name until 2006, when it would change its name to ITT Corporation, the only surviving entity to retain the ITT name.

What Did We Learn, If Anything?

The sample we have considered is small, but perhaps we can glean something by considering some of the reasons for their relative successes or failures:

- Royal Little was more interested in the process of growth through acquisition than the operation of the resulting entity. He delegated almost completely by virtue of his lack of interest in the details of operating management. Although he began with little in the way of a formal strategy than to grow Textron, at the end of his career he carefully considered what he had wrought and enunciated a set of principles, or rules, for growth through acquisition that might be considered the playbook for a successful conglomerate.

- Tex Thornton was also consumed by the process, in the sense that he could assemble a group of overvalued (underperforming) companies and grow the stated earnings of the company without regard to the quality or durability of those earnings. He seemed more intrigued by the relative laxity of the accounting rules and the public's predisposition to be moved by the headlines rather than the substance, or lack of it, underlying his business decisions.

- James Ling was also a student of the manipulation of financial statements, as well as the seemingly endless possibilities of leverage, the opportunity to buy a company with little or no outlay of one's own cash…except when the earnings of the acquired company were insufficient to service the debt undertaken to acquire it. Finally he learned the hard way of the dangers of concentrating business in a single sector. In the final analysis, Ling had no coherent diversification plan to use to screen potential acquisitions according to how they might fit in such a plan.

- Charles Bluhdorn was yet another manipulator of the financial statements, more fascinated by the process than by having a coherent plan with which to assess potential purchases. He would seek companies whose financial situation made them attractive, rather than the underlying business.

- Harold Geneen was a victim of his own ego, believing that he could not only identify and acquire his targets, but that he could do so without regard to the debt he was incurring. Once acquired, he believed that he could personally manage these companies, notwithstanding the fact that they were in an extremely broad array of unrelated businesses.

Warren Buffett

Although we have not examined Berkshire-Hathaway in the same detail as the others, it seems useful to cast a quick glance at the largest conglomerate in the United States. The most continuously successful conglomerate CEO for the past fifty years has been Berkshire Hathaway's Warren Buffett. Since he became chairman of the company in 1965, the stock has increased by 1,826,163 percent (to 2015). He has invested in a wide array of businesses with extraordinary success, preferring to acquire entire companies but willing to acquire partial ownership rather than miss the opportunity to participate in a good company. Buffett's rationale for being a conglomerate is that the business model offers an efficient means of allocating capital for investment. Berkshire Hathaway is not an operating company, but rather a portfolio of effectively managed individual businesses. The role of its headquarters is to accumulate and deploy the cash generated by its subsidiaries, which exceeds that needed to support their ongoing business activities. It is Berkshire Hathaway's experience that managers will always tend to deploy excess cash on opportunities within their own areas of knowledge and expertise, which limits their alternatives. The chairman operates under no such human tendency, but he can search the entire universe of potential acquisitions. The redeployment of excess cash entails a continuous search for attractive investment opportunities, which may or may not be in an existing area of the company's businesses. Investment opportunities are judged on the basis of their intrinsic value, the quality and trustworthiness of their management, and the relative ease of understanding of the nature of the business activity. Charlie Munger, Buffett's vice chairman at Berkshire Hathaway, described their management philosophy this way: "Instead of filling your ranks with lawyers and compliance people…hire people that you actually trust and let them do their job." Berkshire Hathaway has over three hundred thousand employees but no general counsel and no human resources department. Buffett and Munger believe that by focusing on finding trustworthy managers, with a few basic controls you can give them enormous leeway ("Berkshire's Radical Strategy: Trust," May 6, 2014).

Berkshire's management of the company is one of extreme delegation based on trust, believing that trust produces better results than management by directive, meetings, and layers of bureaucracy. It also costs a lot less and avoids single uniform systems that may be inappropriate for substantially diverse portfolio businesses. The manager of each subsidiary has virtually complete responsibility for the success of his or her operations. Headquarters functions and systems are limited to those that cannot be performed by the subsidiaries themselves, or are required either by statute or the board of directors. The current headquarters staff of twenty-five, sixteen of whom appear in the annual report to be female, includes the chairman and vice chairman, the CFO, secretary, controller, vice president, treasurer, and director of internal auditing. The current (2014) total number of employees working for Berkshire Hathaway at the same time was 340,499 ("Berkshire's Radical Strategy: Trust," May 6, 2014; Joe Nocera, March 3, 2015; "Charles Munger: Secrets of Buffett's Success," September 13, 2014; Berkshire Hathaway, 2014).

The result of these acquisition and management philosophies is the fifth largest firm in the United States, with a market capitalization of $337 billion.

Some Tentative Conclusions

If we consider the essential characteristics of the CEOs we have examined, Warren Buffett's approach, and the ups and downs of Singer since the end of World War II, perhaps we can make some tentative generalizations about the nature of conglomerate management that could have guided Donald Kircher in his quest for the Transnational Enterprise.

Diversification Strategy - The Choice of Businesses

- There is a learning curve for an executive entering a new business.

- The more new businesses an executive decides to enter, the more learning curves there will be.

- The more new businesses the company enters, the less likely it is that one can successfully manage them in detail from the top.

- The more businesses you wish to enter, the more you should focus on the quality of the management in the companies you are buying, as they will have the shortest learning curves.

- The management one acquires is at least as important as the product acquired and should be subject to the same critical judgment.

- Buying a business from owners who are looking to cash out leaves you with just the product, not the management talent.

Management Strategy—Nurturing Entrepreneurship

- The management talent you have acquired has been successful because of a highly developed sense of entrepreneurship.

- You should manage in such a way as to feed that entrepreneurship.

- You should set a few clear and measureable objectives and then leave management alone.

- Management has been successful in the marketplace. Otherwise you would not have considered acquiring them.

- You should try to replicate both the motivations (independence) and rewards (stock) of the marketplace.

- You should measure success with the same parameters as the marketplace, such as: operating return on sales, return on capital employed, return on equity, cash flow, and the reliability of plans.

- You should minimize staff oversight and time-consuming interference with operating management.

- You should minimize disincentives, such as accounting systems that charge operations with costs they don't control.

- You should minimize visible signs of corporate excess, such as expense accounts, personal cars, corporate airplanes, etc.

Royal Little's approach to a set of criteria for a conglomerate's acquisitions and his management philosophy contain significant overlap with our conclusions. Hopefully this contributed to his ability to retire at the peak of his success. The others had no such frame of reference, and one wonders whether that wasn't one of the principal reasons for their untimely business demise.

Endnotes

[1] Smithsonian Report, Washington D.C., 1929.

[2] Conforti, Michael, et al. The Clark Brothers Collect, Impressionist and Early Modern Paintings, Williamstown, MA: Sterling and Francine Clark Art Institute, 2006

[3] Cooper, Grace Rogers, The Invention of the Sewing Machine, Washington, D.C.: The Smithsonian Institution Press, 1968. Smithsonian photo No. 1379-A

[4] www.edisonnation.com , December, 2005

[5] Cooper, Idem. Smithsonian photo No. 42490-A

[6] www.Galichon.com

[7] Galichon, idem

[8] www.sewalot, Sussex A., December 2015

[9] The Elizabeth Forum, 2012

[10] Cooper, Idem. Smithsonian photo No. 45525-B

[11] Cooper, Idem. Smithsonian photo No. 48400

[12] Cooper, Idem. Smithsonian photo No. 45572

[13] Cooper, Idem. Smithsonian photo No. 32066-B

[14] Cooper, Idem. Smithsonian photo No.45572-D

[15] Scott, Idem.

[16] Mandore, Robert and Patty, Images of America, Singer Castle, Charleston, SC, Acadia Publishing, 2005.

[17] Scott, Idem.

[18] Cooper, Idem. Smithsonian photo No. 48091-B

[19] Ehrsam, Jacques, Personal collection

[20] Ehrsam, Idem.

[21] Scott, Idem.

[22] Scott, Idem.

[23] Scott, Idem.

[24] Bays, Carter, The Encyclopedia of Early American and Antique Sewing Machines, Paducah KY: Collector Books, 2007.

[25] Bays, Idem.

[26] Scott, Idem.

[27] Scott, Idem.

[28] Scott, Idem.

[29] Scott, Idem

[30] Scott, Idem

[31] This section relies heavily on the extensive biography of Singer by Ruth Brandon (1977).

[32] www.singermemories.com 2015.

[33] www.torquayheraldexpress.co.uk .

[34] This section relies heavily on two primary sources: The Clarks of Cooperstown by Nicholas Fox Weber and The Clark Brothers Collect by Michael Conforti, et al.

35 www.ephemeralnewyork.com , 2015

36 www.wikipediacommons , 2015

37 Conforti, Idem.

38 Conforti, Idem.

39 Conforti, Idem.

40 Conforti, Idem

41 Sir William Orpen (Irish, 1878-1931), Robert Sterling Clark (detail), 1921-22, Oil on canvas, 40 1/8 x 30 in. (101.9 x 76.2 cm). Sterling and Francine Clark Art Institute, Williamstown, Massachusetts, 1955.824, Image © Sterling and Francine Clark Art Institute, Williamstown, Massachusetts, USA (photo by Michael Agee)
Sir William Orpen (Irish, 1878-1931, Stephen Carleton Clark (detail), 1921-22, Oil on canvas, 37 x 30 in. (94 x 76.2 cm). Collection of Jane Forbes Clark. (photo by Richard Walker)

42 Conforti, Idem.

43 Conforti, Idem.

44 Conforti, Idem.

45 Conforti, Idem.

46 Conforti, Idem.

47 Conforti, Idem.

48 Singer Sewing Machine Company, A Century of Service, 1851-1951, Wilmington, DE: Hadley Library, 1951.

49 Private collection of Theodore Ames.

50 Ehrsam, Idem.

51 Mandore, Idem.

52 Mandore, Idem.

53 Singer Sewing Machine Company, Idem.

54 www.nyc-architecture.com .

55 Singer Sewing Machine Company, Idem.

56 This section relies heavily on "The Rise and Fall of the Conglomerate Kings," by Robert Sobel.

57 Unless otherwise indicated, quoted statements in this section are from the Annual Reports of The Singer Manufacturing Company and The Singer Company.

58 Personal collection of the author.

59 www.scotlandsplaces.com/clydebank .

60 Unless otherwise indicated, all of the quotations attributed to Joseph Flavin were drawn from the annual reports of the Singer Company.

61 Special Collections & University Archives: University Libraries, University of Massachusetts.

62 NY Times, May 9, 1980.

63 www.singermemories.com .

64 www.singermemories.com

65 www.scripophily.com .

66 www.kohlberg.com

Photo and Illustration sources:

Scott, John. **Genius Rewarded or, The Story of the Sewing Machine,** New York:John J. Calhoun, 1880.

Conforti, Michael, et al. **The Clark Brothers Collect, Impressionist and Early Modern Paintings.** Williamstown, MA: Sterling and Francine Clark Institute, 2006.

Mandore, Robert and Patty, **Images of America, Singer Castle,** Charleston, SC: Acadia Publishing, 2005.

Bays, Carter, **The Encyclopedia of Early American and Antique Sewing Machines,** Paducah, KY: Collector Books, 2007.

The Smithsonian Institution.

Wisconsin State Historical Society

New York State Historical Association

St. Lawrence County Historical Association

The Elizabeth Forum.

Richard Walker

The Singer Sewing Machine Company Archives

The Hagley Library

The Library of Congress

The SEC Archives

The New York Public Library Digital Collection/public domain

The private collection of Jacques Ehrsam.

The private collection of the Author

Bibliography

(n.d.). Retrieved from "Isaac Merritt Singer": www.nnndb.com.

(n.d.). Retrieved from "Isaac Merritt Singer": www.rootsweb.ancestry.com.

(n.d.). Retrieved from "Isaac Singer": www.en.wikipedia.org.

(n.d.). Retrieved from "American History 102. Photo Gallery": www.us.history.wisc.edu.

(n.d.). Retrieved from "Benjamin Franklin as a Scientist": www.sln.fi.edu.

(n.d.). Retrieved from "Benjamin Franklin: Science Years (Ages 40–49)": www.school-for-champions.com.

(n.d.). Retrieved from "Business Model": www.en.wikipedia.org.

(n.d.). Retrieved from "Business Model": www.quickmba.com.

(n.d.). Retrieved from "Business Model": www.1000ventures.com.

(n.d.). Retrieved from "Elias Howe": www.answers.com.

(n.d.). Retrieved from "Frederick Gilbert Bourne": www.en.wikipedia.org.

(n.d.). Retrieved from "Japanese Sewing Machine Export History": www.google.com/webhp?tab=mw.

(n.d.). Retrieved from "Panic of 1857": www.en.wikipedia.org.

(n.d.). Retrieved from "Panic of 1873": www.en.wikipedia.org.

(n.d.). Retrieved from "Panic of 1893": www.en.wikipedia.org.

(n.d.). Retrieved from "Panic of 1907": www.en.wikipedia.org.

(n.d.). Retrieved from "Product of the Enlightenment": www.asp.org.

(n.d.). Retrieved from "Sears Roebuck and Their Machines": www.ismacs.net.

(n.d.). Retrieved from "Singer Castle Blog & More": www.singercastle.blogspot.com.

(n.d.). Retrieved from "Singer Company Records": www.hagley.org.

(n.d.). Retrieved from "Singer History": www.singermemories.com.

(n.d.). Retrieved from "The Singer Company N.V.—Company History": www.fundinguniverse.com.

(n.d.). Retrieved from "Thomas Jefferson": www.sc94ameslab.gov.

(n.d.). Retrieved from "Thomas Jefferson: Father of Invention": www.earlyamerica.com.

(n.d.). Retrieved from "Types of Business Models": www.master-your-business-model.com.

(n.d.). Retrieved from "United States v Singer Co., 374 U.S. 174 (1963)": www.supreme.justia.com.

(n.d.). Retrieved from "What Did Thomas Jefferson Do as a Scientist?": www.asp.org.

(n.d.). Retrieved from "History and Genealogy of Samuel Clark, Sr. and His Descendants from 1636": www.archive.org.

(n.d.). Retrieved from "Labor Geographies in a Time of Early Globalization: Strikes against Singer in Scotland and Russia in the Early 20th Century": www.sciencedirect.com.

(n.d.). Retrieved from "*Le Chemin de Fer de Thurso et de la Vallee de la Nation* (History of the Thurso and Nation Valley Railway)": www.railways.incanada.net.

(n.d.). Retrieved from "Sir Douglas Alexander, 1st Baronet": www.en.wikipedia.org.

(n.d.). Retrieved from "The Law of Vertical Integration and the Business Firm: 1880–1960": www.papers.ssm.com.

(n.d.). Retrieved from "Sewing Machine Collector. Major 19th & 20th Century USA Manufacturers": www.dincum.com.

"$15,169,779 Earned by Singer in 1948." (June 16, 1949). *New York Times*.

"A Challenge for Anyone Who Feels He Must Go Everywhere." (May 20, 1968). *New York Times*.

Abelson, Reed. (May 14, 1995). "INVESTING IT; Singer's Success Requires Reading Between the Bottom Lines." *New York Times*.

"Agreement Is Set on Singer Merger." (June 20, 1963). *New York Times*.

"Alexander Will Filed." (June 14, 1949). *New York Times*.

Antique and Collectibles Forum, Monarch sewing machine, Posted by damascusannie, March 11,2008. (n.d.). Retrieved from "Japanese Imports from Postwar Japan": www.thathomesite.com.

Askaroff, A. (n.d.). Retrieved from "Isaac Merritt Singer: A Brief History of a Giant—Touched by Fire": www.sewalot.com.

Barmash, Isadore. (May 19, 1974). "A Resurgence in Home Sewing?" *New York Times*.

Barron, James. (October 8, 1987). "Joseph B. Flavin Is Dead at 58; Lead Overhaul as Singer Chairman." *New York Times*.

Bays, C. (2007). *The Encyclopedia of Early American and Antique Sewing Machines, Third Edition, Identification and Values.* Paducah, KY: Collector Books.

Berkshire Hathaway (2014). *2014 Annual Report.* Berkshire Hathaway.

"Berkshire's Radical Strategy: Trust." (May 6, 2014). *New York Times*.

"Bid for Singer Extended." (January 28, 1988). *New York Times*.

"Bilzerian Extends Offer for Singer." (December 31, 1987). *New York Times*.

"Bilzerian Holds 9.9% of Singer." (October 30, 1987). *New York Times*.

"Bilzerian Indicted over Deals." (December 22, 1988). *New York Times*.

"Bilzerian Remains Silent on Financing." (December 23, 1987). *New York Times*.

"Bilzerian Seeks Auction for Singer." (November 28, 1987). *New York Times*.

"Bilzerian Talks on Singer Bid." (November 21, 1987). *New York Times*.

"Bilzerian, Investor End Their Talks." (January 6, 1988). *New York Times.*

Bissell, D. (1999). *The First Conglomerate: 145 Years of the Singer Sewing Machine Company.* Brunswick, ME: Audenreed Press.

Black Monday (1987). (n.d.). Retrieved from Wikipedia: www.en.wikipedia.org.

Bonin, H. &. (2009). *American Firms in Europe 1880–1990, Strategy, Identity, Perception and Performance.* Geneva: Librairie Droz S.A.

Brandon, R. (1977). *A Capitalist Romance, Singer and the Sewing Machine.* New York: J.B. Lippencott Company.

Bucheli, M.M. (2007). "Chandler's Living History: The Visible Hand of Vertical Integration in 19th-Century America Viewed under a 21st-Century Transaction Costs Economic Lens." *Abstract: University of Illinois at Urbana-Chapaign, College of Business,* 12–30.

Business Week. (October 3, 2009). "Three Steps to a Sound Business Model." Retrieved from 2009. Retrieved from www.businessweek.com.

"Business: Gloomy Singer." (September 28, 1936). *Time.*

Callaway, D.T. (n.d.). "Thomas Jefferson: Minister of Enlightenment." Retrieved from www.monticello.org/library

Carlson, L. (2003). *Queen of Inventions, How the Sewing Machine Changed the World.* Brookfield, CT: The Millbrook Press.

Carstensen, F.V. (1984). *American Enterprise in Foreign Markets, Singer and International Harvester in Imperial Russia.* Chapel Hill, NC, and London: University of North Carolina Press.

"Cathedral School Gets $500,000 Gift." (April 13, 1914). *New York Times.*

"Chandler's Living History: The Visible Hand of Vertical Integration in 19th-Century America Viewed under a 21st-Century Transaction Costs Economic Lens." (2007). Retrieved from www.inventors.about.com.

"Charles Munger: Secrets of Buffett's Success." (September 13, 2014). *Wall Street Journal.*

Clark, R.E. (1982). *History and Genealogy of Samuel Clark, Sr. and His Descendants from 1636–1892: 256 Years.* St. Louis, MO: Nixon-Jones Printing Co.

Cole, Robert J. (December 22, 1987). "Amid Doubt, Bilzerian Extends Bid for Singer." *New York Times.*

Cole, Robert J. (December 24, 1987). "Bilzerian Obtains Financing for Bid to Acquire Singer." *New York Times.*

Cole, Robert J. (January 7, 1988). "Bilzerian's Singer Bid Aided by Pickens Loan." *New York Times.*

Cole, Robert J. (November 14, 1987). "Singer Acts to Bar a Bid by Bilzerian." *New York Times.*

Conforti, M.G. (2006). *Clark Brothers Collect, Impressionist and Early Modern Paintings.* Williamstown, MA: Sterling and Francine Clark Institute.

Conglomerate. (n.d.). Retrieved from www.en.wikipedia.org/wiki/Conglomerate.

"Conglomerates—Still Trying." (November 5, 1972). *New York Times.*

Cooper, G.R. (1968). *The Invention of the Sewing Machine.* Washington, D.C.: Smithsonian Institution.

Cowan, A.L. (August 24, 1988). "How Bilzerian Scored at Singer." *New York Times.*

Cowan, Alison Leigh. (May 24, 1987). "Corporate Raider: Paul Bilzerian, a Scrappy Takeover Artist, Rises to the Top." *New York Times.*

Cuff, Daniel F. (October 9, 1987). "Flavin's Successor Is Named by Singer." *New Yotk Times.*

Davies, R.B. (1976). *Peacefully Working to Conquer the World, Singer Sewing Machines in Foreign Markets, 1854–1920.* New York: Arno Press.

Day, Stoddard, & Williams, Inc. (February 1, 1942). "Singer—Producer of a Household Servant." *THE YANKEE FORUM.*

DePew, C.E. *One Hundred Years of American Commerce, American Sewing Machines, Frederick G. Bourne.* New York: The De Vinne Press, 1895.

"Dishonored Dealmaker." (August 5, 2002). *Business Week.*

"Do Patent Pools Encourage Innovation? Evidence from the 19th-Century Sewing Machine Industry." (October 9, 2009). Retrieved from www.papers.ssm.com.

"Donald P. Kircher: Enlistment Record from WW2." (April 22, 2014). Retrieved from www.WW2enlistment.org.

"Douglas Alexander Made a Baronet." (June 10, 1921). *New York Times.*

"Eaton to Buy Singer Division." (May 13, 1986). *New York Times.*

Ehrsam, J. (June 2012). Interview by J. Buckman.

Eichenwald, Kurt. (September 28, 1989). "Bilzerian Gets 4 Years in Jail and Is Fined $1.5 Million." *New York Times.*

"Electronics Unit Bought by Singer." (January 22, 1958). *New York Times.*

"Era of Japan's Miracle Economy." (n.d.). Retrieved from www.sjsu.edu.

"Estate to Sell Stock in Singer." (April 25, 1964). *New York Times.*

"Exclusive: Kohlberg Looking to Sell Singer Sewing Machine Company: Sources." (March 12, 2014). *New York Times.*

Forde, B. (n.d.). Retrieved from www.limaritime.org.

Forde, B. (n.d.). "Frederick G. Bourne." Retrieved from www.limaritime.org/bournehardpage.

Frank, Peter H. (November 10, 1987). "Mesa Gets 9.9% Stake in Singer." *New York Times.*

Friedman, S.M. (2015). *The Inflation Calculator.* Washington, D.C.: Bureau of Labor Statistics.

Frieman, W. (2004). *Birth of a Salesman, The Transformation of Selling in America.* Cambridge, MA: Harvard University Press.

Gaughan, P.A. (2007). *Mergers, Acquisitions, and Corporate Restructurings (Fourth Edition).* Hoboken, NJ: John Wiley & Sons, Inc.

Gay, P.A. (1973). *Modern Europe to 1815.* New York, Evanston, San Francisco, London: Harper & Row.

"George R. MacKenzie's Will." (March 23, 1892). *New York Times.*

Godley, A. (April 10, 2009). "Selling the Sewing Machine around the World: Singer's Internatioal Marketing Strategies, 1850–1914." Retrieved from www.rdg.ac.uk.

Gordon, Sarah A. "Commodifying 'Domestic Virtues': Business and Home Sewing. Retrieved from www.gutenberg-e.org/Gordon/chap4.html.

Gray, C. (January 2, 2005). "Once the Tallest Building, but Since 1967 a Ghost." *New York Times.*

Hagley, M.A. (n.d.). "Singer Company Records, 1851–1990." Singer Company.

Hayes, Thomas C. (August 8, 1987). "Pickens Is Considering a Big Stake in Singer." *New York Times.*

"History of Brother Corporation." (n.d.). Retrieved from www.brother.com.

"History of the Sewing Machine." (n.d.). Retrieved from www.moah.com.

Holson, Laura M. (July 2012). "Dusting Off the Sewing Machine." *New York Times.*

Hounsell, D.A. (1984). *From the American System to Mass Production.* Baltimore and London: The Johns Hopkins University Press.

Hovenkamp, H. (March 2009). "The Law of Vertical Integration and the Business Firm: 1880–1960." In H. Hovenkamp, *Neoclassical Business Firm* (pp. 1–15). Iowa City, IA: University of Iowa College of Law.

"Italian Unit Bought by Singer." (May 1, 1964). *New York Times.*

Jack, A.B. (1957). "The Channels of Distribution for an Innovation: The Sewing Machine Industry in America, 1860–1865." *Explorations in Entrepreneurial History.*

"Jerome Kohlberg, Jr." (2014). Retrieved from www.en.wikipedia.org.

Johnson-Srebro, N. (2001). *Featherweight 221, The Perfect Portable and Its Stitches Across History (Expanded Third Edition).* China: Silver Star, Inc.

"Judge Reduces Bilzerian Term." (October 17, 1992). *New York Times.*

Kilborn, Peter T. (October 24, 1974). "Singer's High-Key Diversification Hits a Sour Note." *New York Times.*

Kircher, D.P. (1964). "Now the Transnational Enterprise." *Harvard Business Review,* HBR 42, No. 2 Mar./Apr. 6–10, 172–176.

Kobler, J. (July 1952). "Mr. Singer's Money Machine." *Saturday Evening Post.*

Kohlberg & Co. (2015). "Kohlberg & Co." Retrieved from www.kohlberg.com.

"Kohlberg Unit Buys Singer Brand and Business." (October 2, 2004). *New York Times.*

Labaton, Stephan. (August 24, 1987). "Business and the Law; States Protect Merger Targets." *New York Times.*

Lewton, F.L. (1929). "The Servant in the House: A Brief History of the Sewing Machine." *United States Museum*. Annual Report: Smithsonian Institution.

LoPucki, Lynn M. (2005). "Global and Out of Control." University of California, Los Angeles School of Law, Public Law & Legal Theory Research Paper Series.

Lyon, P. (October 1958). "Isaac Singer and His Wonderful Sewing Machine." *American Heritage*, 9.

"Malaysian Investor May Bid for SSMC." (February 9, 1989). *New York Times*.

Mandore, R.A. (2005). *Images of America, Singer Castle*. Charleston, SC: Arcadia Publishing.

"Market Turmoil." (October 28, 1987). *New York Times*.

McKenzie, F.A. (1901). *The American Invaders: Their Plans, Tactics and Progress*. New York: Street and Smith.

"McKesson & Robbins Scandal (1938)." (n.d.). Retrieved from www.en.wikipedia.org.

McNeil Jr., Donald G. (May 2, 1978). "Ex-Head of Singer Company Slain in Jersey; Brother-in-Law Is Held." *New York Times*.

"Merger Opposed by Equity Corp.—Company Seeking to Block Friden-Singer Proposal." (September 25, 1963). *New York Times*.

"Milton C. Lightner, 78, Ex-Head of Singer Co. and N.A.M. Dies." (March 26, 1968). *New York Times*.

Miwa, Y.U. (1991). "Economic Effects of the Decentralization Policies in Postwar Japan." *The Postwar Economic Reforms in Japan*.

Moody's. (1987). The Singer Company. *Moody's Industrial Manual*, 4310–4316.

"Moody's Downgrades Ratings of the Singer Company N.V. (Senior to Ba1) and Semi-Tech Corporation (Senior Secured to B1)." (February 19, 1997). *Moody's Investor's Service*.

Mossoff, A.G. (March 6, 2009). "A Stitch in Time: The Rise and Fall of the Sewing Machine Patent Thicket." Retrieved from www.papers.ssn.com.

"Multiple—Textron, Litton, LTV, Gulf & Western & ITT Histories." (2014). Retrieved from www.fundinguniverse.com.

"New Singer Chairman Is a Railroad Retiree." (August 28, 1989).

"No Singer Bid from Allied Signal." (November 18, 1987). *New York Times*.

Nocera, Joe. (March 3, 2015). "How Buffet Does It." *New York Times*.

NY Times. (February 24, 1967). "Singer Earnings at Record Level." *New York Times*.

"Offer from Singer." (November 25, 1987). *New York Times*.

Parton, H. (1867). *History of the Sewing Machine*. Middletown, CT: The Howe Machine Company (reprinted for the Michigan Historical Reprint Series, University of Michigan Library).

"Pays $10 a Share as Extra Dividend." (June 11, 1926). *New York Times*.

Phalon, Richard. (December 30, 1975). "Singer Co. to Phase Out Business Machines Unit." *New York Times*.

Poindexter, J. (January 1969). "A New Stitch for Singer." *Dun's Review*, 28–32.

"Profit of Singer Rose 53% in 1959." (April 14, 1960). *New York Times*.

Reckert, Clare. (January 31, 1976). "Singer Deficits Widen Broadly." *New York Times*.

Rosen, H. (1981). *The System Gribeauval: A Study of Technological Development and Institutional Change in Eighteenth-Century France*. Chicago: University of Chicago, Department of History.

Sage, H.J. (n.d.). "The Enlightenment in America." Retrieved from www.sage-history.net.

Sanders, R. (n.d.). "Facing the Corporate Roots of American Fascism." Retrieved from Robert S. Clark (1877–1956): www.coat.ncf.ca/our_magazine/links/53/clark.

Scott, J. (1880). *Genius Rewarded, or the Story of the Sewing Machine*. New York: John J. Calhoun.

"Semi-Tech Bids More for SSMC." (March 2, 1989).

"Semi-Tech Corp (Profiles)." (November 2015). Retrieved from www.Bloomberg.com/live.

"Semi-Tech Is Winner: $38 a Share for SSMC." (March 23, 1989).

"Sewing Machine Markets in the World—Market Size, Development, and Forecasts." (April 2015). Market Research Store.

"Sewing Machine Venture Is Planned by Singer for China." (July 30, 1989). *New York Times*.

"Sewing: 30 Million Women Can't Be Wrong." (March 2, 1997). *New York Times*.

"Singer Agrees to Sell Education Unit." (July 9, 1988). *New York Times*.

"Singer Agrees to Sell Flight Simulation Unit." (July 9, 1988). *New York Times*.

"Singer Agrees to Sell Motor Products Unit." (July 6, 1988). *New York Times*.

"Singer Agrees to Sell Motor Products Unit." (July 6, 1988). *New York Times*.

"Singer Backs Bid." (January 14, 1988). *New York Times*.

"Singer Board to Meet on Bid." (January 13, 1988). *New York Times*.

"Singer Co. Announces Record Results for Year and Quarter as Corporations Report Earnings and Sales." (February 26, 1969). *New York Times*.

"Singer Co. Is Selling Canadian Pulp Unit to Maclaren, Ltd." (December 24, 1964). *New York Times*.

"Singer Co. Plans Big Stock Dividend." (November 7, 1922). *New York Times*.

"Singer Co. Plans Expansion Move—Accord Set for Acquisition of Panorama Electronics." (July 17, 1962). *New York Times*.

"Singer Co. Wins Merger Backing." (October 15, 1963). *New York Times*.

"Singer Committed to Sale or Merger." (December 1, 1987). *New york Times*.

"Singer Company Earns $8,758,851." (September 18, 1941). *New York Times.*

"Singer Company Raises Earnings." (May 18, 1961). *New York Times.*

"Singer Company Sets Sales Mark." (May 17, 1962). *New York Times.*

"Singer Divestment." (July 29, 1988). *New York Times.*

"Singer Earnings at Record Level." (February 24, 1967). *New York Times.*

"Singer Files for Chapter 11." (September 14, 1999). *New York Times.*

"Singer Funds for Bilzerian." (February 1, 1988). *New York Times.*

"Singer in Agreements to Sell 2 More Units." (July 15, 1988). *New York Times.*

"Singer in Talks." (November 20, 1987). *New York Times.*

"Singer Invites Bilzerian Bid." (December 21, 1987). *New York Times.*

"Singer May Bid Sewing Adieu." (February 19, 1986). *New York Times.*

"Singer Mfg. Co." (June 29, 1960). *New York Times.*

Singer N.V. (2003). *Disclosure Statement and Report.* Willemstad, Curacao, Netherlands Antilles: Singer N.V.

Singer N.V. (2004). *Singer N.V. Announces Closing of Sale of Sewing Business.* Willemstad, Curacao, Netherlands Antilles: Singer N.V.

Singer N.V. (April 2004). *Disclosure Statement and Report.* Willemstad, Curacao, Netherlands Antilles: Singer N.V.

Singer N.V. (September 2001). *Disclosure Statement and Report.* Willemstad, Curacao, Netherlands Antilles: Singer N.V.

"Singer Offer Ends." (February 5, 1988). *New York Times.*

"Singer Plans Fight on Antitrust Suit." (December 24, 1959). *New York Times.*

"Singer Plans German Venture." (September 3, 1965). *New York Times.*

"Singer Reorganizes and Emerges from Bankruptcy." (September 16, 2000). *New York Times.*

"Singer Seeks a New Buyer." (November 27, 1987). *New York Times.*

"Singer Spinoff." (July 15, 1986). *New York Times.*

"Singer to Acquire 80% Stake in German Manufacturer." (November 7, 1997).

"Singer to Buy Back Furniture Operation." (November 14, 1995). *New York Times.*

"Singer to Close Rochester Plant." (February 12, 1972). *New York Times.*

"Singer to Decide on New Partner." (December 2, 1987). *New York Times.*

"Singer to Meet Amid Talk of Change." (December 11, 1985). *New York Times.*

"Singer to Move Uptown, Sell Broadway Building." (November 16, 1961). *New York Times.*

"Singer to Produce Appliances for Sale in Foreign Markets." (May 16, 1963). *New York Times.*

"Singer to Relocate and Offer Stock." (June 11, 1991). *New York Times.*

"Singer Vice President to Be President Jan. 1—Donald P. Kircher." (December 5, 1957). *New York Times.*

Singer, Company. (1951). "A Century of Service, 1851–1951, prepared for the celebration of Singer's 100th anniversary. *Pamphlet.* Washington, D.C.: Singer Sewing Machine Company.

Singer, Company. (1951–1985). *Annual Reports.* New York: The Singer Company.

Singer, Company. (1976). *Elizabeth, The Great Factory.* New York.

"Singer's Offices Move to Jersey." (August 21, 1987). *New York Times.*

"Singer's President Takes Leave." (September 13, 1975). *New York Times.*

"Sir D. Alexander, Singer Firm Head, President for 44 Years Is Dead in Stamford at 84—Made Baronet for War Work." (May 23, 1949). *New York Times.*

Sloane, Leonard. (July 16, 1972). "Sewing-Machine Pioneer in Trouble?" *New York Times.*

Smith, Gene. (February 14, 1976). "Singer Streamlines Corporate Structure." *New York Times.*

Smith, Gene. (May 14, 1976). "Singer Expects '76 Profit; Chief Says 'Worst Is Over.'" *New York Times.*

Smith, Gene. (November 11, 1975). "Xerox Officer to Head Singer." *New York Times.*

Sobel, R. (1984). *The Rise and Fall of the Conglomerate Kings.* Washington, D.C.: Stein and Day Publishers. Reprinted in 1999 by Beard Books.

"SSMC Attracts New Suitors." (February 7, 1989). *New York Times.*

"Status of Major Insider Investigations." (July 28, 1988). *New York Times.*

Sterba, James P. (June 14, 1978). "Singer Co. Is Moving to Stamford to Surprise of New York Officials." *New York Times.*

"Stitches—The History of Sewing Machines." (n.d.). Retrieved from www.inventors.about.com.

Strom, Stephanie. (March 29, 1992). "All About/Sewing; In the Gray 90s, Women Are Heading Back to the Bobbin." *New York Times.*

Sulpukas, Agis. (November 3, 1987). "Takeover Activity Resuming; Singer Gets Hostile Offer." *New Yotk Times.*

"T. Boone Pickens." (n.d.). Retrieved from www.en.wikipedia.org.

"The Lore Persists, but Singer Isn't Sewing Machine Firm Anymore." (August 8, 1987). *New York Times.*

"The Singer Company N.V.: How Did It Find Trouble?" (December 12, 1997). *The Motley Fool.*

The Story of the Sewing Machine: Its Invention, Improvements, Social, Industrial, and Commericial Importance. (1860). New York: New York Times.

Thomson, R. (1989). "Invention, Markets, and the Scope of the Firm: The Nineteenth-Century U.S. Shoe Machine Industry." *Business and Economic History, Second Series.*

Time. (1963). "Personalities: October 25, 1963." *Time.*

Time. (November 20, 1920). "Frederick G. Bourne Left $42,592,813.59: Appraisal of Singer Sewing Machine Man's Riches Puts State Taxes at $1,669,200. Many Small Bequests. Bulk of Fortune, Largely in Stocks, Goes to Seven Sons and Daughters." *Time.*

Time. (October 1, 1934). "Corporations: Singer." *Time*.

Time. (October 25, 1963). "Personalities: Donald P. Kircher." *Time*.

Time. (September 28, 1936). "Business: Gloomy Singer." *Time*.

Tocqueville, A.D. (2000). *Democracy in America*. Chicago: University of Chicago Press.

Turner, J.R. (2003). *Elizabeth, the first capital of New Jersey*. Charleston, SC: Arcadia Publishing.

"Two Suits Accuse Singer Sewing Machine of Excessive Surplus and Ask Dividends." (May 14, 1941). *New York Times*.

United States Supreme Court, United States v. Singer Mfg. Co., U.S.174 (1963). (July 20, 2010). Retrieved from www.caselaw.lp.findlaw.com.

United States v. McKesson & Robbins, Inc. (January 5, 1939). *Securities and Exchange Commission*.

"Vacancy Filled as Singer Elects a New President." (May 9, 1980). *New York Times*.

"Vice President Is Named by the Singer Company." (July 2, 1952). *New York Times*.

Weber, N.F. (2007). *The Calrks of Cooperstown, Their Sewing Machine Fortune, Their Great and Influential Art Collections, Their Forty-Year Feud*. New York: Alfred A. Knopf.

"White Estate Quits Sewing Machine Co." (January 14, 1926). *New York Times*.

Wiggins, Phillip H. (October 8, 1987). "Stocks End Mixed in Wild Day." *New York Times*.

Wikipedia. (November 2015). "Grande Holdings Ltd." Retrieved from www.wikipedia.com.

Wilkins, M. (1970). *The Emergence of Multinational Enterprise: American Business Abroad from the Colonial Era to 1914*. Cambridge: Harvard University Press.

Wisconsin Historical Society. (n.d.). "The Singer Company Archives." *Box 104, Folder 3*.

Young & Rubucam, I. (June 15, 1951). "Progress and Development of the Singer Sewing Machine." Press release. New York.

Young & Rubucam, I. (June 14, 1951). "Singer Announces New Plant." Press release. New York.

Young & Rubucam, I. (June 15, 1951). "Singer Started with $40 Capital." Press release. New York.

Young & Rubucam, I. (June 15, 1951). "The Singer Industrial Sewing Machine in the Needle Trades." Press release. New York.

Appendix A

Letter dated June 1, 1861from Isaac M. Singer to Edward C. Clark and Edward C. Clark's reply, dated June 2, 1861

London, June 1, 1861.

Mr. Clark,

New York.

Dear Sir,

I feel quite low-spirited today. It does seem to me that this man Grey has defrauded in some how to a very large extent but how I cannot tell. Bills for putting up the office is constantly coming in which I thought were all paid, yesterday a bill for £19 and today another for £230 more. What the end will be I cannot tell. My belief is that if we had never had anything to do with foreign countries and had attended more strictly to that of our own, we should be much better off today. Now I should like to know in post I want Mr. Hooper to send me the exact account of profit and loss of the business outside of the one United States of America. Our country - what will become of our country. I am satisfied that the feelings of the English are with the South and are only waiting for our government to something which they may construe into an overt act to lend aid to the South.

I. M. S.

New York, June 2nd, 1862.

I. M. Singer Esq.
    London -

Dear Sir:

I am in very low spirits today and although I regret to do so,
I must inform you of the cause. You are out of the country. I
heartily wish I was. The load here is getting very heavy for me to
bear. On Saturday last, the same day you left New York, I sent down
to the Chemical Bank a note for $5,000 to be discounted. Hopper had
no doubt as to getting the accommodation, as our discounts at the
Bank were very small and money very plenty. On Monday the note was
sent back to us not having been discounted. Hopper went to the Bank
and asked an explanation. The Cashier told him the Directors of the
Bank had seen the publication about you in the Police Gazette and
referred him to the President for further information. The President,
Mr. Jones, said that the Directors had come to the conclusion that
it was not reputable for the Bank to discount any notes for I. M.
Singer. Hopper then told him that the business of the firm had for
several months been entirely under my direction and that you had
been absent from the City - also that you had just sailed for Europe
expecting to be gone a long time and that the Bank ought not to in-
flict such an injury upon me in consequence of any publication about
you - also that the greater part of the publication was absolutely
false and that the whole of it malicious and written for black mail-
ing purposes. Hopper asked the President to present the matter to
the board of Directors again and to have them reconsider their determination. That was on Saturday. Today Hopper went to the Bank
again and was told by the President that the Bank positively would
not discount any more papers for I. M. Singer & Co. The only reason

assigned for this is the discredit of doing business with you on account of the disgraceful situation of your private affairs. The President of the Bank sent a verbal message to me that he sincerely sympathizes with me in the disagreeable situation in which I was placed but that could not alter the decision of the Directors of the Bank.

Now all this is exceptionally annoying to me, as well as disastrous to our business. I hardly dare speak to any old friends when I meet them in the street. The firm of which I am the active manager has been publicly accused of keeping numerous agents in various cities to procure women for you to prostitute. And although this is an infamous falsehood, yet it is mixed up with so much truth that it would be disgraceful to bring into the light of a public trial, that neither I who am most injured in money and reputation nor the agents at the Branch Offices, who are outrageously slandered, dare to appeal to the law for redress. I am constantly expecting to hear of other damages from this cause. There are thousands of persons who are interested in spreading these stories and not one person with whom I have spoken on the subject has any doubt that they will greatly stand in the way of making sales of our machines for family use especially. Our agents all over the country are having the Police Gazette thrust in their faces and it makes the public shy of our agents and reluctant to deal with them. How far this evil influence will extend it is impossible to say.

Now there is one remedy for a part of this mischief, and that ought to be applied as soon as it can conveniently be done. The name of Singer, as it now stands, is a terrible weight upon the firm. When you were present I did not like to express all I felt on that

subject, though I did tell you I believed our business would be considerably injured. Your interests as well as my own imperatively require that the name of Singer & Co. should be merged in that of a
joint stock Company. I believe it would make a difference of at least
$50,000 within a year if that could be done today. I had determined to
say no more on that subject, but the stand taken by the Bank shows me
how the great public regard the matter.

There is only one sensible reason why you should not wish to have
the Stock Company and that is, that it would be a little easier for
you to sell the stock and get rid of it than to dispose of your interest in the firm. There is not much in this idea either, because now,
if you get into debt beyond what you can pay, your interest in the
firm can be sold. The advantages of the Company to you are several.

1st - You would have several persons interested in looking out
for you and would not have to rely entirely on me.

2nd - The real estate of the firm could be put in such a shape
that there never could be any contest about down rights in it.

3rd - Money could be borrowed on a pledge of the stock, or some
of it, as security. It may be very necessary next December to be able
to do this.

4th - You will be able if you wish to sell portions of the stock,
and turn it into other property. Also to transfer such part of your
property as you please to any other country. I think you will here-
after wish to make such a transfer.

5th - Both you and I will at once make more money in consequence
of the change. A new incorporated Company will have no bad name.

I shall enclose herewith a Power of Attorney from you to McKenzie
for the special purpose of authorizing him to act for you in the formation of the new Company. I propose to sell out to Hopper, McKenzie

and a few others, who will be glad to get it, enough of the stock to pay your debts and mine, which are about the same amount. The residue of the stock will belong to us equally, and I will promise to take care of your stock the same as I do of my own.

Now I hope you will not allow any absurd suspicion of my motives to prevent your doing what I ask, and what ought to be done. It is necessary for the good of the business, and for your benefit, and it is very necessary for me, who stand here subjected to all the odium of your private affairs. I am willing to stand by you and your interests and have no idea of abandoning what I deem my duty, because there is disgrace attaching to the performance of it. Still I cannot afford to continue to be looked upon with a kind of compassionate pity by my friends, as is the case now, simply to accommodate a whim or fancy of yours. I think I know what is right and what is best in all these matters, and that you ought not to oppose my wishes on the subject.

From what I have heard from you and from Grey I suppose it will be prudent for you not to make any public display in London. I fear some hostile legal proceedings may be trumped up against you there, though perhaps my apprehensions may be groundless. You will know best what cause exists for troubling you, if any. I have heard there was some other woman there who had some claims. My advice to you is not to stay long in London, but to travel in Belgium, Holland, Germany & Switzerland.

You can arrange with Broderick to send you a letter of credit to any place you may desire on the Continent. You can have remittances in that way sent at any time to any place you name within a few days. This may be for any sum, say £100 or £200 at a time.

I shall, with the aid of McKenzie, do the very best I can in your private affairs here. Ann Spouslee is quite impatient to get that house, but it can't be bought just now, there is no money to spare to do it with. We shall be able to do much better I think in consequence of your having gone. I give it out that you have arranged your business affairs in this country and never mean to return to it. By the next mail I shall probably be able to send you the Annual Statement, which is nearly finished.

Inclosed is the "card" of the business of the last week.

Yours most truly,

(Signed)   EDWARD CLARK

P.S. If you want that letter written which you spoke to me about, let me know it, and it shall be done. My advice, however, is that it will be best to treat that matter squarely. I suppose there will not be much difficulty about it.

Dear Sir: Mr. Clark has read me the portion of this letter which refers to the conversation had by me with the President and Cashier of the Chemical Bank and I assure you it is just as stated by him.

(Signed)   INSLEE A. HOPPER

CPSIA information can be obtained at www.ICGtesting.com
Printed in the USA
LVOW10s1747180816

500937LV00023B/1302/P